START WITH THE SOIL

THE ORGANIC GARDENER'S GUIDE
TO IMPROVING SOIL
FOR HIGHER YIELDS,
MORE BEAUTIFUL FLOWERS,
AND A HEALTHY, EASY-CARE GARDEN

GRACE GERSHUNY

Rodale Press, Emmaus, Pennsylvania

Executive Editor: Margaret Lydic Balitas
Senior Editor: Barbara W. Ellis
Editor: Sally Roth
Production Editor: Nancy J. Ondra
Copy Manager: Dolores Plikaitis
Copy Editor: Laura Stevens
Editorial assistance: Susan L. Nickol and Kimberly Moore
Office Manager: Karen Earl-Braymer
Art Director: Anita Patterson
Book Designer: Jerry O'Brien
Cover Designer: Frank Milloni
Illustrator: Pamela Carroll
Indexer: Ed Yeager

If you have any questions or comments concerning the editorial content of this book, please write to:
Rodale Press, Inc.
Book Readers' Service
33 East Minor Street
Emmaus, PA 18098

Library of Congress Cataloging-in-Publication Data

Gershuny, Grace
    Start with the soil : the organic gardener's guide to improving
soil for higher yields, more beautiful flowers, and a healthy, easy-
care garden / by Grace Gershuny.
        p.   cm.
    Includes bibliographical references (p.   ) and index.
    ISBN 0–87596–567–9 hardcover
    ISBN 0–87596–697–7 paperback
    1. Garden soils. 2. Organic gardening. I. Title.
S596.75.G47 1993
635'.0489—dc20   93–16669

Distributed in the book trade by St. Martin's Press

2 4 6 8 10 9 7 5 3 1 hardcover
2 4 6 8 10 9 7 5 3 1 paperback

To those who have taught me and then returned their bodies to the soil: Hyman Gershuny, Adele Dawson, and Jack Cook—with thanks to the unseen billions who make humus out of humans and keep the cycles of life in motion.

CONTENTS

ACKNOWLEDGMENTS

My preoccupation with soil has been nourished and supported over the years by many people—an attempt to list all of them would be futile. My best teachers have been other organic farmers, especially those I've been fortunate enough to visit in the course of working as an organic certification inspector. My students at the Institute for Social Ecology have kept me searching for better ways to explain it all. One inspiration who deserves direct acknowledgment is Fred Franklin of Orleans, Vermont, who passed away a few years ago—he was a true soil fanatic, and our arguments were great learning experiences.

A few people and organizations have directly contributed to making the information in this book as complete and clear as possible. Stuart Hill, his associates at the Ecological Agriculture Project in Canada, and the staff at ATTRA (Appropriate Technology Transfer for Rural Areas) have provided access to extensive files on soil management. Miranda Smith, Joseph Smillie, and Judith Gillan are colleagues and cherished friends who have shared essential experience and insights. Bill Wolf, president of Necessary Trading Company, was a reliable source of advice. Nancy Ondra, assistant editor at Rodale Press, was prompt and helpful when I was stuck for answers. Joanna Poncavage, senior editor of *Organic Gardening* magazine, contributed her organic fertilizer listing. My editor, Sally Roth, was relentless and thorough in helping me make technical subjects clear to the average reader.

Deep thanks are due my husband, Stewart Hoyt, for helpful questions and moral support when I've needed it most, and our daughter, Opal, for sharing me with the computer. Special friends in Trelawny Parish, Jamaica, gave me a fresh perspective on the whole thing.

INTRODUCTION

Every culture's philosophy includes a special reverence for soil. To some cultures, soil is associated with the homeland—and perhaps with ancestral burial grounds. Most cultures directly acknowledge that they depend on fertile soil as the source of all nourishment. Our reverence for soil has been personified in the form of Mother Earth providing for the needs of her children.

In the times before the agricultural revolution, people lived by collecting what grew naturally where they were; there was no need to worry about replenishing soil fertility. Natural cycles of growth and decay replaced nutrients lost to occasional harvest by humans. As people began to cultivate crops intensively in the same location year after year, they noticed that harvests diminished over time. They discovered that they could maintain good harvests only by giving something back to the soil—by spreading animal and human manure or by allowing fields to lie fallow at intervals.

Although many ancient peoples were aware of the importance of caring for soil, there is strong evidence that soil destruction was a major factor in the downfall of several great civilizations. For example, the Phoenicians thrived on overseas trade of timber and grain, which eventually led to the deforestation of the once-famed cedars of Lebanon. The Phoenician empire became unable to feed its expanding population because its soils were depleted of nutrients necessary for plant growth. They resorted to warfare and conquest to import foodstuffs in an attempt to remedy their problem, but instead were conquered themselves by Alexander the Great.

Such a downfall is not inevitable, however. Great civilizations in China, Japan, and Korea flourished for thousands of years without soil destruction because they embraced agricultural practices that recycled every scrap of organic matter while preventing loss of topsoil from their fields.

Most likely, our ancestors relied on intuition combined with trial and error to evaluate methods of soil improvement. Although they may have noticed that spreading campfire ashes on fields caused increased plant growth, they were unaware of the complexities of plant nutrition. In fact, productivity was considered to be as much a spiritual issue, dependent on the gods, as it was a material issue. They believed that, in addition to fertilizing the soil, the proper rituals and sacrifices had to be performed to ensure a good harvest.

Until the nineteenth century, humus was thought to be an essential plant nutrient—the raw material consumed directly by plants as they grew. Justus von Liebig disproved this tenet by demonstrating that the three "major nutrients"—nitrogen, phosphorus, and potassium—were of prime importance to plant growth. Furthermore, he showed that when these elements in chemically purified form are added to soil, rapid growth and high yields result. Due to his work, von Liebig (a German contemporary of Darwin) is credited with ushering in the age of "scientific agriculture."

Post–World War I industrialists eagerly promoted von Liebig's findings, which opened up new uses for nitrates that were no longer needed for manufacturing munitions. After World War II, the synthetic chemical pest-control industry also grew as a result of the government working to create new markets for the poisons it had developed for military purposes. It is interesting to note that, late in his life, von Liebig wrote that he regretted that his theories on amending the soil had resulted in farmers abandoning the building of soil humus to improve its productivity.

In the twentieth century, a different way of looking at the world—called reductionist science—began to be applied to agriculture and other living systems. The foundation of this science is the idea that everything can be understood by reducing it to its simplest component parts. This theory has, unfortunately, been taken to extremes, and nowhere is this more apparent than in the case of modern, industrialized agriculture. Reductionism has resulted in scientists overlooking or ignoring the living quality of soil because their focus is instead on its content—its simplest component parts—specifically, its inorganic, chemical plant nutrients. Another part of the reductionist mind-set is a disdain for things that cannot be easily quantified—if you can't measure it, it doesn't exist. Reductionism further assumes that we can determine and control all of the factors involved in producing healthy, abundant crops, thereby ending world hunger. While this goal is a noble one and the approach has proved successful in the short term, reductionism is an arrogant belief system. We have overwhelming evidence that there are too many unforseen and ecologically destructive consequences to this worldview.

Criticism of the increasing industrialization of our food system often focuses on the alarming statistics that show widespread soil degradation. The harm resulting from modern, chemical-intensive soil management methods includes:

- **Increased soil erosion.** This is largely caused by economic factors that discourage conservation measures such as terracing, cover cropping, and windbreaks.
- **Widespread pollution of surface and groundwater.** Water pollution due to fertilizer nitrates and phosphates as well as pesticides and herbicides is becoming a real problem, especially in agricultural areas.
- **Loss of large areas of farmland from production.** Many acres of land are no longer suitable for agriculture due to salt buildup resulting from irrigation practices.
- **Increased soil compaction, loss of tilth, and reduced biological activity.** Use of heavy equipment and chemicals that kill earthworms and other soil organisms causes these problems.
- **Overuse of synthetic fertilizers and pesticides.** In many cases, the excessive use of energy-intensive petroleum-based fertilizers and pesticides has destroyed the biological fertility of the soil, so growers use ever-larger amounts of these materials to sustain crop growth.

Following the lead of early pioneers such as Rudolph Steiner, Sir Albert Howard, Lady Eve Balfour, and J. I. Rodale, critics of industrialized agriculture have developed practical alternatives to synthetic fertilizers and pesticides based on a sophisticated understanding of biology and ecology. Their organic farming practices are more than simply a return to the old ways because they are concerned not only with *current* soil health and food supply but also with the *future* of these things.

Scientists have steadily accumulated evidence that plants' pest and disease resistance (their ability to resist attack of pests and diseases) is strongly related to the fertility of the soil in which they grow, with the soil's humus content being of primary importance. Studies have demonstrated improvements in the health of animals whose feed was grown on biologically active soil free from chemical fertilizers. In comparisons between potatoes grown organically and those grown using artificial fertilizers, the organically grown produce has consistently shown superior storage qualities. Organically grown grains generally gave a higher content of dry matter, which improves their storage ability and nutrition.

We have yet to substantiate broad claims for superior nutritional quality of organically grown food, but we do know that crops grown in healthy soil do not have to be sprayed with toxic chemicals to protect them from pests and diseases. And using fewer chemicals translates into both a reduction in the possibility of food contamination and the elimination of the exposure to these dangerous chemicals by factory workers, farmers, and home gardeners.

One of the great "benefits" of modern agriculture has been to free most people from the necessity of tilling the soil for their sustenance. However, increasing numbers of us are discovering that working with soil and growing plants satisfies a need that goes beyond merely supplying healthy food. Gardening is therapeutic—good for the mind, body, and soul. I have personally found that having my hands in the soil is the best therapy for any tension, stress, or grumpy mood that afflicts me. Understanding a little about the delicate complexities of the living fabric of the soil further enhances the joy that I get from close contact with it.

Today, Mother Earth, who has nurtured and sustained us for so long, needs our help. Everywhere you turn, you find reminders of environmental threats and crises. The magnitude of the problems can be overwhelming, and many people have become apathetic because they feel powerless to change things. No one is powerless. If you have access to even a tiny piece of land, you can make a big difference. You have the opportunity to help heal our damaged planet in the only way that can really work—one little bit at a time. The best place to begin is beneath your feet. To help our Earth, we must start with the soil.

HOW TO USE THIS BOOK

Start with the Soil is your handbook to creating and caring for healthy, productive soil. It contains both the science you need to understand the complex cycle of soil life and fertility, and the practical tips on how to put your knowledge to use in the garden. To help you find the information you need quickly and easily, we've divided this book into two parts: "Understanding Your Soil" and "Managing Your Soil."

The first part, **"Understanding Your Soil,"** is the place to look for in-depth information on what soil is and how it relates to plant growth. You'll find out how to identify the physical characteristics of your soil, how soil organisms and humus contribute to soil fertility, and how to balance soil fertility and chemistry for best plant growth. You'll also learn how composting and other techniques can help you improve your soil and build humus and fertility.

The second part, **"Managing Your Soil,"** covers the real how-to aspects of soil care. You'll learn how to create a comprehensive soil-care program, built on the basics you learned in part 1, as well as how to identify and deal with problem soils. Specific chapters on vegetables, flowers, trees and shrubs, lawns, and container plants show you the tips and techniques you need to fine-tune your soil-care program and create the best garden you ever thought possible.

You'll be able to put this book to good use as soon as you get it. During the growing season, the chapters in part 2 will be most helpful. There you'll find specific steps you can take throughout the season to improve plant growth and deal with soil problems. But when you have a chance, it's definitely worth your time to read through part 1 and learn about the interactions between soil and plant growth. You'll be amazed at the world of activity going on right beneath your feet!

UNDERSTANDING

YOUR

SOIL

KNOW YOUR SOIL

Most people have little idea what soil is—other than something they get on their shoes or under their fingernails when they garden. Even those who are aware that soil nurtures plant life may think of it as more or less inert stuff, little more than a medium for nutrients and a structural material to anchor roots. From this viewpoint, soil is something to manipulate by adding this or that chemical element to feed plants. But soil is alive. It's an ecosystem of its own, full of living critters, with physical qualities and chemical interactions that play an important role in its health. When you start to appreciate the living quality of soil and understand how complex and dynamic a substance it is, you begin to treat it differently. In this chapter, you'll learn how to identify your soil's characteristics and find out how those traits affect the growth of your plants. Once you understand the unique qualities of your soil, you're on your way to developing an effective soil-care system for your property, as explained more fully in Chapter 6.

GETTING ACQUAINTED

If you want to get to know someone, you try to find out as much as possible about his background and history. It's the same with your soil. You may not be able to ask your parents or grandparents about how your land was managed, but if you can, that's the place to start. Neighbors and local historical societies can often tell you what kind of use, like an orchard or a dairy farm, your property

3

NAME THAT SOIL

Scientists have developed complicated systems to describe different qualities of soils based on the kinds of minerals they contain, the way in which they were formed, and various physical characteristics. Knowing the names of the soils on your property may not help you grow more vegetables or brighter flowers, but it will give you clues to the soils' characteristics, such as texture and drainage. It's also a great way to impress your gardening friends!

Soil scientists use a classification scheme to categorize soils worldwide into ten major orders. In humid temperate regions such as the Northeast, for example, where forests are the predominant natural vegetation, the soil order of spodosols is common. These soils are generally formed from coarse-textured parent material and tend to be quite acid and low in mineral nutrients. Prairie soils, which have developed under flat, grass-covered areas with modest rainfall, are classified as mollisols. They are among the most naturally productive soils, with high native organic matter and mineral content.

Each order is further broken down into suborders, great groups, and subgroups. Beyond this, soils are described in terms of families, associations, and series, which provide more information about their plant growth characteristics, organic and mineral content, structure, drainage, and color. Series are often named after the places—towns, rivers, or counties—where they are located.

You'll be able to find out the names of soils common to your area in a county soil survey, available at your local Soil Conservation Service office.

had in times past. Was this ever woodland? How long ago was it logged? Did someone have to drain the property to build on it? Was fill used to level the site? Be nosy and find out as much as you can about your land.

DO YOUR HOMEWORK

Your local Soil Conservation Service office is a wealth of information (look them up in the phone book under "United States Government"). Ask them for the most recent soil survey for your county. The survey includes extensive information about your soil type and its suitability for different uses. Drainage characteristics, geological information, and slope are all described in detail. In some cases you can also get an aerial map of your property. Not every county has complete soil surveys available, but you can probably at least get a basic idea of the geology and soil types in your general area.

Beyond your own land, it helps to know about your bioregion—

the area defined by common ecological factors. Elevation, waterways, temperature and precipitation patterns, and the types of vegetation and wildlife that predominate in your region are all important pieces of information. Where do the prevailing winds come from, and how strong are they? Is there a nearby lake that moderates temperatures? Your soil survey will include much of this, but the more you can learn from local naturalists and your own experience, the better equipped you will be to understand what's happening in the ecosystem beneath your feet.

SOIL COMPOSITION

To really understand how your soil affects the growth of your plants, it helps to know a bit about some of its characteristics, such as what it's made of. The basic composition of any soil can be broken

THE MAKING OF SOIL

As a living entity, the soil in each different area is unique. Its individual character begins with a combination of factors, such as the following, that are inherent to the soil's particular geographic region.

Parent material. Underlying rock types from which the soil was formed determine its mineral content and basic textural qualities. Limestone bedrock, for instance, tends to produce soils that have a neutral to alkaline pH.

Topography. Soil may be eroded from slopes and deposited in lowlands. The legendary fertility of river valleys such as the Nile resulted from deposits of rich sediment carried from the highlands.

Age. How long the native rock has been subject to weathering influences the availability of minerals and extent of humus development. Young soils may be low in clay content, which is produced by the chemical effects of weathering on parent rocks.

Glaciation. In the North Temperate region, advance and retreat of the glaciers, most recently a mere 12,000 years ago, has had a significant effect on soil formation and quality.

Climate. Temperature and precipitation affect the rate of organic matter accumulation and the presence of soluble soil minerals. For example, more organic matter accumulates where decomposition is slow due to cooler temperatures.

Native vegetation. Grassland, forests, and transition zones each affect soil development in a different way. Leaf litter from pine forests, for example, increases soil acidity.

down into two major components: solids and spaces. The solids include soil minerals and organic matter; the spaces contain air and water. The exact proportions of these parts vary from soil to soil, and they can have a great influence on plant growth.

THE SOLID PART OF SOIL

About 90 percent of the solid part of the soil is composed of tiny bits of the rocks and minerals from which the soil was formed. These particles are referred to as sand, silt, or clay, depending on their size. Most soils contain a mixture of these three types of particles. These components of a soil are largely unalterable—there's not much you can do to change them.

A Small but Mighty Fraction

The remaining 10 percent of the solid part of the soil is the organic fraction. This small part of the soil has a tremendous influence on the soil's ability to support plant growth. How you manage your soil has a profound influence on the amount and quality of organic matter it contains.

The organic fraction of the soil is a dynamic substance, constantly undergoing change. This vital bit consists of living organisms, including plant roots and bacteria, as well as dead plant residues and other wastes. The total weight of the living organisms in the top 6 inches of an acre of soil can range from 5,000 pounds to as much as 20,000 pounds.

The continual decomposition of organic residues results in the formation of humus and the release of plant nutrients. The fertility of your soil—its capacity to nurture healthy plants—depends on the health, vitality, and diversity of the organisms that live, grow, reproduce, and die in the soil. Through the activities of soil microbes, which can number in the billions in every gram of healthy topsoil, the basic raw materials needed by plants are made available at the right time and in the right form and amount. To improve the fertility of your soil, you must provide hospitable conditions for soil organisms.

The Humus Connection

Soil health and humus are interrelated: Health is the vitality of the soil's living population, and humus is the manifestation of its activities. Humus is produced by bacteria and fungi as they consume organic material in the soil. Dark brown, porous, spongy, and somewhat gummy, humus has a pleasant, earthy fragrance. It keeps your soil healthy and easy to work, and it helps hold water. Chapter 3 discusses the different forms of humus and their role in the soil ecosystem. It also describes ways you can build and maintain vital organic matter and humus in the soil.

SPACE FOR AIR AND WATER

About half the volume of a good soil is pore spaces—the area between particles where air and water can penetrate. The pore space generally contains an equal volume of water, which clings to the surface of soil particles, and air. Keeping a healthy balance of air and water by maintaining a loose, open soil is critical for good root growth and the health of the soil community. All the fertilizer in the world won't solve the problems of dense, compacted soil that is deficient in pore spaces.

PHYSICAL CHARACTERISTICS OF SOIL

The relative amounts of the various soil components have a great influence on whether or not your soil will be in good condition for growing plants. Gardeners often describe a well-balanced soil as being in good tilth. Moisture and aeration are the key physical qualities of good soil tilth. Soil in good tilth holds water without becoming soggy and allows air to penetrate to plant roots and soil organisms. Good tilth also means soil is loose and easy to work, so gardening tools as well as plant roots can readily dig in.

The tilth of your soil depends upon its texture, structure and aggregation, density, drainage, and water-holding capacity. These qualities are interdependent; dense, compacted soil, for example, can lead to poor drainage. You can improve some of these characteristics with proper management; others, you'll just have to live with. There's not much you can do to change the depth of bedrock or the water table, for instance. Part of the challenge of maintaining healthy soil is knowing how to change the characteristics that you can and how to deal with those that you can't.

SOIL TEXTURE

Your soil's texture is a key factor in how well it can hold water and nutrients and allow air to circulate. Texture refers to the relative proportions of sand, silt, and clay particles in a given soil. Clay particles are those smaller than 0.002 millimeters in diameter. Silt particles range in size from 0.002 millimeters up to 0.05 millimeters in diameter. And sand-size particles are those from 0.05 millimeters to up to 2 millimeters in diameter.

Soil texture can range from clay, with mostly very fine particles, to sand, which is mostly the coarse particles. In between, soil scientists recognize ten more groupings (called textural classes), depend-

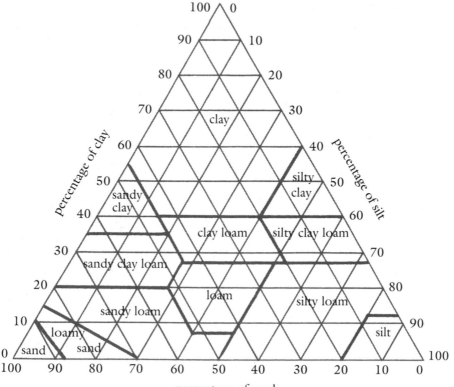

Use this textural triangle to look up the relative percentages of sand, silt, and clay. The area in which the three lines intersect will indicate the name of that soil's textural class.

ing on the relative percentages of the three particle sizes. A sandy clay, for example, has a high content of clay and sand but very little silt. A silty clay, on the other hand, has lots of clay and silt but not much sand. A loam contains a balance of fine clay, medium-size silt, and coarse sand particles. To see how different soil textures are named, see the illustration on the opposite page.

Any extreme is undesirable: Clay soils hold water and nutrients well but can be poorly drained and difficult to work. When they dry out, they form hard clumps and can take on the consistency of concrete. Sandy soils are generally easy to work and well-drained, but they have poor nutrient- and water-holding abilities.

As most gardeners know, the soil often contains many "particles" larger than 2 millimeters in diameter. These fragments are known as gravel, cobbles, or boulders, depending on their size. These larger components are not technically part of the soil texture, but they do have an effect on the soil's physical characteristics. Soils with lots of large particles are commonly said to be stony or rocky, and are generally difficult to plant in. Soil texture also does not take organic matter into account—only sand, silt, and clay.

Evaluate your soil's texture by scooping up a handful of moist soil—add a little water if it's very dry—and squeezing it in your fist. Now open your hand. If your sample falls apart instead of staying in a ball, you've got sand on your hands. If you have a ball of soil sitting on your palm, try to squeeze it upward with your thumb to form a ribbon. If you can't make a ribbon, classify your soil as loamy sand. If you can make a ribbon, make it as long as you can, and measure it.

Now for the fun part: Add water to your ribbon to make a soupy mud in your hand. Rub the forefinger of your other hand in the mud, and decide if it feels mostly smooth, mostly gritty, or equally smooth and gritty. Then match up your observations on the length of the ribbon you made with the information in the table on page 10 to find the texture that best describes your soil.

Knowing your soil's texture will help you make informed decisions on how to manage your garden. You can't effectively change your soil's texture unless you work in huge quantities of sand or clay, and that's not a practical solution for most gardeners. Fortunately, though, management practices like adding organic matter *can* help improve your soil's structure, which has an equally important influence on plant growth.

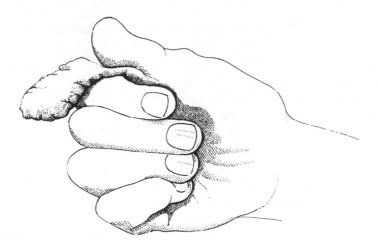

Make a ribbon of soil between your fingers to gauge its texture. Light-textured sandy and silt loams form shorter ribbons than heavier-textured silty clay and clay.

STRUCTURE AND AGGREGATION

The key to soil tilth is good soil structure. Structure refers to the way soil particles are grouped together. Particles may clump together in rounded aggregates (called crumbs or granules); blocky units; flattened, layered structures (called plates); or vertically oriented units (known as columns or prisms). Crumbs are most commonly found in the top layer of soil; the other kinds of aggregates are generally more prevalent in the subsoil. Soils can also be structureless. Structureless soils may be single-grained (having no aggregates) or massive (forming very tight clumps).

EVALUATING SOIL TEXTURE

Sandy loams and silty loams are light-textured soils. Silty clay and clay are heavy-textured soils. Everything else can be categorized as medium texture.

Ribbon Length	Feels Mostly Gritty	Feels Mostly Smooth	Feels Both Gritty and Smooth
Shorter than 1″	Sandy loam	Silty loam	Loam
1″–2″ long	Sandy clay loam	Silty clay loam	Clay loam
Longer than 2″	Sandy clay	Silty clay	Clay

The size of the aggregates that make up your soil and how well they hold together are critical aspects of its tilth. The looser the aggregates, the bigger the pore spaces between them, and the better water and air can infiltrate. Soils with good structure can hold up to twice as much water as those with poor structure and the same texture. Plants grow better in soils with good structure, even when water isn't a problem. Their roots can penetrate the soil easily and get plenty of oxygen and nutrients from the air and water in the pore spaces.

A good crumb or granular structure also has plenty of interconnected pore spaces, which are essential for conducting soil moisture upward from the deeper layers to plant roots. This process is called capillary action, and it works in much the same way as oil being taken up into the wick of a lamp. Adequate soil moisture replenishes the moisture that is lost through plant leaves. It's also crucial because most of the nutrients that plant roots take up are dissolved in the thin film of water that coats the soil particles. The more pores your soil has, the more access your plants' roots have to this nutrient-bearing water film.

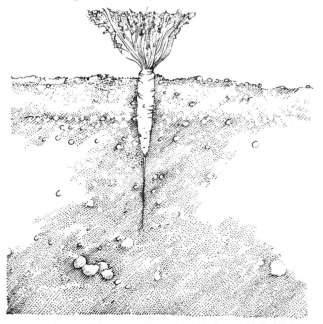

Like oil drawn up by a wick, water is taken up through the soil by capillary action. If soil structure is good, moisture reaches the root zone from deeper soil levels even though the surface dries out.

To check the structure and aggregation of your soil, pick up a handful of soil and see how it crumbles. Heavy, clayey soils with good structure will still crumble easily, and light, sandy soils will retain some shape instead of becoming powdery. Heavy soils with poor structure will resist crumbling or form large clods, while lighter soils will become dusty.

Next, dig a hole about a foot deep and examine the size of the crumbs at different depths. Crumbs can come in many sizes; they aren't single discrete objects like marbles, but more like a bit of moist cake. Look for large crumbs, about ¹⁄₃₂ to ⅜ inch in size. Check aggregate stability by placing a small handful of soil in a glass and gently filling it with water. Do the aggregates keep their shape, or does your sample collapse into a muddy blob? Good structure is indicated by a lot of large crumbs that hold together in a glass of water.

Soil structure is the physical quality that you can improve with good management practices or destroy by abuse. Good soil structure is very much a product of biological activity. Humus, of course, plays a central role in forming rounded aggregates, but many soil creatures—most notably earthworms—secrete the sticky gums that are crucial for holding soil particles together. Adding lots of organic matter and working the soil when it is not too wet are ways to promote and maintain good soil structure. Walking on or tilling wet soil can destroy the soil aggregates and ruin the soil's structure.

THE SOIL COMMUNITY

The living part of the soil is just as critical to plant growth as the physical characteristics discussed above. Soil micro- and macroorganisms are the essential link between mineral reserves and plant growth. The cycles that permit nutrients to flow from soil to plant are all interdependent, and they work only with the help of the living organisms that constitute the soil community. Animals and people are also part of this community when their wastes are returned to the soil for the benefit of the organisms that live there.

Soil organisms—from bacteria and fungi to protozoans and nematodes, on up to mites, springtails, and earthworms—perform a vast array of fertility-maintenance tasks. Organic soil management aims at helping soil organisms maintain fertility; conventional (nonorganic) soil management merely substitutes a simplified chemical system to provide nutrients to plants. Once a healthy soil ecosystem is disrupted by the excessive use of soluble synthetic fertilizers, restoring it can be a long and costly process.

SOIL INHABITANTS

Microscopic creatures form the basis of the soil food web. These microbial decomposers are essential to all life on Earth, since they are responsible for virtually all organic waste recycling. Most contribute directly to humus formation and the release of nutrients from organic matter.

Other creatures, both microscopic and visible, also make important contributions to soil health. Plant roots themselves are major participants in the soil ecosystem. Chapter 2 includes more details about the variety and functions of the living organisms that inhabit the soil community.

Anytime you work in the soil, take notice of how biologically active it is. Try to identify the kinds of macroorganisms you see crawling, skittering, and squirming around. An inexpensive magnifying glass can open up a whole universe of creatures you never knew existed. When you realize how dependent you are on the billions of creatures flourishing in the universe below the surface of the soil, you catch a glimpse of the marvelous interdependence of all life on this planet. When you can comprehend the extent of the responsibility you hold, as the steward of one small piece of it, you are on your way to making a positive contribution to restoring it to health.

SIZING UP YOUR SOIL

The things you can tell from just walking around your garden and paying attention to what you see are of greatest importance for good soil care. A few simple shovel tests will tell you even more about your soil.

The physical condition of your soil is its easiest aspect to evaluate. You don't need precise instruments to get a pretty good feel—literally—for its general tilth. The tests that follow are good indicators of how well your soil-improvement program is working. You may want to repeat them once a year or even more often.

Start by making a map of your property. Even a rough sketch will give you some basis for planning improvements like new trees or perennial beds. Record features such as slopes and contours, water-ways, wet areas, rocky outcrops, and woods. Make note of any signs of erosion you see. Check for soggy places in early spring or after a period of rain. Be sure to indicate current garden areas and buildings.

This map will be a good planning tool for locating future garden areas in favorable sites. It can also give you good clues to dealing with existing problems. Diverting water from an upper slope, for example, may solve or reduce drainage problems on lower-lying sites. A rocky outcrop could indicate that the soil in that area is very shallow and possibly an undesirable site for a garden. Keep your map in a handy place with your other gardening notes. For more details on starting and maintaining a garden journal, see "Keeping Records" on page 24.

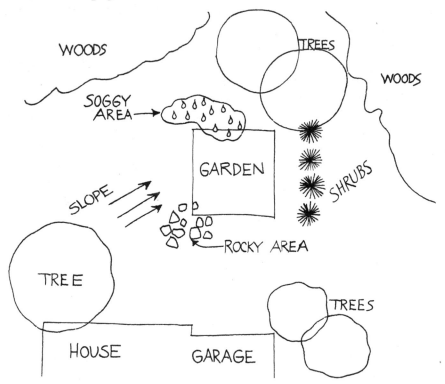

A walk around your garden helps you evaluate your soil. Sketch a map, showing physical features such as slopes and contours, soggy places, rocks, garden areas, and buildings.

A GOOD WORD FOR WEEDS

You may even gain a new sense of respect for your weeds once you have learned to carefully examine them. Weeds, although unwelcome in your vegetable or flower garden, can provide many free soil-improvement services if allowed to pave the way for your desired crops. Perennial weeds are frequently deep-rooted, helping break up hardpans, aerate the subsoil, and bring up mineral nutrients from areas too deep for crop roots. When the weeds die and decompose, these nutrients become available for other plants. Some plants are such reliable mineral accumulators that prospectors can use them to indicate a possible source of deposits such as copper and selenium.

LEARN FROM YOUR WEEDS

Existing vegetation can provide many clues about the status of your soil. Start with a weed identification guide, or consult your local Cooperative Extension office for help in identifying the weeds you find.

Weeds can often be reliable indicators of potential fertility problems. "Indicator Weeds and Soil Conditions" on page 16 lists some common weeds and the conditions they are associated with. (Weeds can even give you a clue to nutrient deficiencies. See how your weeds stack up against the "Nutrient Deficiency Symptoms" table on page 91.)

As you explore the weeds on your land, keep these considerations in mind:

• A few individual weeds don't mean much. Look for consistent populations of the same species. If several species that prefer similar soil conditions predominate, it's a good clue. For example, if you have a lot of plantain, chicory, and coltsfoot, it is a clearer indication of heavy, poorly drained soil than if you find just one of those species.

• Perennial weeds, which regrow each year, are better indicators of soil conditions than annual weeds, which only survive one season.

• Many weeds can tolerate a wide range of conditions, but some are more specific in their requirements. Some indicate more than one factor. For instance, perennial sow thistle and dock both indicate wet areas, but dock prefers more acid soils, while thistle likes a higher pH.

(continued on page 18)

INDICATOR WEEDS AND SOIL CONDITIONS

Name of Weed	Condition(s) Indicated
Bindweed, field (*Convolvulus arvensis*)	Hardpan or crusty surface with light sand texture
Bracken, Eastern (*Pteridium aquilinum*)	Acidic or low lime soil; low potassium; low phosphorus
Buttercup, creeping (*Ranunculus repens*)	Wet, poorly drained clay soil
Buttercups (*Ranunculus* spp.)	Tilled or cultivated soil
Campion, bladder (*Silene cucubalus*)	Neutral or alkaline pH
Chickweed (*Stellaria media*)	Tilled or cultivated soil with high fertility or humus unless weeds are pale and stunted, then fertility is low
Chicory (*Cichorium intybus*)	Soil with heavy clay texture, tilled or cultivated with high fertility or humus unless weeds are pale and stunted, then fertility is low
Cinquefoil, silvery (*Potentilla argentea*)	Dry soil, often with thin topsoil; acidic or low lime
Coltsfoot (*Tussilago farfara*)	Heavy clay soil; waterlogged or poorly drained; acidic or low lime
Daisy, oxeye (*Chrysanthemum leucanthemum*)	Waterlogged or poorly drained soil that has been neglected or uncultivated; acidic or low lime with low fertility
Dandelion (*Taraxacum officinale*)	Heavy clay soil; tilled or cultivated; acidic or low lime, especially on lawns
Docks (*Rumex* spp.)	Waterlogged or poorly drained soil; acidic or low lime
Grass, quack (*Agropyron repens*)	Hardpan or crusty surface
Hawkweeds (*Hieracium* spp.)	Acidic or low lime soil
Henbane, black (*Hyoscyamus niger*)	Neutral or alkaline pH

(continued)

INDICATOR WEEDS AND SOIL CONDITIONS—CONTINUED

Name of Weed	Condition(s) Indicated
Horsetail, field (*Equisetum arvense*)	Sandy light soil; acidic or low lime
Joe-Pye weed (*Eupatorium purpureum*)	Wet or waterlogged soil
Knapweeds (*Centaurea* spp.)	Acidic or low lime soil with high potassium
Knotweed, prostrate (*Polygonum aviculare*)	Tilled or cultivated soil; acidic or low lime
Lamb's quarters (*Chenopodium album*)	Tilled or cultivated soil with high fertility or humus unless weeds are pale and stunted, then fertility is low
Lettuce, prickly (*Lactuca serriola*)	Tilled or cultivated soil
Meadowsweet, broad-leaved (*Spiraea latifolia*)	Wet or waterlogged soil
Mosses (Musci class)	Waterlogged or poorly drained soil; acidic or low lime
Mullein, common (*Verbascum thapsis*)	Neglected uncultivated soil; acidic or low lime; low fertility
Mustard, white (*Brassica hirta*)	Neutral or alkaline pH
Mustards (*Brassica* spp.)	Hardpan or crusty surface; dry, often with thin topsoil
Nettles (*Urtica dioica*)	Tilled or cultivated soil; acidic or low lime
Pigweed, redroot (*Amaranthus retroflexus*)	Tilled or cultivated soil with high fertility or humus unless weeds are pale or stunted, then fertility is low
Pineappleweed (*Matricaria matricarioides*)	Hardpan or crusty surface

(continued)

INDICATOR WEEDS AND SOIL CONDITIONS—CONTINUED

Name of Weed	Condition(s) Indicated
Plantains (*Plantago* spp.)	Heavy clay soil; waterlogged or poorly drained; tilled or cultivated; acidic or low lime, especially on lawns
Shepherd's purse (*Capsella bursa-pastoris*)	Saline soil
Sorrel, garden (*Rumex acetosa*)	Waterlogged or poorly drained soil; acidic or low lime
Sorrel, sheep (*Rumex acetosella*)	Sandy, light soil; acidic or low lime
Sow-thistle, annual (*Sonchus oleraceus*)	Heavy clay soil
Sow-thistle, perennial (*Sonchus arvensis*)	Wet soil; neutral or alkaline pH
Thistle, Canada (*Cirsium arvense*)	Heavy clay soil
Yarrow (*Achillea millefolium*)	Low potassium

SOURCE: Adapted with permission from *The Soul of Soil: A Guide to Ecological Soil Management* by Grace Gershuny and Joseph Smillie. St. Johnsbury, Vt.: Gaia Services, 1986.

• The growth of the weed can tell as much as its presence. Vigorously growing leguminous weeds, such as clovers, are a sign that soil nitrogen is low. Stunted, yellowish non-leguminous weeds may mean the same thing.

TESTING DRAINAGE

A simple perc test will tell you if you have drainage problems. Dig a hole about 1 foot deep and 6 inches across. Fill it with water and allow it to drain completely. As soon as it does, fill it again and see how long it takes to drain again. If it takes more than 8 hours, try the suggestions under "Drainage Problems" on page 150 to improve your drainage.

Each growing season, make note of any changes in the predominant weed species that invade your garden. As time goes on, you should see poor-soil indicators such as Queen-Anne's-lace and mullein replaced by fertility indicators like chickweed and lamb's quarters.

CHECK FOR COMPACTION

Soil compaction reduces the pore space in the soil, minimizing its capacity to hold air and water. A tight, compacted soil is difficult for roots to grow through and is often poorly drained; it's also difficult to dig. If you can't plunge a garden fork into your soil to its full depth without standing on it, assuming you haven't hit a rock or other obstacle, your soil is compacted. Compaction problems can be indicated by poor water infiltration, as shown by a simple perc test (see "Testing Drainage" on the opposite page for details on doing your own perc tests), as well as by poor structure. Another way to judge compaction is to shove a thin (¼-inch) metal rod into the ground as far as it will go until it bends under pressure. Try this in various locations—the sooner it bends, the more compacted the soil.

EXAMINE SOIL MOISTURE

Use the method outlined below to check moisture levels early in the growing season and anytime you are concerned about the availability of water for your plants. Plants will wilt if soil moisture in their root zone drops below a range of 5 percent for sandy soils to 15 percent for clay soils.

If soil moisture levels as determined by the following method are not above the 50-percent range within a 6-inch depth, many garden plants will suffer from lack of water. If your soil dries out to less than 50-percent moisture at this depth two days after a good rain, you have a problem with excessive drainage (refer to Chapter 7 for hints on overcoming it).

To determine how much moisture your soil has:

1. Look for obvious signs of surface crusting and cracking caused by dryness.

2. See how far down you have to dig before the soil gets darker, indicating more moisture. Take handfuls of soil from different

FINDING FIELD CAPACITY

If you're curious about how much water your soil can hold when it is saturated, measure its field capacity. Do this a day or two after a soaking rain, or flood a small area and then wait until the water has soaked down into the lower levels. Now dig up a few samples of soil from areas 2 to 4 inches down—an ounce or two is enough.

Weigh the sample you collected, then dry it by spreading it on a cookie sheet in the oven with the setting on "warm" for a day or so. Now weigh the dry soil. (Be sure to subtract the weight of the container both times.)

Field capacity is expressed as a percentage, calculated as:

$$\frac{(\text{wet weight of soil} - \text{dry weight of soil})}{\text{dry weight of soil}} \times 100\% = \text{field capacity}$$

Good field capacity is another sign of high humus content. Sandy soils may have a field capacity below 10 percent, while the field capacity of clay soils may approach 30 percent.

depths and squeeze them firmly in your hand. If your hand gets wet, your soil is saturated.

3. Using the table on the opposite page, match the behavior of your handful of soil with the appropriate texture and description to see how much water it contains.

ANALYZE ORGANIC CONTENT

You may want to have organic matter content measured when you have your soil tested (see "Testing Your Soil" on page 93 for more information on taking soil tests), but you can visually evaluate it yourself. In general, darker browns mean higher humus content. Look for white threads of fungal mycelia and bits of undecomposed organic matter. If you can recognize garden residues from the previous season within a few weeks of spring planting, you'll need to work harder at stimulating the soil organisms—refer to Chapter 3 for guidance.

COUNT ON WORMS

An earthworm census is another valuable barometer of soil biological activity. Take one during a cool time of day to avoid harming your worms. Here's how to do it:

SOIL MOISTURE

Available Soil Moisture	Feel or Appearance of Soil		
	Light Texture	Medium Texture	Heavy Texture
0–25%	Dry; loose; flows through fingers	Powdery dry; sometimes slightly crusted but easily broken down into powdery condition	Hard; baked; cracked; sometimes has loose crumbs on surface
25–50%	Appears to be dry; will not form ball	Somewhat crumbly but holds together from pressure	Somewhat pliable; will form a ball under pressure
50–75%	Tends to ball under pressure but seldom holds together	Forms a ball; somewhat plastic; will sometimes slick slightly with pressure	Forms a ball; ribbons out between fingers
75% to field capacity (100%)	Forms weak ball; breaks easily; will not slick	Forms a ball; is very pliable; slicks readily if relatively high in clay	Easily ribbons out between fingers; has slick feeling
At field capacity (100%)	Upon squeezing, no free water appears on soil, but leaves wet outline of ball on hand	Upon squeezing, no free water appears on soil, but leaves wet outline of ball on hand	Upon squeezing, no free water appears on soil, but leaves wet outline of ball on hand
Saturated	Water appears on ball and hand	Water appears on ball and hand	Water appears on ball and hand

SOURCE: S.C.S. Information Bulletin No. 199.

NOTE: A soil ball is formed by squeezing a handful of soil very firmly. To form a soil ribbon, use your thumb to push the ball of soil out against the side of your index finger. (See the illustration on page 10.)

1. Measure out a 1-square-foot plot, avoiding places where results would be distorted, such as near a compost pile or under mulch.

2. Now dig down 6 inches, placing everything you dig up in a bucket or pan.

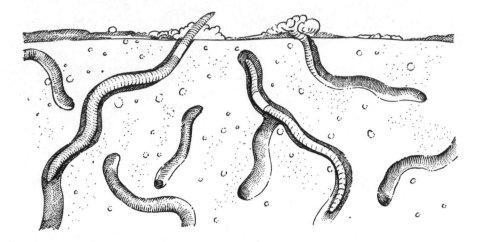

For a quick check of soil biological activity, look to your earthworms. Look for holes and piles of castings, signs that worms have been tunneling through your garden soil.

3. Count the earthworms in the earth in the bucket. You should find at least ten of them in that much healthy soil.

You can also count the number of earthworm holes, with their little piles of castings next to them, that you see in a given area of garden bed. You should see at least five or six per square foot of healthy garden soil.

HEALTHY SOIL MEANS HEALTHY ROOTS

The condition of plant roots is one of the ultimate indicators of soil health. Observe the root systems of weeds as you pull them up. You can also dig up a plant just to examine its roots, being careful to cut off as little as possible of its root mass. Choose the healthiest-looking specimen in the vicinity, and try to answer the following questions:

• Do the roots seem vigorous and well-branched? You want to see roots penetrating as much of the soil area as possible.

• Are there lots of fine root hairs? Finding only a few fine feeder roots might indicate that too little air is available in the root zone.

• Do roots grow freely in every direction, or do they seem to grow sideways at a certain depth? Roots that suddenly turn sideways are a sure indication of a hardpan.

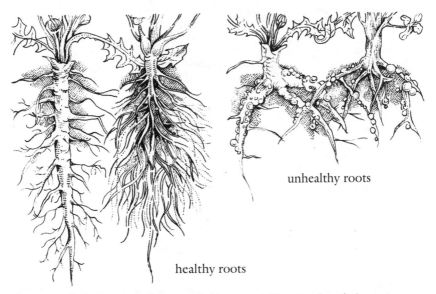

unhealthy roots

healthy roots

Before you pitch those weeds onto the compost pile, examine their roots. Healthy roots are well-branched and far-reaching and have many root hairs. Unhealthy roots in unhealthy soils may be stunted, growing in odd directions, or clubbed by nematodes.

DIGGING DEEPER

To get a real worm's-eye view of your soil, you might feel inspired to dig down even farther—2 or 3 feet. You might not gain much more in the way of essential information from this effort, but you will acquire a more thorough and intimate sense of what's happening beneath the surface. If you need to dig a hole to plant a tree or shrub anyway, you can take the opportunity to make the following observations.

Examine the layers of soil you see, and try to identify different horizons. The thickness and nature of each soil horizon tells a story about how the soil was formed, its drainage characteristics, and biological and chemical activity. How thick is the topsoil? Are there sharply delineated layers below, with differences in color and/or texture? Mottled gray and rust-brown streaks in lower horizons indicate leached, acid soils and possible drainage problems. Brown and red colors are from oxidized iron, a result of acidity.

Other things you'll want to look for include the depth to which plant roots and soil creatures penetrate. Shallow roots may indicate drainage problems or a compacted layer, while lush, deep root sys-

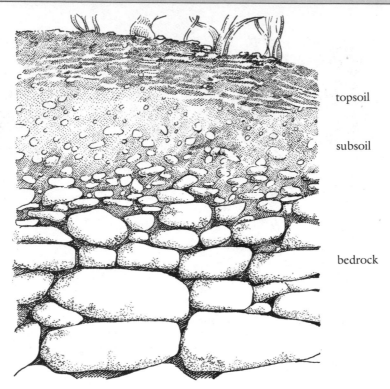

topsoil

subsoil

bedrock

Dig deeper to reveal the soil horizons. A 2- to 3-foot cleanly dug hole will show you how much topsoil you have and what the soil structure and texture are in lower layers, and it will make clear any hardpan or bedrock limitations.

tems with signs of earthworm activity in the lower layers are good signs of healthy soil. Also take note of the depth to any area of bedrock, gravel, or other kind of stone. Shallow soils are obviously difficult to grow good plants in—they may be poorly drained and lack a loose, granular structure.

KEEPING RECORDS

Becoming an astute observer of soil, like any other skill, takes time and practice. An important part of developing this skill involves keeping good records of what you see and comparing them with how your garden does over time. Good records are one of the most important tools you can use to build healthy soil and to improve your garden, too. Below are some tips on recording your observations and using these records in garden planning.

MAP YOUR GARDEN

If you use a bed system, make a scale drawing of each bed. If you have a lot of beds, it is helpful to develop a coding system to identify each one. For vegetable gardens not arranged in beds, divide the garden map into rotation units (see Chapter 8 for information on rotation planning).

Use your original map as a master, which you can photocopy each year to record what you grew and how it was treated. In subsequent years, add new beds or changes to the garden area, or make a new master. Information you should record on your map includes the type of crop grown and how it was fertilized. For this purpose, it's enough just to note the total amount of compost or other organic fertilizer used that year, along with any mineral nutrients applied.

THE GARDEN JOURNAL

There are a lot of things you should try to keep track of as they occur, including weather (especially rainfall); pest, weed, and disease problems; and crop growth and development. It also helps to record your activities, such as planting and transplanting, weeding, pruning, spraying foliar nutrients, fertilizing, and harvesting. Later on, when you want to know when you last fertilized the peppers or pruned your peach trees, you'll know just where to look.

A diary format works well for much of this record keeping and also allows you to reflect on the possible causes of problems and make note of ideas for improvement as they come up. Some people use a large wall calendar to record activities, as well as to remind themselves of what needs doing when. I like to use a loose-leaf notebook for garden records. You can have separate pages for each bed, for example; this lets you quickly find out when a given bed has had a green manure crop or compost application. You can also have a page describing the yearly soil observations you've made, along with copies of your soil test results. If you're really organized you can insert your maps, too.

After a while you will get a sense of how much information you need to write down—at first it may seem a bit overwhelming. Remember that when you want to do some planning it will be much easier to refer back to a few brief facts than to pages of rambling

A loose-leaf notebook makes a handy garden journal. Get in the habit of jotting down observations and activities, and you'll have a valuable record for improving your soil and your garden.

paragraphs. Depending on the size of your garden and how often you work in it, you can jot down your notes each day you do something or just once a week.

If you are considering small-scale farming, especially if you would like to become certified organic, getting into a good record-keeping habit is crucial. The financial viability of any farm rests to a large extent on your ability to make changes based on information in your records. Extensive and detailed records are a key requirement of every bona fide organic certification program. You need to be able to go back at least three years in your soil management history and show what fertility-improvement and pest-control measures you have used. Keep receipts for any purchased fertilizers or soil amendments as well. For more information on organic certification requirements, consult one of the organizations listed in "Organic Certification" on page 261.

THE SOIL COMMUNITY AND HOW TO CARE FOR IT

CHAPTER 2

You can have productive, fertile soil without knowing anything about the fine points of soil chemistry and mineral balancing, as long as you understand the importance of caring for the soil organisms. An astonishing number and variety of creatures—from bacteria and fungi to earthworms and moles—make up the soil community. These organisms are constantly growing, reproducing, and dying in every crumb of soil—billions in each gram of healthy topsoil. In this chapter, you'll find out how these organisms contribute to the health of your plants and what steps you can take to protect and encourage a healthy soil community. For more details on how caring for soil organisms fits in to your comprehensive soil-care program, see Chapter 6.

LIFE IN THE ROOT ZONE

The health of plants, animals, and people all begins with healthy soil. Each organism—above and below ground—has a role to play in the soil ecosystem. Here's what they do.

Producers create carbohydrates and proteins from simple nutrient elements, almost always by capturing energy from sunlight through photosynthesis. Green plants, including blue-green algae, are the producers for the soil community. A few specialized bacteria, known as autotrophs, are also able to synthesize their own food from carbon dioxide and mineral elements in the soil.

Consumers are just about everyone else: all those organisms, big and little, that depend on the food created by green plants.

27

Animals from simple protozoans to humans, as well as non-photo-synthesizing plants such as yeasts and certain other fungi, fall into this category. Primary consumers eat plants directly, while secondary and tertiary consumers feed on other consumers. For example, if you ate a salad for lunch, you acted as a primary consumer. If you had a hamburger, you were a secondary consumer.

Decomposers perform the critical function of bringing the basic chemical nutrients full circle—from consumers back to producers. They are primarily bacteria or fungi and are found almost exclusively in the soil. Microbial decomposers account for about 60 to 80 percent of the total soil metabolism. Without them, life would grind to a halt as we suffocated in our own wastes.

THE WORLD BENEATH YOUR FEET

There is still a great deal of mystery and uncertainty about what happens in the soil beneath us. Despite the many volumes that have been written about soil biology, knowledge of the kinds of organisms that live in soil and how they interact is extremely limited. No doubt many creatures yet unnamed and uncounted contribute to our sustenance. Some of the organisms that we know are critical to soil health include bacteria, actinomycetes, fungi, algae, nematodes, and earthworms.

Bacteria

Bacteria are the most numerous and varied of soil organisms. There are anywhere from a few hundred million to three billion in every gram of soil. Under the right conditions, they grow at an astonishing rate and can double their population every hour. The top 6 to 8 inches of soil may contain anywhere from 200 pounds to 2 tons of live bacteria per acre.

Bacteria vary in their requirements for air, but most beneficial ones need some air to thrive. If enough moisture and food are present, bacteria do best at temperatures of 70° to 100°F and at a pH close to neutral. Bacteria need adequate calcium and a balance of micronutrients, which are essential to the enzymes used to perform their biochemical tasks.

Unfavorable conditions rarely kill bacteria off completely; the bacteria will either stop growing and form spores to wait for better times, or new generations will adapt to the changed conditions

BACTERIA AND BREATHING

The bacteria in the micro-universe of the soil are divided into two types: those that need air and those that don't. The availability of air determines which kinds will flourish and how vigorously they will grow.

Aerobes require air in order to live. The bacteria responsible for turning organic proteins into nitrates and sulfates, as well as many important decomposers, are aerobes. All other soil organisms, including plant roots, are also aerobic. Some bacteria can survive in either aerobic or anaerobic conditions but will only grow and thrive if they have air.

Anaerobes can live happily without air and, in fact, may be killed if exposed to it. The bacteria responsible for diseases like botulism and tetanus are famous examples. Many anaerobes are decomposers, which can generate some foul-smelling waste products, such as the hydrogen sulfide that gives rotten eggs their characteristic odor. Anaerobic decomposition is also known as putrefaction. Anaerobic bacteria can also generate useful by-products such as methane gas, which is sometimes used as an energy source.

through genetic mutation. (This adaptability can work against you when the organism in question causes a plant disease.) If any soil nutrient is in limited supply, bacteria will be the first to consume it. Plants must wait until the bacteria die and decompose to get access to the nutrients.

Bacteria have a virtual monopoly on three basic soil processes that are vital to higher plants: nitrification, sulfur oxidation, and nitrogen fixation.

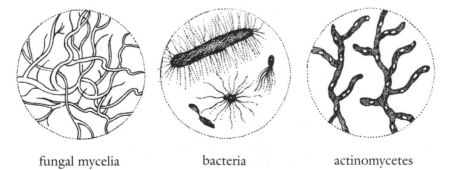

fungal mycelia   bacteria   actinomycetes

It's a whole other world beneath your feet, and these three play a big part in it. Fungal mycelia (*left*) snake through the soil, some of them causing disease and others fighting it. Actinomycetes (*right*) decompose organic matter and form humus. Bacteria (*center*), which occur by the millions in each gram of soil, transform nitrogen and sulfur to a form usable by plants.

Nitrification. Nitrogen occurs in several different forms in the soil, but some of them are unavailable to plants until they are transformed by bacteria. Soil organic matter, for example, holds nitrogen in the form of complex proteins. Bacteria and other organisms help to break down these proteins into the form of ammonium. Some plants, such as acid lovers like azaleas and rhododendrons, readily use nitrogen in this form. Most other plants, however, depend on different types of bacteria to convert the ammonium into a different form, known as nitrate. These bacteria, known as nitrifying bacteria, thrive in warm, well-aerated, evenly moist soil. Extreme conditions, such as cold temperatures, waterlogging, and tight, compacted soil, are harmful to these bacteria and will slow the conversion of ammonium nitrogen into the more accessible nitrate form.

Sulfur Oxidation. Sulfur undergoes similar chemical and biological transformations in the soil. Specialized bacteria turn organic sulfur compounds into sulfates, the form most usable by plants. These bacteria, however, can tolerate a wider range of soil conditions than nitrifying bacteria.

Nitrogen Fixation. Nitrogen-fixing bacteria transform elemental nitrogen from the atmosphere into protein and eventually make it available to other organisms. (To make synthetic fertilizers, humans imitate this process at a high energy cost by burning tremendous amounts of natural gas to synthesize ammonia from atmospheric nitrogen.) Some nitrogen-fixing bacteria live in symbiosis with leguminous plants, such as peas and lupins; you'll find more information on these bacteria in "Nitrogen-Fixing Legumes" on the opposite page. Other nitrogen-fixing bacteria live free in the soil.

Actinomycetes

The characteristic aroma of freshly plowed earth is attributed to actinomycetes. These microbes, which behave like a cross between bacteria and fungi, play a critical role in organic matter decomposition and humus formation. Manure is especially rich in actinomycetes, which is why many people consider manure to be essential for making high-quality compost.

After bacteria, actinomycetes are the most numerous soil organisms. They need a loose, well-aerated soil and a pH between 6.0 and 7.5, and they're more tolerant of dry conditions than either bacteria or fungi. Their intolerance of low pH can be used to advantage in preventing potato scab, a disease caused by an actinomycete.

Nitrogen-Fixing Legumes

The root systems of legumes, such as clover, vetch, and garden beans, should contain a good sprinkling of little bumps called nodules. This is where the beneficial rhizobia bacteria, which fix atmospheric nitrogen, live. If you slice open some of these nodules, they should be noticeably pink or red in color. A green or black color indicates a lack of bacterial activity. (This may be a normal phase if the plant is entering dormancy). The size and number of nodules is directly related to how much nitrogen the plant can fix. Dig up different kinds of legumes and compare the number of nodules you find—alfalfa and clover are normally more heavily nodulated than beans or peas. Using the right bacterial inoculants on your garden legume crops will increase nodulation and the resultant nitrogen fixation.

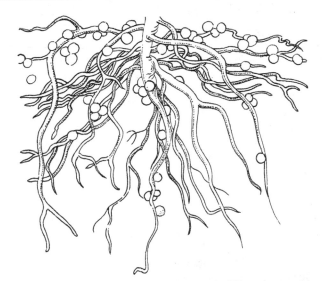

The rounded nodules on the roots of legumes (like peas and beans) are home to beneficial *Rhizobium* bacteria. The bacteria transform nitrogen from the atmosphere into a form usable by the plants.

Fungi

Molds, yeasts, and mushrooms are all fungi. Although they are classified as plants, they do not contain chlorophyll and so must depend on other plants for their nourishment. Yeasts are not common in the soil, but molds and mushrooms play important roles.

FUNGUS ROOT RELATIONSHIPS

One significant group of fungi are called mycorrhizae, a term meaning "fungus root." These fungi enter into symbiotic relationships with plant roots of many kinds, and they are thought to be essential for the health of many trees, including pines and beeches. The mycorrhizal fungi are able to convert otherwise insoluble nutrients, most notably phosphorus, into biological forms usable by the host plant. In turn, they receive carbohydrates from their host plants. Many crop plants are known to enter into mycorrhizal associations. These relationships are most important for plants growing on poor soils, where the fungal ability to extract nutrients from rock particles comes in handy. Mycorrhizae are also believed to protect roots from soil pathogens.

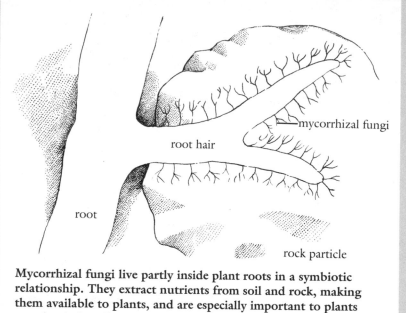

Mycorrhizal fungi live partly inside plant roots in a symbiotic relationship. They extract nutrients from soil and rock, making them available to plants, and are especially important to plants growing in less-than-ideal soils.

Molds may be as numerous as bacteria in soil. In fact, under conditions of poor aeration, low temperature, and acidity, molds outnumber bacteria because they tolerate these conditions more easily. Some molds are detrimental to plant growth. Many plant diseases are caused by soil-dwelling molds, such as *Fusarium,* which causes Fusarium wilt in peas, tomatoes, and melons, and

Rhizoctonia, which causes bottom rot and stem rot in lettuce and cabbage-family plants. The majority of fungi, though, are beneficial to plants and humans. Molds in the genus *Penicillium,* for example, are well-known for their contributions to human medicine. In the soil, molds are especially important for organic matter decomposition and humus formation. Other types of beneficial fungi, known as mycorrhizal fungi, live in association with plant roots and help the roots absorb nutrients from the soil.

Algae

Algae are single-celled plants, usually containing chlorophyll, and are slightly less numerous in the soil than fungi. Blue-green algae are common in many kinds of soils, but are particularly important in wet soils because of their tolerance for high moisture levels and ability to fix atmospheric nitrogen. All algae growth is greatly stimulated by farm manure.

Nematodes and Other Microfauna

Microscopic soil animals, including nematodes, protozoa, and rotifers, are known as microfauna. Nematodes, also commonly called threadworms or eelworms, are extremely widespread and numerous

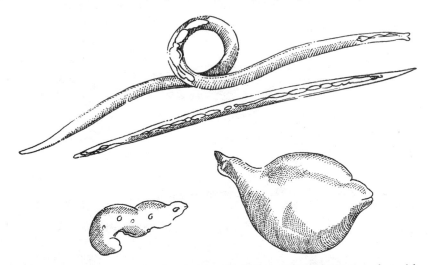

Most soils are full of nematodes, many of which are beneficial types that aid in decomposition and pest control. Others feed on and damage plant roots. Nematodes vary widely in size, but they are all too small to be seen without a microscope.

in most soils. Although they are often thought of as troublesome plant pests, the most common kinds help break down organic matter or prey on bacteria, algae, or other soil animals. Some parasitic nematodes are used as biological control agents for soil-dwelling pests such as cabbage root maggots.

Protozoans are one-celled animals. They are larger than bacteria and often use them as a food supply. Another group of microorganisms, the rotifers, is common in wet soils; they feed by spinning around and sweeping food particles into their "mouths."

Earthworms and Other Macrofauna

Larger soil animals—those we can see without a microscope—make up the macrofauna of the soil. Many animals, from tiny spiders to burrowing prairie dogs, make their homes in the soil. Of the macrofauna, the earthworm is most closely identified with soil health (see "The Noble Worm" on the opposite page). Other small soil animals include mites and spiders, beetles, springtails, flies, termites, ants, centipedes, and slugs, as well as the larval forms of many butterflies and moths.

Many of these animals play an important role in breaking down organic materials into smaller pieces and simpler compounds. Earthworms and other burrowing creatures help to aerate the soil

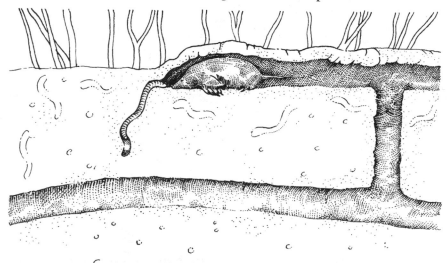

You may not be pleased with the tunneling work of small mammals like gophers, voles, and moles, but these creatures do their part for the soil community by mixing and aerating soil and preying on pests.

THE NOBLE WORM

A good earthworm population is a sign of healthy soil. Unparalleled as soil excavators, earthworms spend their lives ingesting, grinding, digesting, and excreting soil. As much as 15 tons per acre goes through all the earthworm bodies in that piece of ground every year! Earthworm casts, the lumpy, soil-like excretions of the worms, are richer in nutrients and bacteria than the surrounding soil. The casts may add up to as much as 8 tons per acre in cultivated fields. No wonder Charles Darwin extolled earthworms as the "intestines of the soil."

The contributions of worms to drainage and aeration, soil aggregation, and transport of nutrients from the subsoil is significant as well. The miles of tunnels they excavate as they eat are vital to air and water circulation, and the mucous secretions that lubricate their route help hold soil particles together to create a good crumb structure. Because earthworms like cool temperatures, they retreat to deeper soil levels during hot weather and bring back nutrients from the subsoil when they come up again.

The earthworm *Lumbricus terrestris* is the most common of about 200 known species. Interestingly enough, it's not native to North America, but came with the Europeans and turned out to be better adapted to cultivated conditions than its native predecessor. Earthworms, unlike the types used for worm composting, prefer cool temperatures—about 50°F is optimum. They need good aeration and enough but not too much moisture. Some species can tolerate fairly acid soils, but most require adequate calcium supplies and thus a more neutral pH.

During northern winters, earthworms migrate as much as 3 to 6 feet below the surface. A sudden cold snap can catch them off guard, however, and kill them before they reach shelter—a good reason to mulch gardens in the fall. Earthworms are also sensitive to many pest and weed control chemicals, as well as most highly soluble synthetic fertilizers, which are very salty.

The best way to attract and nourish earthworms is to feed them lots of organic matter. Peel back a layer of mulch that has been in place for at least a few days, and you will see the evidence of their activities—little piles of castings next to their tunnel entrances—and the worms themselves, working on your behalf.

with their tunnels, and they move organic matter from the soil surface down into the root zone. Some animals are significant as plant pests. Mammals such as gophers and other burrowers may be a nuisance when they decide your broccoli looks good to them; however, they, too, contribute to the soil ecosystem by keeping pest populations in check, mixing soil, and depositing droppings.

THE ROLE OF PLANT ROOTS

Plant roots themselves play an important role in soil ecology. The area immediately surrounding plant roots, known as the root zone or rhizosphere, is where it's all happening. The largest numbers and kinds of organisms are found in the uppermost layers of the soil, closer to fresh sources of air, water, and food. But biological activity happens even at fairly deep levels, especially where earthworms and other animals burrow and deep-rooted plants grow. A soil such as that found under permanent grass sod, totally permeated by fibrous masses of roots, has a healthier, more robust microbial population than a soil used for cleanly cultivated row crops.

Connecting Plant to Soil

There are many ways in which plant roots interact with the rest of the soil community. Most of the important soil processes, especially nitrogen fixation and mycorrhizal associations, take place in the root zone. Roots serve as homes for nitrogen-fixing bacteria and

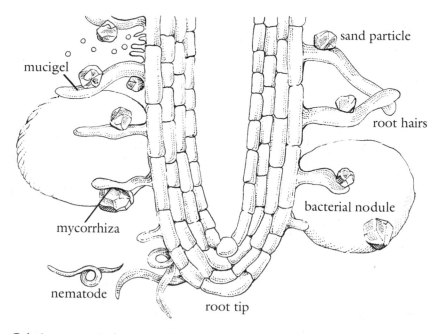

Gelatinous mucigel surrounding the root connects the plant to the soil. It's here that nitrogen fixing and other chemical and microbe interactions take place.

phosphate-scavenging mycorrhizal fungi, which help enrich the supply of these nutrients for the whole soil community. The outer coating of the growing root tip, called the mucigel, is a gelatinous substance secreted by the root and a rich mass of microbes and chemical nutrients that connects the plant to the life of the soil.

Growing roots are also continually sloughing off dead tissue, an excellent food for microorganisms. (For this reason, the roots of a green manure crop often contribute more organic matter than the part of the plants you see above the surface.) Roots also give off certain biochemical compounds called exudates, which can inhibit competing plant species by a process called allelopathy. Winter rye, for example, gives off exudates that suppress couchgrass growth. Black walnuts, which produce the exudate juglone, are well-known for their allelopathic nature.

FEEDING AND CARE OF SOIL BEASTIES

The billions of organisms that make up the soil community are dependent on you for their health and well-being. If you provide for their basic needs and cultivate properly to avoid disturbing them too much, the soil organisms will thank you with a healthy, productive soil that your plants will thrive in.

THE BASIC DIET

Like all living things, the creatures of the soil community need food, water, and air to carry on their activities. A basic diet of plenty of organic material, enough moisture, and well-aerated soil will keep their populations thriving.

Food

Soil creatures thrive on raw organic matter with a balanced ratio of carbon to nitrogen, about 25 to 30 parts carbon to 1 part nitrogen. Carbon, in the form of carbohydrates, is the main course for soil organisms. Given lots of it, they grow quickly, scavenging every scrap of nitrogen from the soil system to go with it. That's why adding lots of high-carbon materials to your soil can cause nitrogen deficiencies in plants.

In the long term, carbon is the ultimate fuel for all soil biological activity, and therefore of humus formation and productivity. A balanced supply of mineral nutrients is also essential for soil organisms, and micronutrients are important to the many bacterial enzymes involved in their biochemical transformations. See Chapter 3 for more information on supplying organic matter to your soil organisms.

Air

Air is crucial for soil health, although certain bacteria can live without it (see "Bacteria and Breathing" on page 29). No amount of fertilizing can compensate for lack of air. Plant roots can't take full advantage of available nutrients if they are suffocating. Much effort in soil management is directed toward improving soil aeration. Later on, we'll explore techniques you can use to increase air penetration in your soil.

Water

Water is also strictly essential, but too much water can mean too little air. The ideal biological environment consists of a thin film of moisture clinging to each soil particle, with lots of air circulating between the particles. Rain and irrigation add needed soil moisture, but good soil structure is required to conduct moisture upward from reserves in lower soil layers. For more details on how soil structure relates to soil moisture, refer back to "Structure and Aggregation" on page 10.

CHOOSING CULTIVATION TOOLS

Knowing how to work the soil benignly is as important for ecologically aware gardeners as knowing how to make compost. When left undisturbed, soil communities tend to reach a balance that preserves nutrients and organic matter. Human invasion of the soil with gardening implements upsets that balance. Tillage and cultivation have a profound impact on drainage, aeration, and structure. The history of agriculture has demonstrated many of the consequences of destructive practices on soils.

The best way to work the soil is not to work it at all. Gardeners who follow Ruth Stout's "no dig" system are practicing a form of no-till gardening. (See "Further Reading" on page 263 for a listing of Ruth Stout's no-till gardening book.) Avoiding tillage does not mean avoiding work, however. Stout's methods involve large quantities of mulch, which must be gathered, transported, and spread. Although perennial gardening and edible landscaping are increasing in popularity, annual plants—including most garden vegetables— require you to disturb the soil.

Tilling the soil and cultivating to control weeds affect the entire soil community, not just the intended crop. If you do have to disturb the soil, there are several things you can do to minimize the damage to the soil community.

Avoid deep tillage. Keep organic residues in the top 2 to 3 inches of soil, so microbial activity can quickly get to work to decompose them.

Protect soil structure. Avoid breaking up soil aggregates and ruining capillary action by pulverizing the top layers too finely or working the soil when it is wet.

Keep the soil loose. Avoid compaction caused by frequent passes with heavy equipment, walking on the soil, and working soil when it is wet.

Tools for Hand Tillage

In this age of mechanization, it is easy to forget that the most effective and sometimes even the easiest way to work the soil is with hand tools. Well-designed hand tools, properly used, are a pleasure to work with. They don't consume nonrenewable fossil fuels, they're quiet, and they're less likely to damage soil than are machines. They also offer the bonus of healthy exercise—who could ask for more?

You can work surprisingly large areas of land using only hand tools. Most of the world's agriculture, in fact, is performed without benefit of internal combustion engines. Start by choosing the right tools and learn the best way to use them.

Spades and spading forks are good primary tillage tools, for preparing new garden sites or turning over established beds. Squared-off, flat-bladed spades are better adapted to most garden digging than are curved-bladed shovels. Keeping your spade sharp will reduce the amount of work entailed in using it. Spading forks are indispensable for loosening and aerating garden beds and incorporating many green manures.

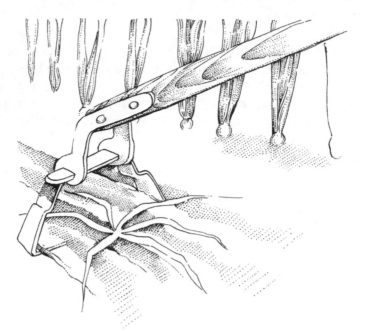

A stirrup hoe slices off young weeds with a swinging motion, saving time and labor.

Hoes are primarily cultivating tools, although heavier types may be used for chopping, digging, forming raised beds, and similar jobs. Cultivation hoes—such as oscillating stirrup hoes or scuffle hoes, colinear hoes, and swan-neck hoes—make the job nearly effortless if you catch weeds when they are young. Keep a good sharp edge on your hoe.

Wheel hoes, illustrated on the opposite page, are nifty tools for more serious gardeners; they can accept a large selection of attachments, including larger oscillating hoes. They cleanly slice off weeds just below the surface, using a back-and-forth motion. If you plan your bed spacing to accommodate wheel hoe implements, you can cultivate several acres of vegetables with this tool.

Rotary Tillers

Rotary tillers are versatile tillage tools, very effective at pulverizing soil, incorporating organic residues, and preparing a smooth seedbed—which is why they are so popular with gardeners. The tillers use a set of blades turning at high speeds to smash up soil and anything else in their path. Self-powered garden tillers come in many

Wheel hoes use a back-and-forth motion to decapitate weeds just below the soil surface. In larger gardens, this tool is a back saver.

sizes, from small, inexpensive front-tined models that are light-weight and easily portable to heavy-duty rear-tined types suitable for managing up to 5 acres. Tractor-driven models are increasingly being made for lawn and garden tractors.

Overuse and misuse of these machines is dangerous to healthy soil. Tillers can cause compaction through the downward force of their blades beating on the soil. Even worse, though, overzealous tilling can destroy the soil structure, leaving it in the form of a fine powder that can easily be blown about by the wind. Tilling also sev-ers the top layer of soil from contact with the lower layers, prevent-ing capillary action from bringing up crucial soil moisture to plant roots.

To avoid those problems, use your tiller carefully. Here are some guidelines to preserve your soil community:

• Restrict use of your tiller to jobs that require it, like incorporating green manures and crop residues. Don't use it for routine cultivating or just to mix in soil amendments or cover seeds. For those jobs, use a rake instead.

• Keep tiller passes to the minimum necessary to accomplish the job.

• Finish off seedbeds with a hand rake, rather than tilling until the surface is finely pulverized.

Other rotary tools, such as the rotary spader, are gaining interest among vegetable growers. Used extensively in Europe, this tool offers all the versatility of the rotary tiller but works with a digging action, like a bunch of little shovels going around. This requires less force on the soil and is less damaging than regular rotary tillers.

Harrows

Farmers use harrows to break up the clods formed by plowing and to smooth out a seedbed. These useful tools are also available for lawn and garden tractors. Harrows can serve quite well as primary tillage tools, especially if the soil is already in good tilth.

A harrow attachment for your garden tractor breaks up clods and rakes the soil smooth without causing severe damage to the soil community.

Disc harrows come in various sizes and configurations, from fairly massive ones capable of cutting through tough sod (which can also damage soil structure with their weight) to small, closely spaced discs used for fine seedbed preparation. They are very useful for chopping in green manures and crop residues.

Springtooth, spiketooth, or drag harrows are like big rakes, their teeth dragging along the surface to make air passages and to lightly bury surface debris. Springtooth harrows and variations on the theme are commonly used for cultivating jobs as well. Homemade drag harrows, consisting of pieces of chain dragged behind a tractor, work well for mixing manure and compost into the soil surface. These harrows are also good for covering seeds of green manures and other broadcast crops.

CHAPTER 3

HUMUS AND SOIL HEALTH

Fragrant, earthy humus is the cornerstone of the soil ecosystem. This crumbly, dark brown stuff that makes our gardens grow is totally a product of soil biological activity. From a soil organism's viewpoint, humus is ideal material to live in. It's chock-full of nutrients, offers a favorable pH, is porous and spongy to permit air penetration, and can hold moisture without becoming soggy. In this chapter, you'll learn how preserve the humus that's already in your soil and how to add more to keep your soil healthy and productive. To find out more about how building soil humus fits into your overall soil-care program, see Chapter 6.

ALL-NATURAL HUMUS

If anyone has succeeded in synthesizing humus in a laboratory, it's a well-kept secret. Humus is a mixture of complex compounds. Some of it is made up of gums and starches synthesized by soil organisms, primarily bacteria and fungi, as they consume organic debris; the rest is plant residues such as waxes and lignins that don't readily decompose.

Just as wine can vary widely in quality, so can humus. Its qualities will reflect different origins and composition. And just as different wines are suitable for different culinary purposes, the various types of humus serve varying soil functions. Some of the benefits humus provides to soil include the following:

• **Water retention.** Humus can hold the equivalent of 80 to 90 percent of its weight in water. Soil that is rich in humus is more drought-resistant.

• **Good soil structure.** Humus is light and fluffy. It allows air to circulate easily and makes soil easy to work. Also, the sticky gums secreted by microbes in the process of forming humus hold soil particles together in a desirable crumb structure.

• **Early soil warming.** Humus is usually a dark brown or black color, which helps warm the soil quickly in the spring.

• **Nutrient retention.** Humus holds mineral nutrients safe from being washed away in rain or irrigation water, yet in a form that is readily available to plants. Ample reserves of humus provide additional plant nutrients in times of need.

• **Balanced pH.** Humus moderates excessive acid or alkaline conditions in the soil, a quality known as buffering.

• **Trapped soil toxins.** Humus can immobilize many toxic heavy metals, preventing them from becoming available to plants or other soil organisms. (See Chapter 7 for more information on dealing with contaminated soils.)

ORGANIC MATTER OR HUMUS?

Although some people use the terms interchangeably, not all organic matter is humus; humus is a form of organic matter that has undergone some degree of decomposition. There is no hard-and-fast dividing line, but instead there is a continuum with fresh, undecomposed organic materials (manure, sawdust, corn stubble, kitchen wastes, or insect bodies) at one end and stable humus, which may resist decomposition for hundreds of years, at the other.

After you add organic matter to the soil, it is broken down by soil organisms into various compounds, including different forms of humus. Humus that can still decompose readily is known as effective or active humus. It consists of a high proportion of fulvic acids, simple organic acids that are soluble in either acids or bases. Although this type of humus is an excellent source of plant nutrients, which are released as soil organisms break it down further, it is of little consequence for soil structure and long-term tilth. Active humus is mainly derived from the sugar, starch, and protein fraction of organic matter.

COLLECTING COLLOIDS

One of the most important characteristics of humus is its colloidal nature. Colloids are substances composed of a lot of tiny particles suspended in a gel-like mass, giving them a large surface area in proportion to their weight. Physically, colloids tend to be sticky and absorbent. Protein, which makes up all living cells, is a colloid. Other examples of colloids are milk, mayonnaise, rubber, and gelatin. Clay is also a colloid, and the clay component of the soil behaves similarly to humus.

Colloids are covered with many negatively charged particles. This makes them able to hold on to positively charged chemical particles, many of which are important soil nutrients. In the soil, colloids are important temporary storage sites for these nutrients, including calcium, magnesium, potassium, and others. As plants take up the nutrients dissolved in the soil solution, more nutrients are released from the colloids, ensuring a steady supply for the plant roots. Humus can hold many more times the amount of plant nutrients as other soil colloids, making it critical for building and maintaining soil fertility. The colloidal nature of humus also helps it to act as a buffer to soil acidity, meaning it can minimize changes in soil pH. This is beneficial for plants and soil organisms, both of which can be harmed by rapid pH changes.

Humic acids characterize more stable or passive humus. Humins, which are highly insoluble and may be so tightly bound to clay particles that microbes can't penetrate them, are the main constituents of the most stable humus. Because stable humus resists decomposition, it does little to add nutrients to the soil system, but it is essential to improving the soil's physical qualities. Carbon-14 dating has revealed that very stable humus complexes may survive unchanged for thousands of years. Stable humus originates from woodier plant residues that contain lots of cellulose and lignin.

HOW HUMUS WORKS

The status of soil organic matter and humus is constantly changing, due to the activities of all the creatures in the soil community. These creatures are most active under optimum conditions for soil biological activity: plenty of moisture, well-aerated soil, and warm temperatures. The fresh supplies of raw organic matter you add to the soil keep the process of organic matter decomposition and humus formation moving.

Anything that harms or disrupts a member of the soil community can lead to a form of indigestion of the soil. For example, if large amounts of nitrate fertilizer flood the soil system, the bacteria responsible for converting protein fragments into nitrates will be suppressed, in turn "backing up" the whole organic decomposition process. They'll recover after a while, but if this process is repeated year after year, the capacity of that soil to digest fresh organic matter will be seriously damaged.

HUMUS AND FERTILITY

The process by which organic matter and humus break down and release nutrients into the soil is called mineralization. Humus is the product of organic matter mineralization, but it, too, can be mineralized under the right conditions. Mineralization is fastest when conditions are perfect for bacteria to reproduce: high aeration, adequate moisture, good pH, and balanced mineral nutrients.

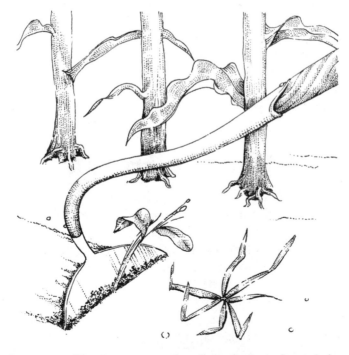

The simple process of hoeing your garden gives a boost to bacteria by bringing in air. As the bacteria go to work mineralizing humus in the soil, your plants get an extra dose of nutrients to speed up sluggish growth.

Take advantage of the extra nutrients released from mineralization by cultivating and irrigating when your plants need a growing boost. If your garden seems to be growing sluggishly in midsummer, speeding up the process will help stimulate growth by releasing nutrients. Cultivation speeds up the process by introducing air. If soil is dry, irrigation will also stimulate mineralization. Dark mulch or row covers will increase soil temperature and encourage faster release of nutrients to plants.

It's important to understand the concept of "enough" when you choose to stimulate mineralization. Too quick a release of nutrients from organic matter can cause problems that parallel those of overfertilizing: plants can take up excess nitrate nitrogen (causing weak, succulent growth), or nutrients can leach into groundwater. Regularly adding organic matter to soil will lead to the formation of new humus and help to replace the reserves lost to mineralization. Humus tends to accumulate fastest under conditions unfavorable to mineralization: cool temperatures, low pH, and poor aeration. Too much humus can be just as bad as not enough. The extreme example of going too far is a peat bog, composed of almost pure humus. Once again the key is balance: An active, healthy biological population will continually be mineralizing humus at the same time that humus is being formed. As you become attuned to the signs of biological activity and health in your soil, as well as the rhythms of growth and rest in your garden, you will develop a better sense of "enough" when it comes to humus formation and decay.

BUILDING HUMUS

The most direct way to increase humus in your soil is to put it there yourself in the form of compost. (The details of how to make and use compost are in Chapter 4.) But good gardening practices and soil improvement also depend on building humus by adding organic matter to the soil. Mulch, green manures, sheet composting, and wise use of uncomposted manure all add humus to the soil and keep the soil community happy and thriving.

MULCHING

Mulch is most often used to suppress weeds and protect soil from temperature extremes. But it's even more important as a means

Supplement the nutrients in mulch with an application of compost. Peel back the mulch and spread compost, then replace the mulch and renew if necessary.

of building soil humus. For perennials and trees, it is practically essential. Permanent mulch will decompose gradually as it is mixed into the soil by the activity of earthworms, who love its cool, moist environment. Mulch applied to annuals can be worked into the soil at the end of the growing season, or left to protect it over winter and worked in the next spring.

Many gardeners rely solely on mulch as a source of soil organic matter and nutrients, adding fresh materials in the course of the growing season as lower layers decompose. Supplement the nutrients in mulch and improve the carbon:nitrogen ratio at soil level by peeling back the mulch and spreading some compost or other organic fertilizer beneath it.

Mulch not only feeds the soil, it also improves the biological habitat. It keeps temperatures a little cooler in summer and a little warmer in winter, which is especially helpful for earthworms. Mulching is vitally important in dry climates to preserve soil moisture. In vegetable gardens, it helps protect crops from having soil splashed on them when it rains, preventing the spread of soilborne disease. Finally, mulch can provide a quick soil cover to protect newly tilled and seeded land from erosion.

Sometimes mulching isn't appropriate. Mulch can worsen drainage problems and lead to increased fungal diseases in plants growing on heavy, wet soils. Regardless of what kind of soil you have, always be careful to leave a gap between mulch and plant stems for air circulation. Pests like slugs and snails may make their home in mulch, and field mice love to nest in it. If you're a northern gardener, wait till soil is fully warm before applying mulch to annual gardens, especially around heat-loving plants such as tomatoes and melons.

You can usually find appropriate mulch materials in your neighborhood, free for the hauling. The most common materials are hay, straw, leaves, and sawdust, but any dry, fluffy organic waste can be suitable, including cardboard and newspapers. See Chapter 9 for more details about mulch materials.

GROWING GREEN MANURES

A green manure is any crop that is grown for the purpose of feeding soil organisms as opposed to being harvested for human or animal consumption. Green manures require very little cash outlay—just the price of some seed—and produce organic matter right where you need it, without transporting and spreading. Even fast-growing annual weeds such as pigweed and lamb's quarters (shown in the illustration on the opposite page) can function as free green manures—just be sure to work them in before they set seed!

Benefits of Green Manures

Green manures are an easy way to increase soil fertility and organic matter. The fibrous, matted root systems of perennial crops such as clover or clover-grass combinations are excellent for building up soil organic matter reserves. Fast-growing annual grasses, such as sudan and millet, also work well. You'll find more information on choosing and using specific green manure crops under "Selecting a Green Manure" on page 53.

Deep-rooted green manure crops, such as alfalfa and sweet clover, absorb nutrients from the subsoil and eventually make them available to more shallow-rooted crops. All legumes, from peas and beans to clover and vetch, contribute substantially to nitrogen, phosphorus, and potassium nutrition of crops that follow. Alfalfa is renowned as the heaviest nitrogen producer. In general, perennials

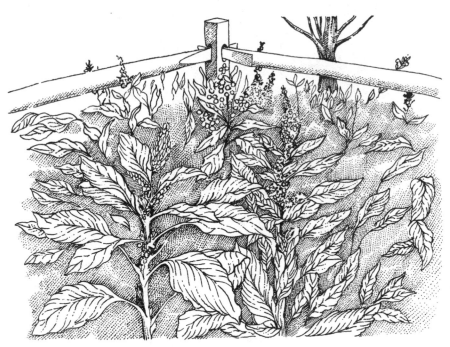

If weeds like pigweed and lamb's quarters take over a corner of your garden, consider it a free planting of green manure. Then, before they have a chance to set seed, till or dig them under to build organic matter.

and biennials such as sweet and red clover fix more nitrogen per given area than annuals such as beans or peas. Nonleguminous plants such as grasses and buckwheat also contribute to nutrition, especially if incorporated when young and succulent.

Green manures also protect soil from exposure to wind, sun, and rain, and so they prevent erosion. When used to protect soil from erosion, these plantings are usually called cover crops. Winter cover crops help trap snow, which insulates the soil from extreme cold and contributes moisture for the following growing season. Some gardeners prefer to plant a crop like oats that will be killed by cold weather; the soil will be protected, but the cover crop won't regrow in the spring.

Use green manures as smother crops to help rid your garden of troublesome weeds. Some species actually suppress weed growth through root exudates. (For more details, see "The Buckwheat–Winter Rye Cure for Couchgrass" on page 54.) They also help prevent buildup of insect pest and disease populations, which often cannot live on the green manure plants.

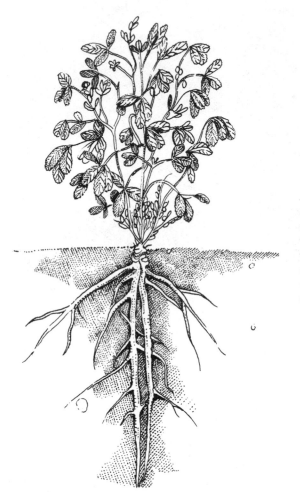

Alfalfa is a well-known soil improver, breaking up compacted soils with its deep roots and working with bacteria to fix nitrogen from the air into a form usable by plants.

Green manures in small gardens. Green manures are generally most useful in vegetable gardens or for preparing the soil for perennial plantings and orchards. If your garden is small, there are some tricks you can use to maximize the benefits of green manures. Interplanting clover between widely spaced rows of crops like corn or squash is a great way to protect the soil and add extra nitrogen, without interfering with the growing food crop. Mow taller-growing green manures periodically and use them to mulch the crop.

You can also undersow a fast-growing food crop with a green manure. Undersow after the food crop is up and growing, so the green manure becomes established before the crop is harvested. If you have late broccoli or greens, for example, undersow winter rye in time for it to get established, while the food crop is still growing.

Integrate certain green manure species, such as low-growing clovers, into a perennial garden as "living mulch." In established orchards, you can interplant green manures between trees, especially when they're still young. One New York orchardist sprinkles a handful of fava beans around each of her young trees in the spring to provide an extra nitrogen boost with minimal effort.

Gardener beware. If your timing is off, some green manures can come back to haunt you. If you don't till in winter rye early enough in the spring, it will regrow vigorously and have to be eradicated like any weed. If you allow buckwheat to go to seed, it, too, will show up again the next season, although rarely vigorously enough to be much of a problem.

Some green manures are more of a challenge to work into the soil, especially with hand tools, than others. Clovers and other leguminous crops, which contribute the most organic matter and nitrogen, also take the most energy—mechanical or human—to turn under.

In arid areas of the high plains, where soil moisture reserves are limited, green manures can sometimes deplete the water that following crops will need to grow. Eventually, however, the increased organic matter they create will help these soils conserve more moisture.

Selecting a Green Manure

Green manures differ widely in adaptability to climate and soil conditions. Buckwheat, for instance, will grow virtually anywhere. Alfalfa, on the other hand, is more finicky about drainage, pH, and mineral balance than most. Use the guidelines that follow to help you find the crop that fits your soil needs and conditions.

Many of these crops are even more useful when combined with others having complementary qualities. Field peas with oats or barley, and winter rye with hairy vetch are popular combinations. Alfalfa or clover and various grasses are often combined in hay mixes; the grass stimulates the legumes to fix more nitrogen than they would if planted alone. Grains and grasses also offer physical support and shelter to slower-growing legumes.

Non-leguminous crops. Non-leguminous crops do not support nitrogen-fixing bacteria, but they are generally fast-growing and produce lots of leafy green material. Non-leguminous crops include buckwheat, small grains, grasses, and brassicas.

Buckwheat is one of the most commonly grown green manures. It germinates easily, tolerates depleted, acid soils, and grows quickly. Although it makes little contribution to organic matter, it is able to scavenge phosphorus from insoluble soil fractions and is an excellent smother crop for weeds. It is very frost-tender. When incorporating it, mow or scythe the buckwheat and let it dry for a day or so before working it into the soil. Its succulent stems can create somewhat anaerobic conditions if incorporated when green.

THE BUCKWHEAT–WINTER RYE CURE FOR COUCHGRASS

Couchgrass (*Agropyron repens*), known variously as quack grass, twitchgrass, and witchgrass, is one of the gardener's most dreaded weeds. Spreading vigorously by underground runners, it is virtually unstoppable by normal cultivating methods and positively thrives on being chopped up and replanted with a rotary tiller.

Deal this pesky weed a real one-two punch with a combination of buckwheat and winter rye. (You can use other small grains, but rye is the most effective against couchgrass because it produces exudates, which actually suppress the weed's growth.) In order for this to work, you have to devote a whole growing season to cleaning up a patch of land, but it's worth it. Here's how to do it:

1. Sow a thick crop of buckwheat as early as possible, after all danger of frost is past. Be careful to get even coverage—any holes in the buckwheat canopy will allow the couchgrass to gain a foothold and come back in force the next year.

2. When the buckwheat reaches its stage of maximum leaf coverage—just after it starts to bloom—cut it down, till it in, and replant another buckwheat crop right away.

3. When the second crop of buckwheat begins to flower, cut it down, till it in, and replant the plot with winter rye.

4. Allow the rye to grow over winter, and work it in as early as possible in the spring. The couchgrass roots will have exhausted their nutrient reserves trying (unsuccessfully) to compete with the buckwheat, and they'll have little defense against the aggressive rye.

Small grains, such as millet, oats, barley, rye, and wheat, can serve many purposes when used as green manures. Millet is a fast-growing warm-season crop that works well as a smother crop. Oats will grow in cooler seasons, but will not overwinter in the North. They are often used as a "nurse crop" for slower-germinating, fine-seeded legumes like clover and alfalfa, shading the tender seedlings from sun and wind until they get established. Mow the oats when they reach the flowering stage, and the legumes will be ready to grow on their own. Rye, wheat, and barley all make excellent winter cover crops. Wheat and barley are less tolerant of low pH than rye.

Grasses such as sudan, sorghum, annual ryegrass, and brome have good, fibrous root systems that contribute to organic matter. Sudan and sorghum are fast-growing warm-season grasses, similar to millet. Annual ryegrass and brome make good winter cover crops. All are tolerant of a wide range of soil conditions.

Brassicas (also known as cabbage-family crops) include rape, kale, typhon, oil radish (canola), and mustard. Some of them make nutritious livestock fodder and are commonly grown for their oil-rich seeds. They grow rapidly in cool spring and fall conditions and work well as a smother crop but will not survive a northern winter. They tolerate many soil conditions but prefer a pH close to neutral. Avoid growing them in areas where you will plant other cabbage-family crops such as broccoli because they can harbor common pests and diseases. (For more hints on planning crop rotations, see "Crop Rotation: The Why and How" on page 192.) Brassicas can easily become a weed problem if allowed to go to seed.

Legumes are excellent for green manures. Besides contributing lots of organic matter, they can even return more nitrogen to the soil than they took from it, giving you a net nitrogen gain. Commonly grown legumes include alfalfa, clovers, beans and peas, and vetches.

Alfalfa is the champion nitrogen fixer. If allowed to grow for two years or more, it will fix up to 200 pounds per acre—more than you need for an average vegetable garden. Alfalfa is very deep root-ed; this makes it valuable for bringing up subsoil nutrients. It's unsuitable for shallow, poorly drained soil. It demands a near-neutral pH and adequate phosphorus and potassium to do well. If you are growing alfalfa or some other legume-grass sod as part of your garden rotation, mow the tops regularly and use them for mulch.

There are many different types of clovers, of which the most

ADDING AMENDMENTS WITH GREEN MANURES

If your soil is in need of mineral nutrients, a good time to spread rock powders is when you seed your green manure (see Chapter 5 for more details about using rock powders). Many green manures are able to use otherwise-unavailable nutrients in rock powders, to the benefit of the crops that follow. Other fertilizer materials, such as manure, compost, and high-analysis organic wastes, are most valuable if spread when you incorporate a green manure crop into the soil, especially if the green manure is coarse and mature. As they break down the organic matter, soil organisms will tie up the nitrogen, preventing it from leaching or evaporating into the atmosphere until it is gradually released for your main crop in the next growing season.

common are red, alsike, sweet (yellow and white), white Dutch, crimson, and ladino. Many are biennials: They flower and seed in the year after they are sown, then die off. Their maximum contribution to organic matter and nitrogen fixation is in the spring after they are planted.

The sweet clovers are excellent subsoilers, like alfalfa, but are better able to extract their phosphorus and potassium from insoluble rock sources. They like a near-neutral pH. Alsike is the most tolerant of acid soils, and red clover is also somewhat tolerant. Crimson clover is well-adapted to hotter southern conditions. White Dutch clover is a low-growing perennial that tolerates traffic well, and it is often used between permanent beds as a living mulch.

Beans and peas are large-seeded annual legumes. Fava beans, cowpeas, field peas, and soybeans are popular choices. Some people use old garden pea or bean seeds in their green manure mix rather than taking a chance of poor germination in the garden. Fava beans and field peas germinate easily and grow well under poor conditions. Soybeans and cowpeas are warm-season crops, helpful for protecting southern gardens during summer rest periods. These crops are commonly grown in combination with a small grain, such as oats or barley.

Vetches are annual vining plants with a spreading habit; they are good nitrogen fixers and biomass producers. Hairy vetch is a favorite for northern gardeners, since it overwinters well, and is often used in combination with winter rye. Common and purple vetches are less cold-tolerant but are useful even in the North where a winter-killed cover crop is desired.

Other legumes used for green manures include lupines, black medic, trefoil, hairy indigo, and lespedeza. Lupines are annuals sometimes grown as cattle fodder, which overwinter where winters are mild; they can be among the highest biomass producers in southern areas. Hairy indigo and lespedeza are good southern summer cover crops that help improve poor soils. Hairy indigo is resistant to root knot nematodes and can be valuable in rotations where this pest is a problem. Trefoil and black medic are both forage crops, similar to alfalfa but better able to tolerate wet, acid soils.

Planting Green Manures

Considering all the benefits they have to offer your garden, green manure crops are remarkably easy to grow. Simply prepare as smooth and even a seedbed as possible for your green manure, especially for the finer-seeded legumes. After sowing, rake or till lightly to cover the seed. Avoid deeply tilled, fluffy seedbeds—the seeds will germinate much better if they are pressed firmly into the soil, allowing moisture to be wicked up around them. Water if necessary. If you are sowing during a dry season, a light sprinkling of mulch to conserve moisture can greatly increase your chances of success.

Sow your green manure by hand, covering the area as evenly as possible with the right amount of seed. If you have a large area to plant—at least ¼ acre—you may find it worthwhile to invest in a hand-cranked broadcast seeder (illustrated on page 58) that consists of a canvas pouch (worn around your neck) with an adjustable opening for setting seeding rates. Lawn seeders may also be suitable for the job.

Working In Green Manures

To make your green manure crop available to the soil organisms, you'll need to chop up the plant material and mix it as thoroughly as possible into the top few inches of soil. To determine the best time to work in your cover crop, see "Getting the Timing Right" on page 62. Hand tools are often sufficient for buckwheat and young small grains. If the cover crop has died over winter, you can simply rake away the dry residue to expose the soil, and plant your transplants without further preparation.

A canvas broadcast seeder cranks out seeds for green manures at a customized rate, allowing you to cover large areas quickly.

When it's time to work the green manure into the soil, some form of power equipment is generally advisable on all but very small patches. For most gardeners, rotary tillers are the best available power tools to use for green manuring.

Before incorporating a tall-growing green manure into the soil, mow it or cut it down and allow it to dry for a couple of days first. This will make the stems more likely to crumble as you till, rather than getting tangled up in the tines. They'll also be in better condition, assuming there is adequate soil moisture, for microbes to attack them. If growth is really tall and rank, rake it aside before you till, then use it for mulch rather than trying to grind it into the soil.

Even a heavy-duty garden tiller will have tough going on a thick, well-established planting of a grass-legume mixture. In this case, plowing—as shallowly as possible—may be the best alternative. Although plowing disrupts the soil community and can cause soil compaction, these problems are offset by the high level of organic matter the soil will gain from the sod. Sometimes you can hire someone with a tractor-driven tiller or rotovator to work in a new patch of sod. Disc harrows are often the farmer's tool of choice for working in a green manure crop.

Use a garden fork to incorporate an early-season crop of an annual green manure. Mix thoroughly into the top few inches of soil, and wait several days before planting.

Wait at least a few days to allow the green manure to decompose before planting a main crop. Some organic acids harmful to germinating seeds are often produced in the early stages of decomposition.

SHEET COMPOSTING

Sheet composting is another means of building humus. It involves spreading the organic materials directly where they will be needed, to decompose in place. When you work in a green manure crop, you're practicing a variation of sheet composting.

Traditional sheet composting requires lots of organic material and a garden plot that you are willing to leave unplanted for a year or two. To prepare the plot, first mow or cut down any existing vegetation and leave the trimmings on the plot. Then spread your other organic material in an even layer over the area. Use whatever you

(continued on page 62)

GREEN MANURES

Type	When to Sow	Seeding Rate (lbs. per 1,000 sq. ft.)	Where Adapted in United States
Legumes			
Alfalfa	Spring	1	All
Beans, fava	Spring or fall	6	All
Beans, soy	Spring	5	All
Clover, alsike	Spring to late summer	0.5	North
Clover, crimson	Fall	1	South to Central
Clover, ladino	Spring to late summer	0.5	All
Clover, red	Spring to late summer	0.5	North to Central
Clover, sweet (yellow or white)	Spring to summer	0.5	All
Clover, white Dutch	Spring to summer	0.5	All
Cowpeas	Spring	5	South to Central
Hairy indigo	Spring	0.5	Deep South
Lespedeza	Spring	1	South
Lupine, white or blue	Spring	1	All
Pea, field or Austrian	Spring or fall	5	All
Trefoil, birdsfoot	Spring	0.5	All
Vetch, hairy	Spring to fall	1.5	All
Nonlegumes			
Barley	Spring or fall	2.5	All
Brassicas (kale, radish, etc.)	Spring to fall	0.5	All
Bromegrass, smooth	Fall	1	North
Buckwheat	Spring to summer	2–3	All
Millet, pearl	Spring to summer	1	All
Oats	Spring or fall	2.5	All
Rye, winter	Fall	2.5	All
Ryegrass, annual	Spring or fall	1–2	All
Sudangrass; sorghum	Spring to summer	1	All
Wheat, winter	Late summer	2–3	All

Comments

Perennial; deep-rooted; needs good drainage; neutral pH

Annual; edible bean

Annual

Tolerates wet, acidic soil

Winter annual

Tolerates traffic; wet or droughty soil

Perennial; good phosphorus accumulator

Needs good drainage and neutral pH; yellow clover tolerates dry conditions

Perennial; tolerates traffic

Annual; drought-resistant

Needs warm, well-drained soil; resists root knot nematode

Good for restoring eroded, acidic soil

Tender annual; good biomass producer

Annual; best combined with grain crop

Comparable to alfalfa but tolerates poor soil

Best combined with rye; good biomass producer; winter-hardy

Needs pH 7–8; use spring varieties in North

Fast-growing, cool season; do not allow to set seed

Cold-hardy winter cover crop

Tender; good smother crop; phosphorus accumulator

Fast-growing warm-season smother crop; tolerates low pH

Tolerates wide pH range; avoid heavy clay; good "nurse crop" for legumes

Suppresses weed growth when turned under

Widely adapted; rapid grower

Tolerates poor drainage; rapid biomass producer in hot weather

Needs pH 7–8 and good fertility

GETTING THE TIMING RIGHT

As your green manure crop grows, its nutrient composition changes. The stage of growth at which you work it into the soil has a major effect on the value it provides to your soil community. The tricks are to know what your soil needs most, to choose the most appropriate species, and to understand the characteristics of the crop you're working with. On the opposite page, you'll find a discussion of the general characteristics of all green manure crops at the different growth stages. To find out about how long a specific crop will take to reach the final stage, look on the seed label for the number of days to maturity.

When buckwheat and other green manures bud and flower, they have reached midseason growth. They'll decompose more slowly than early-season growth, but add more organic matter to the soil.

have in abundance: grass clippings, hay, straw, leaves, apple pomace, kitchen scraps, garden plant residues, or any other organic material suitable for composting. (For more ideas of suitable materials, see "Gathering Raw Materials" on page 75). For a heavier material like apple pomace or kitchen scraps, the layer should be up to 3 inches thick. Lighter materials, such as grass clippings, can go in a layer up to about 6 inches deep. And with very loose materials like leaves, hay, or straw, you can apply a layer as much as 8 inches deep.

Early Growth

This stage occurs just at or before plants reach full vegetative cover. When plants are tilled in at this stage, the young, succulent growth decomposes quickly (provided there is plenty of moisture and aeration) and releases mineralized nutrients for the crops that follow. Carbon:nitrogen ratios are low, so microbes lock up little of the nitrogen, leaving it immediately available to crops. Decomposition is fairly thorough, leaving little contribution to stable humus.

Midseason Growth

Plants at this stage are budding or flowering but have not yet set seed. Growth is coarser, and more powerful cultivating equipment may be required to incorporate it into the soil. Plants decompose more slowly and may not provide surplus nutrients to the crops immediately following. Carbon:nitrogen ratios favor maximum microbial growth, and the nutrients they use will become available later in the season. Plants tilled in at this stage contribute more organic matter to the soil, improving structure and tilth.

Late Growth

Plants that reach the late growth stage have set seed. In most cases, you'll want to avoid allowing green manures to form seed. Their mature growth is difficult to work into the soil, and they break down very slowly, offering minimal nutrients to following crops. On poorly drained soils, though, working in the coarse growth of a mature green manure crop can help to improve soil aeration. The slow breakdown of the material will also contribute to the formation of stable humus in any soil.

Once you've spread the material, you can usually just let it rot in place for a season and then work it in, either in the fall, before planting a winter cover crop, or the following spring, when preparing the plot for a main crop. But if you apply wet, high-nitrogen organic materials like apple pomace or kitchen scraps, it's best to work them into the soil immediately. Alternatively, you could cover them with a layer of high-carbon mulch, like leaves or straw, and let them break down on the soil surface before working them in.

Work in perennial green manures and those in late-season growth with a rotary tiller. Till lightly to incorporate it into the first few inches of soil.

Compared to regular composting, sheet-composting is a labor-saving method for adding lots of organic matter to your soil, but it does have some disadvantages. Wet, smelly materials, for example, are very difficult to sheet compost effectively. And since sheet-composted materials need time to be broken down by soil organisms, they won't provide immediate fertility for a crop. Sheet composting also is not suitable for wet or poorly aerated soils, because a lack of air in the soil will slow down decomposition and leave you with a large mess to handle. But if you have the time and the materials on hand, sheet composting can be a great way to build soil fertility.

ADDING ANIMAL MANURE

Like mulching, planting green manures, and sheet composting, applying animal manures to your soil is an effective way to build soil humus. You can apply fresh manure right to the soil and treat it as

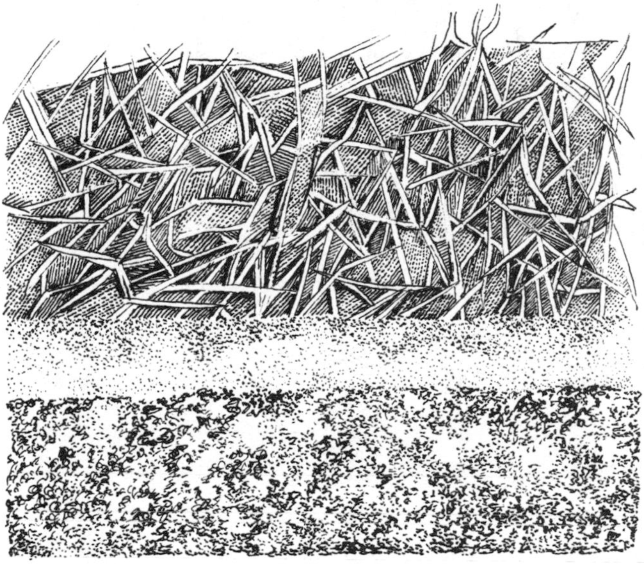

high-carbon layer

high-nitrogen layer

soil

If you spread a wet, high-nitrogen material like apple pomace or kitchen scraps on top of the soil, either till it in right away or cover it with a thick layer of high-carbon mulch (like straw) to prevent nitrogen loss.

you would sheet compost, or compost it in a pile before applying it. The best way to handle the manure depends on several factors, including what animal it came from, how old it is, and how it was stored before you got it. For complete information on using animal manures to build soil fertility, see "Manures" on page 118.

CHAPTER 4

COMPOST: GARDENER'S GOLD

Compost is magical stuff—complex, much studied, but still a little mysterious. It's unequaled as a soil conditioner and a source of plant nutrients. From humble beginnings—a pile of weeds, grass clippings, kitchen scraps—the natural process of decay leads to dark, rich, crumbly compost.

This decomposition and recycling occurs in soil everywhere, effortlessly—in lawns, forests, parks, prairies, cornfields, wetlands, and, of course, gardens. Billions of decomposer organisms flourish in decaying material. They reduce plant tissue, manure, and other animal and plant residues into simpler compounds, which in turn become nourishing fare for food-producing plants. The process of decay is the vital link that completes the food cycle. Without it, life on Earth would grind to a halt.

Cultivating the soil or clearing plant debris from the garden hastens the breakdown of organic matter. Rain leaches out nutrients, and "trash" that has been removed has no chance to decay and enrich the soil. This is why it's important to continually replenish organic matter in the soil. One of the best ways to do this is by making and spreading compost. In this chapter, you will learn several different techniques for producing compost for your garden. For complete details on using compost as part of a complete soil-care program, see Chapter 6.

THE BENEFITS OF COMPOST

Composting is a low-cost, nonpolluting alternative to sending household food and yard wastes to the landfill. If your community has a municipal composting program, you can most likely donate your leaves and clippings, although many municipalities won't accept grass clippings. But why should you give away this green gold? On the compost pile, yard wastes will recycle themselves quickly. Some food wastes from the kitchen can be tossed on the pile, too, to become a resource rather than a liability.

BETTER SOIL

Humus, the main component of finished compost, is essential for creating an ideal soil structure. It increases the soil's permeability to air and water, and helps the soil retain moisture during droughts. Soil high in humus holds together, resisting erosion by wind or water.

Compost provides ideal conditions for microorganisms to proliferate, offering them abundant raw materials and an increased supply of air and water in the soil. And it stimulates biological activity by inoculating the soil with billions of beneficial microbes.

Compost helps to moderate soil conditions that are either too acid or too alkaline. Because it is composed of a number of complex organic molecules, compost is able to neutralize, to some extent, both excess acidity and alkalinity in the soil solution—regardless of the pH of the compost's original ingredients. This quality is known as buffering.

IMPROVED FERTILITY

Compost is a well-balanced source of most of the nutrients needed by plants, in a form that is available gradually throughout the growing season. Depending on what went into the compost, a given batch may be high or low in certain elements, but most compost offers at least some of everything—especially essential micronutrients.

As it breaks down into humus, compost improves the ability of soil to store many nutrients by increasing its cation exchange capacity (CEC). Humus particles have many negatively charged sites all over their surface. Positively charged cations are held on these sites, protected from leaching away in water, but still available to plant roots. As plants give off hydrogen ions, a waste product that is also positively charged, it is exchanged for needed cation nutrients like calcium, magnesium, and potassium on the humus particles. (For more information on CEC, see "Cations Simplified" on page 99.)

A HEALTHIER GARDEN

Removing garden residues for composting is part of the good housekeeping that makes a healthier garden. Otherwise, plant material left to rot on the surface of the soil could provide a haven for overwintering pests and diseases.

Adding compost to the soil improves plant disease-resistance. In some cases, it can even combat diseases that are already present, through the action of natural antibiotics produced by compost organisms. Compost tea has been found to prevent certain fungus diseases such as mildew, and researchers are now able to produce custom composts that can suppress specific disease-causing organisms such as *Pythium,* a fungus responsible for damping-off problems.

Compost can help detoxify soils that have become contaminated with pesticides, heavy metals, and other pollutants. The composting process itself can break down many harmful compounds. Research has shown that few pesticide residues remain in wastes that have undergone thorough composting. Adding large amounts of humus-rich materials such as leaf mold and peat moss to soils that contain unacceptable levels of heavy metals can help bind the metals into forms that are not available to plants—a process called chelation. (For more information on heavy metals in soils, see "Inorganic Contamination" on page 174.)

HOW COMPOSTING WORKS

The alchemy of composting requires only a supply of raw organic matter, a tool for handling it, and a place to pile it. Other accessories can make things a little easier or more aesthetically pleasing but are rarely essential.

bacteria

fungi and
actinomycetes

earthworms

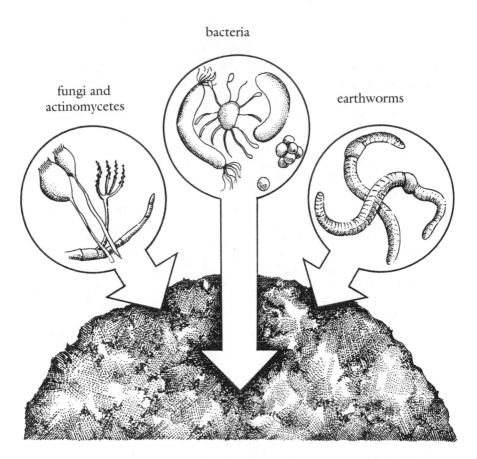

In cooler parts of the compost pile, fungi and actinomycetes proliferate, and earthworms go to work. As the compost pile begins to heat up, warmth-loving mesophilic bacteria predominate. When temperatures get hotter still, thermophilic microorganisms take over.

The basic principles of composting are simple: Combine your ingredients to provide a good nutritional balance, keep the pile well-aerated and moist, and let the compost microorganisms do the rest. An active compost pile, turned once a week or so, will heat up inside to as much as 170°F, speeding the process of decomposition. But if you're willing to wait for your finished compost, you don't even have to turn it.

The compost heap has its own ecosystem, with various organisms playing a central role during different steps of the cycle. As the pile heats up, mesophilic bacteria—those that prefer some warmth—

LAZY COMPOST

If you have the space but not the time or stamina to play with your compost, you can take the passive approach. Compost made the lazy way will heat up at first, but it won't reach as high a temperature as actively turned compost. The maximum temperature of lazy compost will be about 120°F (compared to up to 160°F for actively turned compost), so you can't count on it to kill weed seeds or disease organisms. But some research shows that disease-fighting fungi are more common in compost made at cooler temperatures. The slower process also conserves nitrogen, as long as the pile is protected from the weather.

Build a passive pile on a base of brush on a well-drained site. Add ingredients as you accumulate them, keeping a good carbon:nitrogen balance throughout the pile. As you build up each 4- to 6-inch layer of mixed ingredients, moisten each layer if needed, and cover lightly with soil. Once the pile has reached the right size (at least 3 feet in each dimension), cover it with a layer of straw or leaves and leave it to decompose for six months to a year. The final product may contain undecomposed bulky organic matter. Screen it out and use it to start a new pile.

proliferate. When temperatures get above 120°F, thermophilic, or heat-loving, microorganisms do more of the work. At cooler temperatures, fungi and actinomycetes predominate. Earthworms and other visible macroorganisms also do their jobs at cooler temperatures and on the edges of heating piles.

You can choose from a wide selection of materials and methods to compost successfully, but in all cases the basic principles are the same. Once you understand what the microbes need to flourish, you will know what to do.

FEED THE DECOMPOSERS

The first step to successful composting is providing the right mixture of basic ingredients. Raw organic matter, the basic food for compost organisms, is composed of carbohydrates (carbon) and proteins (nitrogen) in differing proportions. Keeping your small friends well-fed means providing these two food groups in the right balance.

Carbohydrates, which provide energy and cell-building compounds, must make up the bulk of their diet. Protein, which is essential for growth and reproduction, is needed in smaller quantities. A ratio of 20 to 30 parts carbon to 1 part nitrogen is ideal.

Keeping the right balance of carbon and nitrogen in your pile is a big part of successful composting. In general, carbonaceous materials are yellow or brown and dry, bulky, or fluffy. Dry leaves, straw, hay, and sawdust are all high in carbon. Nitrogenous materials tend to be green and wet, succulent, dense, or sticky. Materials such as fresh manure, grass clippings, fish wastes, and soybean meal are especially rich in nitrogen. Some materials, such as rotted manure and food scraps, already have the correct proportion of carbon to nitrogen. As you gain experience, you'll become more skilled at evaluating the approximate carbon:nitrogen ratio of new materials by how they look, smell, and feel.

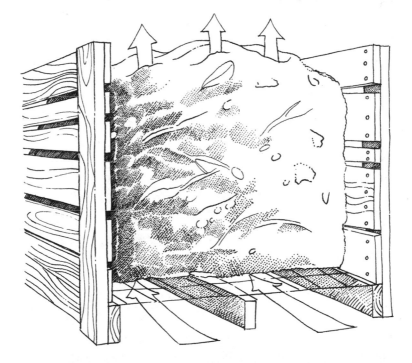

The aerobic organisms that work your compost pile need air to live. Build your heap on a wire mesh bottom or a foundation of brush, so that air is drawn up through the pile.

ONE GOOD TURN
DESERVES ANOTHER

Turning your pile once a week is a good schedule for fast compost. A manure fork is the traditional tool to lift, shake, and mix compost. But if your pile is big or your muscles are small, the thought of turning can be daunting.

To avoid the need for turning the pile, bury perforated drainpipe at intervals within your pile, both horizontally and vertically. Natural convection will circulate air through your pile. Some gardeners use sunflower stalks, which have a central air channel, for this purpose.

Another time-honored trick is to layer poles horizontally into the heap. Withdraw a few every day or so during the major heat buildup. You can also stab the pile with the tines of a pitchfork to open air channels. There is even a tool on the market that has a small umbrella-like mechanism. You insert it into the pile, pull up slightly to open the blades, and twirl it around to make an air pocket.

Turning is the traditional method of adding air, but pipes provide a labor-saving alternative. Place perforated drainpipe horizontally and vertically within the pile to increase air flow.

Compost organisms need other elements, too, such as calcium, phosphorus, sulfur, and micronutrients. Since all organic matter contains small amounts of these elements, as long as the right carbon:nitrogen ration is maintained, these elements are sure to be adequately supplied.

AERATE YOUR COMPOST

Most home composting systems depend on aerobic organisms, which require air to live. Proper aeration is critical to successful composting. A nutritionally imbalanced heap can still decompose—but not if it doesn't get enough air. Fortunately, there are several things you can do to make sure your pile is well-aerated. Start with a well-drained site. A waterlogged pile can't breathe. Compost that sits in a puddle, even for a short time, will wick up the water into all the essential air spaces in the pile. You'll also need to provide air passages beneath the pile. Layer brush or other coarse materials underneath, or make a wire mesh bottom for your bin, so that it sits a few inches off the ground. A mesh bottom is especially effective because air is drawn up through the pile in a chimney effect.

The bulky carbonaceous materials you use in your compost pile create air passages throughout the pile, improving air flow as well as supplying food. Straw is highly prized by some gardeners for its aerating qualities. Be especially careful to avoid large layers of leaves or other ingredients that tend to form impenetrable mats when wet; these include paper, grass clippings, and baled hay. Shred leaves and other coarse debris to fluff them up and avoid problems of matting.

Turning is the traditional method of aerating compost, and frequent turning is the key to quick, hot compost. The more often you turn the pile, the faster the raw materials will decompose and the higher the generated temperatures will be.

KEEP THE PILE MOIST

Your compost pile should be about as moist as a damp sponge. If you can squeeze water out of it, it's too wet. If you're mixing coarse, dry carbonaceous materials with wet, sloppy nitrogenous ones in the right proportions, your ingredients will contain a good moisture level. Here are some other ways to regulate the moisture level in your compost:

• Locate your pile in a well-drained site. But in arid climates, consider digging a shallow composting pit to help trap more moisture.

• If your ingredients are a bit on the dry side, sprinkle each layer with a hose or watering can until there is a good sheen over everything.

• Shape your pile according to your climate conditions. In a wet climate, round the top to shed the rain. In a dry climate, make a shallow depression on top to trap water.

• Use a covering of loose hay or straw to shed excess rainwater and protect your pile from the drying effects of sun and wind. Some gardeners cover their piles with plastic or build bins with lids. A shady, sheltered location offers the same benefits and permits greater air circulation through the pile.

• Check the moisture content when turning the pile. If the pile is soggy, add more absorbent materials, such as leaves or dried grass clippings. If it is dry, give each 6- to 8-inch layer a good sprinkling as you rebuild the pile.

SIZE UP YOUR PILE

Composting works best when the temperature inside the pile stays at about 140°F or higher. Things heat up fast with the right mix of materials, air, and water. But to keep things cozy and cooking, you'll need a pile of a certain size. If the pile is too small, the heat generated by the mesophilic organisms will be quickly dissipated before the pile can reach the right temperature for the thermophilic organisms. A pile must be at least 3 feet high, 3 feet wide, and 3 feet long to provide the necessary mass. A pile that is too big will be hard for you to turn and can become anaerobic in the middle. If you have enough materials, make two medium-size piles instead of one gigantic one.

Bacteria go dormant and compost stops cooking when the temperature drops below 55°F. If properly built, the interior of a compost pile will stay well above that temperature, even in freezing weather. Northern composters sometimes insulate their piles with leaves, straw, or even an enclosure of hay bales to keep things cooking. Decomposition will slow for the winter months, but a pile built in the fall and kept covered should be reasonably finished in spring.

ACTIVATE YOUR COMPOST

Bacteria and fungi are the unseen inhabitants of whatever materials you include in your compost. But they may not be the right mix of the right types for the best composting.

The more diverse your compost ingredients, the more likely

you are to have a good balance of bacteria. The best way to inoculate your pile with the right cultures is to sprinkle a thin coating of good topsoil or finished compost saved from a previous batch over each layer of materials you add. Special commercial compost activators, such as Bio-Dynamic or BioActivator, can also boost your pile's productivity.

GATHERING RAW MATERIALS

Many people find that they can provide all the compost they need from totally "home-grown" sources: household food wastes, newspapers, grass clippings, shrub prunings, weeds, and garden refuse. If you keep poultry, rabbits, or other livestock, you are fortunate in having an assured source of manure. (Dogs and cats don't count—see "What Not to Compost" on page 76 for more details.)

A little looking around is usually all it takes to discover a wealth of compost materials available free for the hauling. Friends, neighbors, and relatives are the best place to start. Ask for the same things you would use at home: leaves, grass clippings, newspaper, and kitchen scraps. Be sure to find out if herbicides or pesticides have been used; avoid adding chemically treated clippings to your compost pile.

Some diligent composters offer to cart away kitchen scraps after every social call. Supply your friends with a 5-gallon plastic pail, complete with tight-fitting lid. This will hold a week's worth or more of goodies. Add a layer of peat moss or sawdust on the bottom to help absorb moisture and odors. Offer to pick up the full one regularly, and leave a fresh empty one in its place—just like a diaper service.

COLLECT FROM THE COMMUNITY

Restaurants and grocery stores, as well as other retail businesses such as florists, throw away a lot of organic refuse. If you are willing to pick it up on a regular schedule, you're likely to find at least one business that will save scraps for you. Food processors, especially if they are small, can sometimes make organic wastes available to home gardeners. Places like cider mills, breweries, sawmills, and flour mills always have wastes to dispose of. Try the small businesses first.

Many communities have composting facilities for at least part of their trash. If yours is one of them, they probably make finished compost available free or at low cost to gardeners. Park services and power companies may also be able to supply chipped or shredded wood wastes.

Horse owners are often more than glad to supply you with horse manure. Check with local farms, race tracks, or riding stables. In addition to manure, farms can be a source of spoiled hay for compost or mulch.

WHAT NOT TO COMPOST

There are a few things that you should keep out of your compost pile if you want the best results. Large or durable items like chunks of wood, bones, shells, and cardboard, for example, will just get in the way. Sometimes they can be used if they are crushed or shredded first.

Feces of humans, dogs, and cats can carry communicable diseases. A small amount of dog manure is no big deal, but cat manure can be especially worrisome for pregnant women and children. Hot composting will kill most pathogens, but certain viruses may be able to survive even prolonged heat. To be on the safe side, avoid adding these materials to your compost pile.

Diseased plants and weeds that have set seed can cause trouble, unless your pile is hot enough to kill the disease organisms and

TOXIC RESIDUES

Toxic residues are an unfortunate fact of life in many organic wastes, especially those from industrial processes. Although most pesticides (including insecticides, herbicides, fungicides, and any other biocides) will degrade when composted properly, there are some that persist. No research exists about the possible dangers of their breakdown products. It's best to avoid heavily sprayed plant wastes, such as highway trimmings where herbicides have been applied.

Some materials known to contain toxic residues or heavy metals include leather meal, cottonseed meal, and paper mill sludge. Glossy, colored printed matter can be a problem in large amounts, although printers are switching to less-toxic inks and paper treatments, and black inks are mostly safe. Recent evidence shows that even colored inks do not pose a hazard of heavy metal accumulation in the quantities used by the home gardener.

seeds. Better not to risk contaminating your whole garden with them. Noxious weeds such as couch grass, Johnsongrass, bishop's weed, comfrey, and Jerusalem artichokes, which reproduce readily from the tiniest bit of surviving root or rhizome, are hard to kill completely, even in a hot pile. Avoid adding them to your compost heap.

Large amounts of fat, oil, or grease will give your microbes indigestion. Smaller amounts may attract rodents and other pests. Oils take time to break down and can slow the composting process. Meat scraps and other animal wastes can also attract unwanted visitors and may create unpleasant odors.

GETTING THE RIGHT MIX

Carbon makes up the bulk of your compost pile. Use as much carbonaceous stuff as you can find—leaves, hay, and straw are all good materials for supplying plenty of carbon. The more carbon you return to your soil, the more you will be building humus. Too much carbon can be easily remedied by adding a little more nitrogen-rich material to balance it. See "Nitro Boosters" below for some suggestions of good nitrogen sources that will help to balance a high-carbon pile.

Use highly nitrogenous materials like grass clippings and fresh manure sparingly. In order to achieve the desired carbon:nitrogen ratio, all you need is a thin covering of a rich nitrogen source over

NITRO BOOSTERS

For compost, the best sources of nitrogen are manures, especially poultry and bird or bat guano. Animal residues (such as fat and meat scraps) have a high nitrogen content, but they also attract pests, so avoid using them in your pile. Vegetable matter that comes from leguminous plants, such as alfalfa, beans, and peas, has a relatively high nitrogen content. So does fresh, green growth, such as young weeds, grass clippings, and green brush. Spoiled grains also are high in nitrogen.

Synthetic nitrogen carriers such as urea or sodium nitrate are a bad idea because these materials can disrupt microbe populations. Moreover, their manufacture consumes vast quantities of natural gas. If you need a concentrated nitrogen source, there are many naturally derived alternatives available commercially. (For more details on nitrogen sources, see Chapter 5.)

COMPOST TROUBLESHOOTING

Remember to check your pile now and then, especially when you turn it. It's easy to solve most problems by adjusting the mix. Here are some commonly encountered compost problems and some tips for remedying them.

Problem	Remedy
Wet, foul-smelling pile	Turn pile and add high-carbon, absorbent materials such as dry leaves and newspaper; protect from rain
Center is dry and materials have not decomposed	Turn pile, thoroughly soaking each layer as it is built; cover with plastic to retain moisture
Pile is damp and warm only in the middle	Increase amount of material in pile; moisten
Pile is damp and sweet-smelling but does not heat up	Add high-nitrogen materials such as fresh manure or green grass clippings; turn pile
Matted, undecomposed layers of leaves or grass clippings	Break up layers with garden fork or put through shredder, then relayer into pile
Large, undecomposed items	Screen out undecomposed items and use as base for next pile

several inches of a carbon source. Too much nitrogen can be harmful if the materials don't allow good air penetration because they are wet and heavy—as is often the case. This can create the foul odors of putrefaction. Excess nitrogen may also be washed out in rainwater, adding to pollution, or dissipated as ammonia gas, creating another unpleasant smell (although it's usually only temporary). A high nitrogen content creates very high temperatures, which can dry out the pile and oxidize the humus into a less stable and less beneficial form.

It's a good idea to become familiar with the carbon:nitrogen (C:N) ratios of various bulky organic materials. That way, you'll be able to decide what is needed to balance your compost ingredients. Keep in mind that anything that has partially decomposed, such as an old pile of sawdust, has a lower C:N ratio than a similar but fresh material. "Carbon:Nitrogen Ratios of Bulky Organic Materials" below shows the C:N ratios of many common compost ingredients. A good balance of these high-carbon and high-nitrogen materials, along with adequate moisture, will provide ideal conditions for microbes to break down the organic matter into rich humus. If your pile doesn't heat up, if it smells bad, or if the organic material doesn't break down, something is lacking in the mixture. If your compost shows any of these symptoms, check out "Compost Troubleshooting" on the opposite page for hints on how to restore the right balance for proper decomposition.

FINE-TUNE THE MIX WITH MINERALS

If you know that your soil requires an extra dose of some particular mineral nutrient, the best way to provide it is through your

CARBON:NITROGEN RATIOS OF BULKY ORGANIC MATERIALS

Materials with a C:N ratio of 30:1 or lower are considered to be high in nitrogen (nitrogenous). Materials with higher C:N ratios are high in carbon (carbonaceous).

Material	C:N Ratio
Vegetable wastes	12:1
Alfalfa hay	13:1
Seaweed	19:1
Manure, rotted	20:1
Apple pomace	21:1
Legume shells (such as peas and soybeans)	30:1
Leaves, dry	50:1
Sugarcane trash	50:1
Cornstalks	60:1
Oat straw	74:1
Chaff and hulls of various grains	80:1
Straw	80:1
Timothy hay	80:1
Sugarcane fiber (bagasse)	200:1
Sawdust	400:1

SOURCE: Reprinted with permission from *The Soul of Soil: A Guide to Ecological Soil Management* by Grace Gershuny and Joseph Smillie. St. Johnsbury, Vt.: Gaia Services, 1986.

compost. By adding mineral amendments directly to your compost, you provide additional nutrients for microbes and turn rock powders into more-usable forms. And you save an extra step when it's time to fertilize the garden.

Rock or colloidal phosphates are excellent materials for enriching the mineral content of your compost. They also contain significant amounts of calcium and micronutrients. Other rock powders such as granite dust and greensand, both sources of potassium and micronutrients, are beneficial in compost. All these materials are more easily used by plants when first processed by compost organisms.

Many people add lime to their compost in order to increase its pH. This is not often necessary or beneficial. Direct contact between lime and any high-nitrogen source is not a good idea because lime reacts with nitrates to liberate ammonia gas. If you need lime, apply it directly to the soil or mix it with the finished compost.

The microbes inhabiting your compost heap can often benefit from the calcium in the lime, but other forms of calcium, such as eggshells or finely pulverized oyster, crab, or clam shells, will serve as well. Bonemeal and wood ashes are also rich in calcium. Use ashes sparingly to avoid overdosing the system with soluble potassium and salts. If your compost is intended for acid-loving plants such as rhododendrons, camellias, and blueberries, avoid adding ashes, pulverized shells, or eggshells.

Seaweeds are especially valuable sources of potassium, iodine, boron, and a host of balanced micronutrients. To boost your compost's content of these micronutrients, add seaweed extract (known as kelp extract) when you water the pile. Aquatic weeds, such as water hyacinths, and autumn leaves are also richly endowed with a wide assortment of nutrients. If you plan to apply your compost to a soil that is lacking in potassium, consider adding hay to your compost pile—it is rich in this nutrient.

HEAPS, BINS, AND OTHER COMPOST STRUCTURES

The easiest structure to use for compost is no structure at all. If you have the space, you can just leave a passive pile in a discreet corner of your yard for a year or two until it's ready (see "Lazy

Compost" on page 70), or you can turn it by forking it from one place to another, moving the pile a few feet each time.

Easily movable structures made of wire mesh are usually called pens, while more substantial wooden or concrete containers are called bins. Make your own, or try one of the many kits on the market. Many gardeners place wire pens right in the garden, where they are convenient for weeds and garden debris and handy for spreading when the compost is finished. Recycled hardwood pallets provide a quick and easy compost bin—just stand them up, pound in fenceposts to hold the corners together, and line the inside with chicken wire to keep varmints out.

Completely contained barrel or drum composters are ideal for small yards in urban areas, where space, appearance, and sanitation are important. The basic design consists of a plastic or metal barrel mounted on a stand that allows it to turn. A drawback is that at a

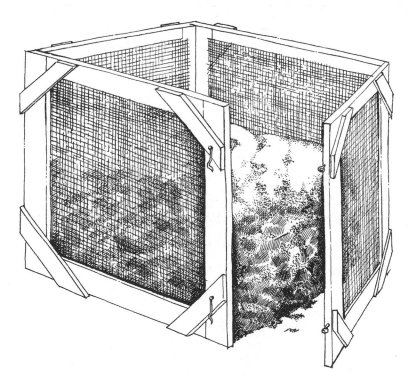

This flexible compost bin costs little if you use recycled materials, and it can be moved around the yard to where you need it. To turn the pile or remove compost, undo the latches for access.

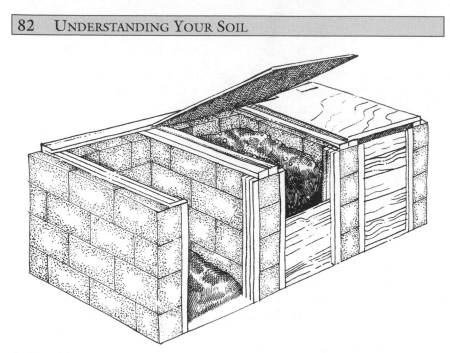

A three-bin system is a convenient way to make a big batch of compost. You can keep slow-decomposing yard wastes in one bin, kitchen scraps and other materials in a faster-composting balance in another bin, and finished compost in the third. Or use one bin for finished compost, and turn your compost-in-progress from one of the remaining bins to the other.

A compost barrel, homemade (as here) or store-bought, keeps the pile out of sight—a consideration for city gardeners. When your compost needs aerating, the crank makes it easy to turn the barrel.

certain point you have to stop adding fresh ingredients to allow the composting process to complete, which takes about two weeks.

LET WORMS DO THE WORK

Did you know you can compost even in an apartment? Earthworm boxes, made from a few boards or a plastic trash can, can be set up indoors. If you're careful about constructing and maintaining the box, it will cause virtually no odors and can be used all winter long. One square foot of surface area is needed to digest each pound of waste material generated per week.

For an average household, a suitable size for a worm box is about 2 feet wide, 2 feet long, and 1 foot deep. You can buy a commercially available worm bin or make your own out of untreated lumber. A plastic storage bin of roughly the same dimensions or larger is also suitable. No matter what type of container you use, make sure that it has holes in the bottom for good aeration and drainage. Drill at least six ⅛-inch holes in the bottom and some more holes around the sides.

You can compost with worms outdoors or indoors. If you place your bins outdoors, make sure you set them in a shady spot so the worms don't get too warm. In cold climates, the worms may not live over the winter. In these areas, you may want to sink your worm container 1 to 2 feet into the ground, or you can surround the container with bales of straw and cover it with a layer of loose straw. You can also just stick with indoor worm composting. Set the container in a comfortably warm, out-of-the-way place.

OUTDOOR WORM COMPOSTER

You can make a simple earthworm composter from a stationary barrel or drum. (Some people use standard plastic trash cans with lids.) Cut out the bottom, and bury the barrel 1 to 2 feet deep in the ground in a shady spot. Cut some holes in the aboveground part for ventilation to encourage the earthworms, who are the real compost turners here, to invade. Then layer your material in the barrel until it's full, put the lid on, and leave it alone for a year or two. The earthworms will come up into your composter from the soil below and return to the soil to overwinter, leaving behind their nutrient-rich castings.

INDOOR WORM BARREL

Here's a simple design for an indoor worm barrel that you can make out of materials available at your local building supply center. This setup is large enough to handle a steady supply of kitchen scraps and produce plenty of worm castings for your house and garden plants.

Metal knitting needle, sharp awl, or ice pick
10- to 20-gallon plastic trash can, with lid
Water
Gravel
Scrap wood
Plastic dishpan or a sheet of plywood covered with plastic

1. If you are using the knitting needle, heat its tip by holding it over a stove burner. Be sure to use a pot holder to protect your fingers. If using the awl or ice pick, you do not need to heat them.

2. Use the knitting needle, awl, or ice pick to poke about 24 holes into the lid of the trash can and the same number around the bottom of the can about 3 inches from the base. Air will enter through the holes in the lid, and water will drain from holes above the base. If using the knitting needle, open a window or do this step outdoors, and avoid breathing the fumes created when the hot needle pierces the plastic.

3. Pour 3 inches of water into the bottom of the trash can—to just below the ring of holes.

4. Fill the trash can with 6 inches of gravel.

5. Lay the scrap wood across the top of the gravel. This wooden barrier will prevent mixing gravel with the compost when you renew the worms later.

6. Place the trash can on the plastic dishpan or on a tray of plastic-covered plywood to catch any spills.

WORM CARE AND FEEDING

Once you have a container for your worms, you'll want to prepare their bedding. Make a mix of topsoil and manure, then mix that with an equal amount of wet peat moss. Add an equal measure of hay, leaves, shredded newspaper, or dried grass clippings, and soak overnight. The next day, squeeze out the water and fluff up the bedding material. Place it in a 4-inch layer over 1 to 2 inches of pebbles

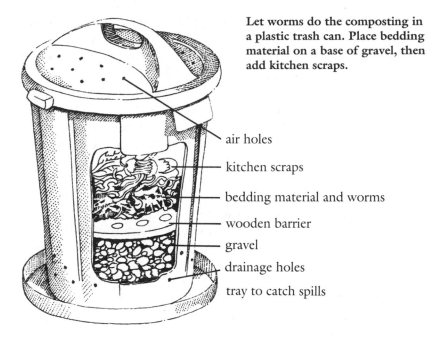

Let worms do the composting in a plastic trash can. Place bedding material on a base of gravel, then add kitchen scraps.

air holes

kitchen scraps

bedding material and worms

wooden barrier

gravel

drainage holes

tray to catch spills

or sand for drainage, and wait a day to see if it heats up. If it does, wait another couple of days for the bedding to cool before introducing your worms. They will not thrive in high temperatures. (For this reason, it's also essential to keep your worm farm out of direct sunlight!)

When the bedding is cool, it's time to add the worms. Ordinary earthworms (*Lumbricus terrestris*) are not the best species for making compost because they prefer temperatures cooler than those found within most compost piles. Worms commonly sold for fish bait—red worms (*Lumbricus rubellus*) and brandling worms (*Eisenia foetida*)—are better. (To find out where to buy worms, see "Worms" on page 261.) Two pounds of worms, which can number 1,200 to 2,400, is enough to get you started.

Release the worms on top of the bedding. Once they've burrowed in, feed them some kitchen leftovers, going easy on onions, garlic, and other strong seasonings. It's best to avoid meat scraps or heavy grease. Worms always appreciate coffee grounds and grains. Feed lightly—2 to 3 pounds at a time—until you get a sense of how quickly they consume what you give them. Spread their food on top of the bedding. You can add a layer of hay or straw on top, and peel it back when it's feeding time.

Worms need the same amount of moisture as other compost creatures. You shouldn't need to add water after putting in the initial bedding; if you've set it up right, any excess water from garbage should drain away harmlessly.

Every month or so, add another couple of inches of bedding material as the worm population increases. Give the whole bin a turning and fluffing at the same time. Wait a couple of days before feeding again to let your worms recover from being disturbed. In three months, you can remove some of the extra worms and start another colony. Or you can let the worms alone; their population will naturally adjust to the size of their container.

The real payoff to composting with worms is the product they leave behind. Every six months or whenever the bin seems too full, remove the worm compost by scalping, as shown in the illustration below: Scrape off a thin layer of compost from the top of the bin, and let the worms retreat from the light to a deeper level. Repeat the process until they are concentrated in a small area. Add fresh bedding and food to regenerate the colony. The compost itself will be practically pure worm castings — one of the richest, most balanced nutrient sources you can offer your garden.

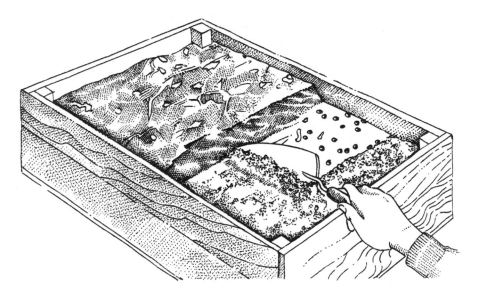

"Scalp" your worm box to remove the nutrient-rich worm droppings (castings), using a hand trowel to scrape off a thin layer from the top of the box. Work slowly to give the worms time to retreat to lower layers.

USING FINISHED COMPOST

When compost from your worms or from a conventional pile is finished, it will smell pleasant—earthy, sweet, and fragrant. It'll be a uniform dark brown or black color, with a moist, crumbly, spongy texture. If you had a hot compost pile, the temperature of the pile will drop, and further turning will not stimulate it to heat any more. Original materials will be largely unidentifiable (except for the occasional corncob or eggshell).

For most uses, compost should be well-finished—that is, aged long enough so that the decomposition process has stabilized. Unfinished compost has been found to retard germination and growth of many plants, such as lettuce, tomatoes, and other vegetable seedlings. But some plants, such as corn and squash, seem to thrive on partly finished compost. Use finished compost when applying it in seed-starting mixes or shortly before sowing. You don't need to be as cautious when applying compost for fall soil preparation or mulching.

If you want to be sure your compost is aged well enough, perform a germination test. Put a few seeds of lettuce or radishes in a tea made by soaking a couple of tablespoons of your compost in a cup of water, and put an equal number of seeds from the same packet in a cup of distilled water. Soak overnight. Lay each batch on a paper towel, and keep them both warm and moist in a plastic bag for a few days until they start to sprout. If the distilled-water-treated seeds germinate better, let your compost age longer; before using it in germinating mixes, store it for a few months in a sheltered location or in bags that allow it to breathe.

Use well-finished compost at any time of year, in as large an application as you wish. There is little loss of nutrients by leaching, and it will not burn plants. Even small amounts will help stimulate soil microbial activity. Later in this book, you'll find details on how to use compost for specific purposes with plants such as vegetables (Chapter 8), flowers (Chapter 9), lawns (Chapter 10), and trees and shrubs (Chapter 11). Whenever you add compost, work it into the surface of the soil as much as possible, to give the microbes a chance to get to it. Adding it before you apply mulch is also a good approach.

Keep in mind that you'll be adding a shot of nutrients with the compost. For some applications, this may not be beneficial: In late summer, the added nitrogen will stimulate tender, cold-sensitive growth in woody shrubs and trees. Remember, too, that the release of nutrients from compost depends on the rate of microbial activity. If your plants are suffering from cold, wetness, or drought, adding compost may not provide the nutrient boost you anticipated because these conditions make the microbes sluggish, too. For information on how to evaluate commercial composted products, see "Compost-Based Fertilizers" on page 106.

BALANCING SOIL CHEMISTRY AND FERTILITY

One goal of organic soil care is to reduce or even eliminate your need for purchased fertilizers. As you get a feel for your soil and your garden, learning to stimulate the nutrient-producing microorganisms in your soil and keeping them thriving with plenty of organic matter and compost, you'll find less and less need to pay for products in bags.

There's no substitute for long-term soil building, but purchased organic fertilizers and amendments do have their place. They can help correct soil imbalances and deficiencies and maintain overall nutrient levels in your soil. These materials also play an important role in restoring damaged or abused soil and can help you handle problems such as drought stress, water stress, transplant shock, and cold soil. In this chapter, you'll learn how store-bought or homemade fertilizers and amendments can make your soil and your garden more productive. See Chapter 6 for details on how these materials fit into your total soil-care program.

HOW DOES YOUR GARDEN GROW?

Before you can decide what nutrients may be needed to restore and maintain your soil's health, you have to find out what it's lacking. Your own observations are a good place to start. The information you gathered about your soil in Chapter 1 will help you evalu-

89

ate your soil's condition. Your plants can also give clues to nutrient deficiencies or other soil problems. A soil test is another good way to find out exactly what's going on in your garden.

LISTEN TO WHAT YOUR PLANTS ARE SAYING

The condition of your plants can tell you a great deal about nutrient problems. Some deficiency symptoms are easier to diagnose than others. Lots of things can cause problems that look like nitrogen deficiency, for example. For clues to what your plants might be lacking, see "Nutrient Deficiency Symptoms" on the opposite page.

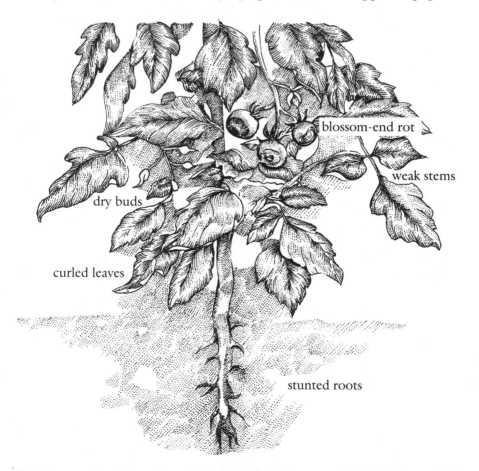

blossom-end rot

weak stems

dry buds

curled leaves

stunted roots

This tomato plant shows signs of distress that point to a calcium deficiency. Curled, unusually dark green leaves, dry buds, weak stems, stunted brown roots, and blossom-end rot are all symptoms of too little calcium.

NUTRIENT DEFICIENCY SYMPTOMS

When a plant is not getting the mineral nutrients it needs, it gets sick. By observing the symptoms of its illness, you can often determine which nutrient is in short supply. Keep in mind that some of these problems may be due more to a mineral imbalance than to an actual lack of the nutrient in question. Before deciding to add a particular nutrient, especially a micronutrient, to your soil, it is a good idea to verify your diagnosis with a soil or plant tissue test.

Nutrient	Deficiency Symptoms	Where Likely to Occur
Macronutrients		
Nitrogen (N)	Pale or yellow leaves, starting with older ones; stunted growth; nitrogen-deficiency symptoms are normal during fruiting	Light, heavily leached soils, or in fast-growing crops that aren't well-fertilized
Phosphorus (P)	Purplish undersides of leaves and stem; pale, dull leaves with yellow, streaked margins; poor flowering and fruiting	Cold, wet conditions; acidic or alkaline soils; excess aluminum
Sulfur (S)	Pale or yellow leaves, starting with new growth	Rarely a problem if there is minimal soil organic matter
Calcium (Ca)	Leaves curled or scalloped, may be abnormally dark green; stems weak; buds dry or drop early; roots stunted and brown; lettuce tip-burn; tomato and pepper blossom end rot	Acidic soils; excess potassium; temporary problems may be due to drought or excess moisture
Potassium (K)	Lower leaves spotted, mottled, or curled; scorched leaf margins; weak stems; fruit shriveled; reduced disease resistance; poor storage qualities	Light, acidic, highly leached soils; excess calcium or magnesium
Magnesium (Mg)	Loss of color between leaf veins; leaves thin, brittle, curled, bronzed, or purplish red color; twigs weak with brown spots on petioles	Light, acidic, highly leached soils; excess calcium or potassium

(continued)

NUTRIENT DEFICIENCY SYMPTOMS—
CONTINUED

Nutrient	Deficiency Symptoms	Where Likely to Occur
Micronutrients		
Boron (B)	Yellow leaves, larger veins remaining green, starting with growing tips; short, slender stems	Light, acidic, highly leached or alkaline soils; excess calcium or potassium
Copper (Cu)	Similar to iron deficiency; collapsed spots on young leaves; poor maturation and keeping quality	Muck or peat soils; excess phosphorus, zinc, or nitrogen
Iron (Fe)	Shoot tips and terminal leaves die back from the tip; leaves pale or don't form; twigs die back or have brown spots; sour fruit; soft onions	Alkaline soils; excess phosphorus or aluminum
Manganese (Mn)	Leaves mottled, blotched, with dead spots; poor bud formation with dead margins and tips, early drop; twigs die back or have brown spots; early tree defoliation; striped corn leaves	Alkaline soils; excess iron, copper, zinc, calcium, or magnesium; toxicity may occur on some acidic soils
Molybdenum (Mo)	Buds die; stems are short; leaves are thick, curled, and brittle; fruit, tubers, and roots are discolored, cracked, and misshapen; corky core of apples; poor nitrogen-fixation in legumes	Very acidic soils; excess sulfur or copper
Zinc (Zn)	Similar to nitrogen deficiency, with rolled leaf margins; cabbage-family crops have narrow, whip-tailed leaves; poor nitrogen-fixation in legumes	Wet, heavy soils; excess phosphorus, nitrogen, calcium, or aluminum

SOURCE: Reprinted with permission from *The Soul of Soil: An Ecological Guide to Soil Management* by Grace Gershuny and Joseph Smillie. St. Johnsbury, Vt.: Gaia Services, 1986.

Before you rush to fertilize, rule out other causes of plant stress. Remember that cold, wet soils and drought slow down biological activity and therefore nutrient availability. If the problem is caused by an insect or disease, fertilizing may help your plants recover, but more immediate relief may be needed.

TESTING YOUR SOIL

If you detect signs of trouble that you can't solve by the usual means, or if your garden isn't performing as well as you think it should, you may need to find out what's going on chemically. That's where soil testing comes in.

The most common tests are for pH, magnesium, phosphorus, potassium, calcium, and often nitrogen levels. Optional tests may include sulfur and such micronutrients as boron, zinc, manganese, iron, and copper. Because most organic fertilizer materials contain a reasonable range of essential micronutrients, these specialty tests are only worthwhile if you have cause to suspect a deficiency problem. Some labs will provide a measurement of your soil's organic matter level and nutrient holding capacity and indicate percentages of various minerals to help evaluate whether they are in balance. Labs may also test for possible soil hazards, such as aluminum, sodium, and heavy metals.

A single soil test is a good way to get acquainted with the details of your soil. But once you start, make soil testing a regular part of your gardening calendar. Test at about the same time every year. Procedures and results may vary from one lab to another, so use the same testing service each year so that you can compare results. You're most likely to get recommendations for your particular soil conditions from a lab based closer to home. By reviewing the results year to year, you'll know if you're making progress in building fertility. Once your soil-building program and nutrient reserves are well-established and your garden is flourishing, you may decide that yearly testing is unnecessary.

You can get a professional test done through your state's Cooperative Extension Service or through any of a number of private soil-testing laboratories (see "Soil-Care Supplies" on page 260 for their addresses). If you're scientifically inclined and want immediate results, a home soil test kit may be for you.

To get the most accurate view of your soil, prepare a separate sample from each area—lawn, flower bed, and vegetable garden, for

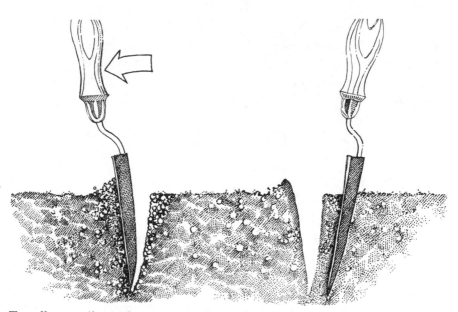

To collect a soil sample, use a trowel to make a cut in the soil and gently rock the trowel to loosen the area right in front of it. Then make another cut about 1 inch behind the first cut, arcing slightly to taper on either side. Now remove the inch-thick slice of soil, being careful to keep it intact.

example. If one area has been fertilized regularly and another has been neglected, or if you'd like to put some flower beds in a corner that has just been cleared of brush, it's worth it to pay for separate soil tests. Or you can take a combined sample by collecting soil from all over your yard and garden and mixing it together for a single test.

Exam Time

Spring is a popular time for testing, but it's a busy season for soil labs, and you may lose precious time waiting for results to come back. If you test in early spring, some nutrients may test low due to sluggish biological activity in cold soil.

Testing in the summer gives you an idea of nutrient availability at the peak season for biological activity, so you won't end up adding more fertilizer than you really need. It also allows you to spread certain rock powders such as lime in the fall or winter.

Fall is a good time to test soil, too, when you're taking care of end-of-the-season cleanup. A fall test gives you a better picture of nutrient reserves left after the season's production. But don't put it

WHY BOTHER?

As a gardener, how much faith should you put in soil test results? Any test is, at best, a rough approximation of what occurs in your soil. You may be sampling to a depth of 6 inches, but many plant roots go deeper, finding subsoil nutrients that may not be present in the upper layers. Nutrient availability changes depending on weather and time of year. The sampling procedure itself is imprecise, and different soil-testing laboratories use different techniques and chemical extractants to test for the same nutrients.

In developing recommendations, a lab compares its results with experimental data based on similar tests done on comparable soils. This provides information about how much fertilizer was needed to increase the crop response, rate of growth, or total yield. Much of this experimental work is incomplete, and the research is often done on soils lower in organic matter than might be found in a well-managed garden.

So why bother getting your soil tested at all? Soil testing can help you monitor how your soil changes over time. Many tests, such as those for pH, calcium, magnesium, and potassium, are reliable indicators of possible deficiencies. Perhaps most important, comparing test results with your own records and observations gives you more confidence in your ability to manage the soil.

off too long, or you'll run into the same cold-soil problem as you would in early spring.

In nontemperate climates such as the Deep South and the West, your timing will be different. If your garden goes through a resting phase, a time when it's too hot or too dry to grow most crops, test at the start of that season. You will then have some time to plan your fertility improvement program for the peak growing season.

Keeping Track of pH

Monitoring soil pH can help you maintain proper mineral balances. The process is relatively easy and accurate. Good-quality pH meters are available through garden supply catalogs, starting at about forty-five dollars. The testing procedure involves adding a soil sample to distilled water (available at local grocery or drug stores) and placing a sensitive probe in the solution.

You can also test pH using litmus paper or any inexpensive home soil test kit. These tests are less accurate than the precise readout of a pH meter, but they're fine for most home garden uses.

Do a quick check of soil pH using sensitive litmus paper. Following the directions on the package, mix up a slurry of soil sample and distilled water, insert the test strip, and match it to the color chart supplied.

SOIL pH AND FERTILITY

The pH scale, from 1 to 14, is a measure of the acidity or alkalinity of soil, determined by the concentration of hydrogen ions in a water or salt solution. A pH of 7.0 is neutral. Acidity is indicated by a pH below 7.0, and pH values of over 7.0 indicate alkalinity. But determining soil pH is more than just a finding a number—it is a way of finding out valuable information about your soil's fertility.

The pH of your soil has a great effect on what nutrients are available to your plants. The solubility (availability to plants) of most nutrients is highest at a slightly acid pH; the optimum range is 6.3 to 6.8. This pH range is also ideal for many soil organisms, including earthworms and bacteria. As the pH approaches strong acidity or strong alkalinity, some nutrients become insoluble (unavailable to plants) while others become more soluble and may even be released in toxic amounts. Extreme acidity and alkalinity will also disrupt the soil organisms, interfering with the breakdown of organic matter and the resulting release of nutrients.

Keeping your soil at a balanced pH is a major part of maintaining soil health and fertility. If you have an acid soil, amendments like calcitic and dolomitic limestone can raise the soil pH. If your soil is alkaline, you can add various forms of sulfur or acidic organic matter, like peat or pine needles. For details on managing soils that are excessively acid or alkaline, see "Acid Soil" on page 163 or "Alkaline and Saline Soils" on page 167.

USING YOUR TEST RESULTS

When you send in your soil test, it's a good idea to ask the lab to recommend organic amendments. If your lab report only gives recommendations for chemical fertilizers, you'll need to figure out organic alternatives by using tables that give an analysis of nutrients available in organic materials. Sometimes it is easy to find an organic substitute using these tables, but keep in mind that these tables don't always indicate the total amount of nutrients available if the organic material is used over time in healthy, biologically active soil. As a result, the application rates recommended may seem higher than necessary. This may also be the case for labs that use such tables as the basis for their "organic" recommendations. The best way to find out about a recommendation that puzzles you is to ask the lab for an explanation.

IT'S A MATTER OF CHEMISTRY

An understanding of basic soil chemistry will help you make the most of your soil test results. Most chemical interactions—in the soil or anywhere else—take place between particles that carry either a positive or a negative charge when dissolved in water. Positively charged particles are called cations (pronounced "CAT-ions"), while anions ("AN-ions") carry a negative charge. These particles may be a single element, such as calcium, or a compound, such as nitrate (nitrogen and oxygen). The behavior of nutrients in the soil ecosystem is determined by whether they exist as cations or anions.

A BALANCING ACT

Soil fertility requires nutrients to exist not only in sufficient quantities but also in balanced form. Too much of one nutrient may lock up or interfere with the absorption of another. Phosphorus is the classic example; it will become immobilized in very acid soils by high concentrations of zinc and iron and in alkaline soils by too much calcium.

The ideal proportion of anion nutrients is the balance that is normally found in humus—100 parts carbon:10 parts nitrogen:1 part phosphorus:1 part sulfur. The ratio of nitrogen to phosphorus is important to proper plant nutrition because inadequate nitrogen

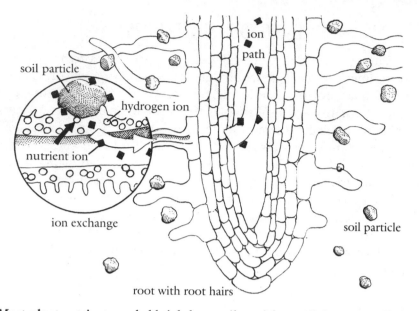

ion path

soil particle

hydrogen ion

nutrient ion

ion exchange

soil particle

root with root hairs

Most plant nutrients are held tightly to soil particles until they are needed by the plants. As the roots give off hydrogen ions, these ions take the place of nutrient ions. The released nutrient ions may be taken up directly by plant roots or dissolve in the soil solution first.

slows the growth of roots and, therefore, their ability to reach phosphorus supplies.

Micronutrient problems are often a result of imbalances. New information is continually being discovered about previously unknown interactions between major and minor nutrients in the soil ecosystem. The "cookbook" approach to soil fertility (adding one amendment for nitrogen, another for phosphorus, and yet another for potassium) can lead to soil imbalances and reduced availability of micronutrients. The best nutrient sources contain a balance of many different nutrients.

Understanding Anions

Reserves of anion nutrients are held in the organic portion of the soil and are released to plants through the decay of organic matter or through air and water. Soil anions, which form acids in solution, continually change in form and quantity. As the major building blocks of proteins and carbohydrates, anions are required in larger quantities than are cation nutrients. It is helpful to think of anions as large, soft, and changeable in form, while cations are small, hard, and durable. Elements that form soil anions include nitrogen, carbon, phosphorus, and sulfur.

Nitrogen. Nitrogen tends naturally towards the gaseous state as its most stable and plentiful form. Although plants cannot use atmospheric nitrogen directly, certain soil microbes such as rhizobia (bacteria that live on the roots of legumes) are able to capture it from the air and transform it into a biologically useful form: the nitrate anion. The nitrate form, which is present in the soil solution, is extremely transitory and will fluctuate significantly from day to day and even at different times of day.

Carbon. Carbon is the major constituent of plant (and animal) tissue. It is the food consumed by plants more than any other mineral. Although abundant in the organic fraction of the soil, carbon is taken in by plants almost entirely from the atmosphere, as carbon dioxide. Some of the carbon dioxide reacts in the soil to produce carbonate and bicarbonate anions. Some of these anions are used by plants or are leached out of the soil; others join with cations to form chemical compounds such as calcium carbonate and magnesium bicarbonate.

Phosphorus. Although more mineral-like than other anion nutrients, phosphorus is easily immobilized in the soil through its tendency to form insoluble compounds with calcium and other minerals. It is most readily available to plants when released gradually through the decomposition of organic matter. Its relative immobility means that distribution of phosphorus throughout the soil is only accomplished through the movement of earthworms and other soil organisms. Otherwise-insoluble soil phosphorus reserves can become available to plants through the activities of soil microbes.

Sulfur. Sulfur, an essential component of protein and fats, acts a lot like nitrogen in the soil ecosystem and is particularly important for nitrogen-fixing microorganisms. Sulfur deficiency is rarely a problem, especially where adequate soil organic matter levels are maintained. Acid rain, containing sulfur compounds released by coal-burning industrial plants, also adds sulfur to the soil.

Cations Simplified

Cation nutrients tend to be metallic mineral elements, important for both plant and microbial nutrition as components of enzymes. The major cation nutrients are calcium, magnesium, and potassium. These nutrients are essential for uptake and metabolization of the anion nutrients.

Calcium. Calcium is essential for nitrogen uptake and protein synthesis in plants. It also has a role in enzyme activation and cell reproduction.

Magnesium. Magnesium is an essential part of the chlorophyll molecule. It's necessary for phosphorus metabolism and enzyme activation.

Potassium. Potassium is essential for carbohydrate metabolism and cell division. It regulates the absorption of calcium, sodium, and nitrogen.

Cation nutrients are generally water-soluble and enter the soil either through the recycling of organic matter or by addition of mineral nutrient sources such as limestone. Cations are called base elements because they form bases in solution. In humid climates, where there are over 30 inches of precipitation a year, cations tend to become leached out of the topsoil, although they leach more slowly if they are stored by soil colloids such as clay and humus. Soils in arid climates, conversely, are usually rich in minerals and so are extremely productive when irrigated.

Cation exchange capacity (CEC) is a measurement of the amount of cation nutrients a soil is able to store on its clay and humus particles. These tiny particles, known as colloids, have a large number of negatively charged sites all over their surfaces. Positively charged cations are held on these sites, largely protected from leaching away in water but still available to plant roots. Plants give off hydrogen ions, a waste product that is positively charged, in exchange for needed nutrients like calcium, magnesium, and potassium. Nutrients held in colloidal exchange sites may not show up in soil tests because they are not dissolved in water, but they are still available to plants through direct contact between roots and soil colloids.

CEC is measured by how many thousandths of a gram of hydrogen can be held by 100 grams of dry soil. This means that if 100 grams of dry soil can hold 50 thousandths of a gram of hydrogen, that soil has a CEC of 50. Different kinds of clays have CECs that range from as little as 10 to as much as 100, while the CEC of pure humus can approach 200. Very sandy soils have a CEC of 5 or less.

Think of your soil's CEC as a kind of nutrient savings account. As nutrients are withdrawn, whether by removing crops or through the prolonged action of water leaching down through the soil, it is important to replace them to maintain your reserves. A soil with a high CEC but depleted nutrients will require greater applications of mineral nutrients to restore its fertility than will a similarly depleted but low CEC soil. A high CEC soil with an acid pH will require a larger amount of calcium, in the form of limestone, to correct it than will a low CEC soil with the same pH. If you have your soil tested by a lab, the report will often tell you the CEC of your soil. Knowing your soil's CEC will help you better understand and interpret your soil test recommendations.

Micronutrients

Sometimes called "trace elements," micronutrients, in minute quantities, are essential for plant, animal, and microbial enzyme functions. Most of the important micronutrients, such as copper, iron, manganese, and zinc, are cations. Boron and molybdenum are the most important anion micronutrients. To learn how these micronutrients function in plants, see "Some Important Micronutrients" on page 102.

Micronutrients occur as part of large, complex organic molecules in chelated form. The word *chelate* (pronounced "KEY-late") comes from the Greek word for claw, which indicates how a single nutrient ion is held in the center of the larger molecule.

The finely balanced interactions between micronutrients are complex and not fully understood. We do know that balance is crucial; when any micronutrient is present in excessive amounts, it will become a poison, and certain poisonous elements, such as chlorine, are also essential micronutrients. Unless a specific micronutrient deficiency has been diagnosed by a soil test, the best way to provide adequate supplies is by building soil organic matter and applying balanced sources of minerals such as rock powders and seaweed.

FERTILIZER OR AMENDMENT?

What's the difference between fertilizers and soil amendments? These terms are often used interchangeably, but there is a distinction. A fertilizer's primary purpose is to provide nutrients to plants. It can be a simple topdressing of rotted manure, a concoction of organic matter from your own recipe, or a store-bought bag with a magic formula. A manufacturer may not legally label a product as a

SOME IMPORTANT MICRONUTRIENTS

Nutrient	Desired Amount in Soil (ppm)*	Function in Plants
Iron (Fe)	25,000	Chlorophyll synthesis; oxidation; constituent of various enzymes and proteins
Manganese (Mn)	2,500	Synthesis of chlorophyll and several vitamins; carbohydrate and nitrogen metabolism
Zinc (Zn)	100	Formation of growth hormones; protein synthesis; seed and grain production and maturation
Copper (Cu)	50	Catalyst for enzyme and chlorophyll synthesis, respiration, and carbohydrate and protein metabolism
Boron (B)	50	Protein synthesis; starch and sugar transport; root development; fruit and seed formation; water uptake and transport
Molybdenum (Mo)	2	Essential for symbiotic nitrogen fixation and protein synthesis

SOURCE: Reprinted with permission from *The Soul of Soil: An Ecological Guide to Soil Management* by Grace Gershuny and Joseph Smillie. St. Johnsbury, Vt.: Gaia Services, 1986.
*Approximate values indicate relative proportions.

commercial fertilizer unless it has a minimum nutrient content, which varies from state to state.

The term soil amendment usually refers to a material added primarily to enhance soil physical qualities or microbial activity. A soil amendment may contain mostly organic matter, such as compost, or very slow-release minerals, such as greensand. In some states, these products may not be legally labeled as fertilizers because most of their nutrients are not immediately available to plants or, like the calcium in lime, are not considered to be important plant nutrients. The boundaries can become blurry when you talk about compost and other nutrient-rich organic materials, which feed both plants and soil organisms.

NATURAL, SYNTHETIC, OR ORGANIC

Ask a gardener what "organic" means. Ask the federal government. Ask a representative of the fertilizer industry. Most likely, you'll get three different answers. Confusion over what's natural, what's synthetic, and what's organic is nothing new. And it still isn't settled.

The use of the word *organic* on a label, according to fertilizer industry guidelines, may simply mean "containing carbon." The term *natural* on a label refers to anything of plant, animal, or mineral origin, regardless of what industrial manipulation it has received. Fish waste that is treated with acids to stabilize it and combined with soluble potassium superphosphate (made by treating rock phosphate with sulfuric acid) would also be considered natural by this definition.

Federal legislation covering organic foods gives some guidelines about which kinds of fertilizer materials are and are not acceptable for organic production. It forbids synthetic materials, but makes exceptions in some instances, leaving it to an advisory board to come up with a list of specific permitted products. It will be a couple of years before we have the national list, but fortunately you can make your own judgments by keeping some basic information in mind.

Organic certification programs have, in fact, started to move away from a strict natural-versus-synthetic criterion for evaluating fertilizers. Organic farmers and gardeners have come to recognize that the ecological profile of a material—the effect it has on soil health and environment—is more important than whether it was dug from the ground or is a by-product of industry. For example, some organic waste products can contain unsafe residues of pesticides, heavy metals, and other contaminants that you wouldn't want to add to your garden. On the other hand, elemental sulfur, which is used to control plant diseases and to neutralize soil alkalinity, may be naturally mined or derived from industrial stack scrubbers. Although the latter is technically synthetic because it results from a chemical refining process, the two forms of sulfur are virtually indistinguishable.

Lynn Coody, one of the founders of Oregon Tilth, a private certification group, has developed a decision-making model based on the criteria outlined in federal law. The following criteria detailed by Coody are the questions most organic farmers and gardeners would ask of a new material.

- What effects will it have on plant growth and health?
- Is it safe for me to handle?
- Will it affect the safety of the food I grow?
- What will it do to (or for) soil organisms?
- Can it lead to air or water pollution?
- Does its mining, manufacture, or transport harm the environment?
- How energy-intensive is it to make?
- Does it help recycle an existing organic waste product?
- Is there a feasible alternative that may be more environmentally benign?

Bill Wolf, president of Necessary Trading Company, a distributor and manufacturer of products for organic gardeners and farmers, poses a simple test that anyone can perform: Ask the earthworms. He advises people to dig up a handful of earthworms from their garden or compost pile and place a sample of the fertilizer in question in the same container. Then watch the worms. Observing whether they head straight for the fertilizer or whether they get as far away from it as they can will tell you something about its attractiveness to soil organisms.

Choosing the Right Fertilizer

"Feed the soil, not the plant" is fundamental to organic soil management, but standard fertilizer recommendations are based only on plant responses to the fertilizers. They fail to consider such things as effects on earthworms and other soil organisms, groundwater pollution, pest and disease resistance, and quality of the harvest.

Most commercial fertilizer labels include only the familiar three numbers, such as 20-10-10, that stand for three major nutrients—nitrogen (N), phosphorus (P), and potassium (K). These three numbers are commonly known as the NPK analysis of that fertilizer. You may sometimes see them called nitrate, phosphate, and potash: These terms refer to the same nutrients, but in different chemical forms—the forms in which they usually occur in synthetic fertilizer formulas.

Organic materials almost always contain other nutrients besides the big three. You can get into trouble if you substitute materials

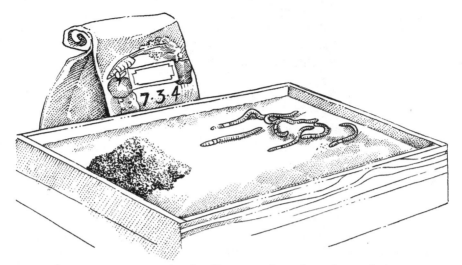

With all the commercial garden fertilizers out there, how do you know what's good for the health of your soil community? Ask the earthworms! Put a handful of worms in a container with a handful of fertilizer and watch to see whether they move toward it. If they do, they like it, and they'll be happy when you spread it on your garden!

based only on their NPK analysis. For example, wood ashes are rich in potassium, but they also contain a lot of calcium, a nutrient that is overabundant in some soils. Some commercial organic fertilizer products are sold with a guaranteed nutrient analysis. If you compare the NPK numbers on a bag of chemical fertilizer with those on a bag of organic fertilizer, you may wonder why the organic bag's NPK numbers are so low. Most organic materials vary considerably in their composition. Their nutrients are low in solubility, so they are released slowly, over time. While this is desirable from the soil's point of view, commercial fertilizer labels may legally claim only the immediately available nutrient content. Those fertilizers based on organic materials may therefore have a much higher total nutrient content than is stated on the label. "Commercial Organic Fertilizers" on page 108 will give you an overview of some of the most commonly sold organically acceptable products.

It's tempting to look for a recipe that will give you the equivalent organic fertilizers to plug into application rates recommended for chemical fertilizers. Some gardeners hope they can just substitute more benign products and still get impressive results. But knowing what to add requires you to know your soil and your garden by observation instead of picking numbers from a chart. "Selecting

Organic Fertilizers" on page 124 will give you an overview of the most commonly used organic fertilizer materials and their suggested application rates for different soil fertility levels.

BALANCED FERTILIZERS

Compost and most manures contain fairly balanced proportions of essential plant nutrients. Before deciding you need to use any of the materials listed in the following pages, take into account the nutrient value of your compost. You can conservatively estimate the NPK analysis of homemade compost at about 1-1-1; it might well be higher, but the difference won't upset soil mineral balances.

Adjust these figures depending on your compost ingredients. For example, if you've used a lot of potassium-rich materials like seaweed or legume hay to build your pile, figure on a 2 percent potassium content. You can use the nutrient-rich materials described in the following section to supplement your compost, creating your own boosted blends similar to those sold in bags at fancy prices.

Compost-Based Fertilizers

Your first choice in store-bought organic fertilizers is a quality commercial compost—as long as it's low enough in moisture to justify the cost. The materials in compost are relatively stable, won't harm soil organisms, and may contain cultures of beneficial microbes. Also, if any of the compost ingredients contained toxic contaminants, they're more likely to have been broken down or locked up in complex organic molecules.

Locally produced composts made by municipal yard waste facilities or nearby food processors may be available to you in bulk. Buying from local sources eliminates long-distance transport and helps to recycle local wastes—and it allows you to know exactly what you're getting. Store-bought compost should look, feel, and smell like good homemade compost—if it's too wet, smells like ammonia, or has recognizable raw materials or mushrooms in it, reject it.

In some cases, raw materials are so contaminated that even composting can't make the finished product safe to use in your home garden. Mushroom compost, the spent bedding from commercial mushroom production, may contain pesticide residues that have not undergone composting. When in doubt, ask the seller for a laboratory analysis showing a clean bill of health for the product.

HOW TO READ LABELS

First, look at the guaranteed analysis—the three numbers that represent the percentage of soluble nitrogen (N), phosphorus (P), and potassium (K) in the bag. The key word here is *soluble*. Most organic materials are of low solubility, so the numbers on a bag of reputable organic fertilizers tend to be in the single-digit range. They'll provide ample nutrition over time, but very little will immediately dissolve in water.

If any of these numbers is higher than 10, your suspicions should be aroused. Only a few very concentrated organic waste products, such as fish and meat meal or blood meal, can have this high an analysis of nitrogen. The same is true for phosphorus and potassium. In some cases, borderline-organic materials such as Chilean nitrate or soap wastes have been used to boost nitrogen or phosphorus analysis, but these numbers should still be less than 12. Unless you are a candidate for organic certification, this is not a big problem. If your soil is really not able to supply adequate nitrogen or phosphorus, these products can be excellent stopgap measures to get it going.

In most cases, you'll want to avoid "organic" fertilizers that have high analyses (close to 20-20-20). These high-analysis fertilizers are generally based on standard chemical fertilizer formulations using urea, monoammonium phosphate, muriate of potash, and other highly soluble materials, with something recognizably organic such as fish meal or dried manure added as window dressing. If the label lists the ingredients, usually in fine print, this will tell you right away. Incredible as it seems, listing the ingredients is not always required on fertilizer labels—the conventional wisdom being that all that really matters is the NPK analysis.

Blends with a Boost

Many companies put out a line of compost-based blends, adding various "boosters" for special applications or to ensure that the product meets the NPK analysis on the label. The source of these added nutrients is important, especially if you're concerned about organic certification. Some nutrient sources, like cottonseed meal and leather meal, can be a problem because they contain residues of pesticides or other toxic residues. Other materials, like soap phosphate, may be questionable. Find out what's in that bag, and make sure you want it in your garden. If you are concerned about the suitability of a material, check with an organic certification group to see what restrictions they place on fertilizer materials.

Products boosted with extra nitrogen, such as Fertrell Super N and Erth-Rite C, are intended to promote lush vegetative growth.

(continued on page 116)

COMMERCIAL ORGANIC FERTILIZERS

This is a sampling of the more widely available commercial fertilizers, their ingredients, guaranteed analysis, and cost per pound. Many more products are on the market, many of them only regionally distributed. Note: Most organic certification groups place all commercial organic fertilizers in a "regulated" category because of the difficulty of verifying label claims.

Product Name and Manufacturer	Guaranteed Analysis	Ingredients*
Agway Nature's Way Organic Plant Food Agri-Cycle Inc. 7201 Rawson Rd. Victor, NY 14564	4-5-4	Composted poultry manure; feather meal
All-Natural Organic Flower and Garden Food A. H. Hoffman Inc. 77 Cooper Ave. Landisville, PA 17538	7-5-1	Bonemeal; meat-and-bone meal; blood meal; ground cocoa shells
Baa Baa Doo Pecos Agricultural Corp. P.O. Box 1712 Pecos, TX 79772	2-2-1	Composted dehydrated sheep manure
Compostost Bricker's Organic Farms Inc. 824-K Sandbar Ferry Rd. Augusta, GA 30901	Varies	Composted paunch manure (contents of cow stomachs from slaughterhouses); granite meal; cricket manure; blood meal
Coventry Gardens Natural Organic Tomato and Vegetable Food Earth Conscious 7737 N.E. Killingsworth St. Portland, OR 97218	3-5-5	Dried poultry waste; Sul-Po-Mag; bonemeal; soft rock phosphate; blood meal; kelp meal

*This information comes from label information and contact with companies.

†Cost will vary; this unit price is based on 10- to 25-pound bags.

Cost per Pound ($)[†]	Sources	Comments
.40	Agway stores	Lawn blend also available
1.42	Lawn and garden centers	Ornamental blend and single-ingredient products also available
.06	Lawn and garden centers	Composted dehydrated cow manure (Pure-Tex) also available
.23	Stores in mid-South; company catalog	Cricket manure product (4-3-2) also available
1.42	West Coast retail stores	Citrus, avocado, azalea, and lawn blends also available

(continued)

COMMERCIAL ORGANIC FERTILIZERS—
CONTINUED

Product Name and Manufacturer	Guaranteed Analysis	Ingredients*
Door County 100% Organic Fish Compost Door County Compost Inc. Washington Island, WI 54246	1-1-1	Composted fish waste; wood chips
Earth-Safe Organics Tomato and Vegetable Food Plus Calcium Carl Pool Corp. P.O. Drawer 249 Elmendorf, TX 78112	4-6-5	Blood meal; feather meal; fish meal; bonemeal; sylvite (mined mineral form of potassium chloride); gypsum
Earthgro's Best Natural Organic and Mineral Vegetable and Flower Food Earthgro Inc. R.R. 207, P.O. Box 143 Lebanon, CT 06249	4-6-4	Composted manures; cocoa bean hulls; yard waste; feather meal; bonemeal; Sul-Po-Mag; Chilean nitrate
Erth-Rite Garden Food Erth-Rite Inc. (formerly Zook and Ranck Inc.) R.D. 1, Box 243 Gap, PA 17527	3-2-2	Composted manure; leaves; peat humus; rock phosphate; seaweed; greensand; feather meal; Chilean nitrate; Sul-Po-Mag; humates; aragonite; slag
Fertilaid Microkey Sciences Inc. P.O. Box 27701-450 Houston, TX 77227	4-2-0	Composted slaughterhouse waste (mostly from poultry and fish); vegetable matter
Fertrell Super Fertrell Co. Box 265 Bainbridge, PA 17502	3-2-3	Composted poultry manure; cocoa waste; bonemeal; oyster or crab meal; leather tankage; animal tankage; soybean, cotton or peanut meal; rock phosphate; greensand

*This information comes from label information and contact with companies.

†Cost will vary; this unit price is based on 10- to 25-pound bags.

Cost per Pound ($)[†]	Sources	Comments
.65	Mail-order from Jung Seed Co., 335 S. High St., Randolph, WI 53957; garden centers	Began as University of Wisconsin project
2.00	Lawn and garden centers in Texas area, Southwest, and California	Ornamental blend and single-ingredient products also available
Varies	Garden centers	Lawn, fall, high-acid, and starter blends also available
.46	Hardware stores and garden centers; company will ship	Lawn blends and single-ingredient products also available
.22	Farm supply stores in California, Idaho, and Texas; garden centers in Texas; company will ship	Sold as soil conditioner/activator
.25	Mail-order from Growing Naturally, P.O. Box 54, Pineville, PA 18946, and Necessary Trading Co., P.O. Box 305, New Castle, VA 24127; companies will ship	Ingredients vary with availability; also recommended for lawns; other blends available

(continued)

COMMERCIAL ORGANIC FERTILIZERS—
CONTINUED

Product Name and Manufacturer	Guaranteed Analysis	Ingredients*
Gardener's Best All-Purpose Fertilizer Gardener's Supply Co. 128 Intervale Rd. Burlington, VT 05401	5-5-5	Whey meal (by-product of cheese making); peanut meal; Chilean nitrate; sulfate of potash magnesia
Green Earth Organics Natural Fertilizer Green Earth Organics 12310 Highway 99 S., Unit 119 Everett, WA 98204	6-4-4	Feather meal; blood meal; bonemeal; langbeinite; dolomitic lime; kelp meal
Greenview Certified for Flowers and Vegetables Agri-Cycle Inc. 7201 Rawson Rd. Victor, NY 14564	3-4-3	Composted poultry manure
Natural Guard Tomato and Vegetable Plant Food Natural Guard P.O. Box 8432 St. Louis, MO 63132	5-10-5	Chilean nitrate; bonemeal; muriate of potash
Naturall Organic Natural Fertilizer for Gardens CFS Specialties Division R.R. 2, Box 24 Cashton, WI 54619	2-4-4	Composted poultry manure; mined potassium sulfate
Nature's Best All-Natural Organic Garden Fertilizer KOOS Inc. 4500 13th Court Kenosha, WI 53140	5-5-5	Bone phosphate; hydrolyzed feather meal; sunflower seed hull ash

*This information comes from label information and contact with companies.

†Cost will vary; this unit price is based on 10- to 25-pound bags.

Cost per Pound ($)†	Sources	Comments
.99	Custom-made for Gardener's Supply; company catalog	Other products available in catalog
.56	Stores in Northwest; company catalog	Ornamental and lawn blends also available
.50	Hardware stores and garden centers	Custom-made for Greenview, a division of Lebanon Chemical Corporation
1.25	Independently owned lawn and garden centers	Single-ingredient products and lawn blend available
.25	Stores in Midwest; company will ship	Lawn blend also available
.75	Garden centers and hardware stores	Lawn blend also available; sold as Green Thumb brand in True Value hardware stores

(continued)

COMMERCIAL ORGANIC FERTILIZERS—
CONTINUED

Product Name and Manufacturer	Guaranteed Analysis	Ingredients*
Nature's Choice Organic Garden Fertilizer NK Lawn and Garden Co. 7500 Olson Memorial Highway Golden Valley, MN 55427	3-4-3	Dried poultry manure
Nature's Cycle Organic Garden Fertilizer EKO Systems Corp. P.O. Box 9168 Missoula, MT 59807	4-5-2	Composted dried poultry waste; blood meal; bonemeal
Necessary Starter Fertilizer Necessary Trading Co. P.O. Box 305 New Castle, VA 24127	3-5-3	Composted poultry manure
Plant Right All-Natural Organic Fertilizer Agri-Cycle Inc. 7201 Rawson Rd. Victor, NY 14564	3-4-3	Composted poultry manure
Pure-Tex Pecos Agricultural Corp. P.O. Box 1712 Pecos, TX 79772	2-1-2	Composted and dehydrated cow manure
Ringer Vegetable Garden Restore Ringer Corp. 9959 Valley View Rd. Eden Prairie, MN 55344	8-5-5	Hydrolyzed poultry feather meal; wheat germ; soybean meal; bonemeal; sunflower seed hull ash; brewer's yeast; microorganisms

*This information comes from label information and contact with companies.
†Cost will vary; this unit price is based on 10- to 25-pound bags.

Cost per Pound ($)[†]	Sources	Comments
.50	Home and hardware stores and garden centers	Lawn blend also available
Varies	Stores in Northwest	Lawn blend also available
.32	Company catalog	Lawn blend and single-ingredient products also available
.36	Garden centers; mail-order from Harris Seeds, P.O. Box 22960, Rochester, NY 14692	Lawn blend also available; products sold under various labels
.05	Lawn and garden centers	Also recommended for lawns and ornamentals
2.00	Retail stores; company catalog	Lawn and specialty blends also available

(continued)

COMMERCIAL ORGANIC FERTILIZERS—
CONTINUED

Product Name and Manufacturer	Guaranteed Analysis	Ingredients*
Scotts Next Generation All-Natural Vegetable Plant Food O.M. Scott and Sons Co. 14111 Scottslawn Rd. Marysville, OH 43041	3-6-3	Hydrolized poultry feathers; bonemeal; muriate of potash
Sustane Sustane Corp. 1107 Hazeltine Blvd. Chaska, MN 55318	5-2-4	Composted turkey litter
Vermont Organic Fertilizer Vermont Organic Fertilizer Co. 26 State St. Montpelier, VT 05602	5-3-4	Whey meal (by-product of cheese making); Chilean nitrate; cocoa shells; sulphate of potash

SOURCE: Adapted and printed with permission of *Organic Gardening* magazine. Copyright © 1991 Rodale Press, Inc. U.S.A. All rights reserved. For a one-year subscription, send $25 to *Organic Gardening*, 33 E. Minor St., Emmaus, PA 18098.

*This information comes from label information and contact with companies.

†Cost will vary; this unit price is based on 10- to 25-pound bags.

Extra phosphorus is added to blends intended for use in establishing new plantings, planting of perennials and bulbs in fall, and stimulating blooming of flowering plants. Potassium is added to blends to enhance fruit set or to balance a compost that may be a bit low in this nutrient. Other nutrients sometimes mentioned on fertilizer labels include sulfur, calcium, and magnesium. Some nutrients are known to be important for special purposes, such as sulfur for turf enhancement. Some companies add trace mineral supplements such as kelp meal and greensand.

Blended products can differ considerably from each other in terms of nutrient content, as well as in their effects on soil health and the environment. Examine the ingredients and make sure you feel comfortable about putting them in your soil. Creating your own

Cost per Pound (\$)[†]	Sources	Comments
.86	Retail stores	Ornamental and lawn blends also available
.21	For sale mostly to commercial landscapers and farmers; by mail from Gardener's Supply Co., 128 Intervale Rd., Burlington, VT 05401	—
.95	Lawn and garden centers; by mail from Gardener's Supply Co., 128 Intervale Rd., Burlington, VT 05401, and Seventh Generation, 49 Hercules Drive, Colchester, VT 05446	—

blend from generic ingredients is usually much less expensive than paying for the convenience of a specially formulated blended product.

Uncomposted Fertilizers

Dried and pulverized waste products of food- or fiber-processing industries are available to home gardeners as uncomposted organic fertilizers. In some cases, livestock feed ingredients such as soybean meal and alfalfa meal are sold as fertilizers.

Most of these products are generic: Blood meal or alfalfa meal packaged by Company X is not likely to be different from that sold by Company Y. Similarly, mineral fertilizers of finely ground rock powders tend to be comparable from brand to brand, although the quality of some rock mineral deposits is known to vary. Kelp meal and fish meal may differ depending on the species used and how it is processed.

Make your own custom blend of fertilizer by adding materials high in nitrogen, phosphorus, potassium, sulfur, calcium, or magnesium to your best compost. Mixing your own fertilizer usually costs less than buying it in bags, and you have control over what goes into the mix and into your garden.

Manures

Manure can vary widely in nutrient analysis, depending on what animal it came from, how that animal was fed, and how the manure was handled. Manure from "factory farms" is sometimes sprayed with larvicides to reduce fly populations. It can also contain pesticides, antibiotics, and hormones, which will readily decompose but can have harmful short-term effects on the soil community. It's best to know the source of your manure, if at all possible, and to avoid using manure that you suspect might be contaminated.

Fresh manure generally contains a large dose of soluble nitrates and phosphates, which can easily wash away and pollute groundwater. Fresh poultry, rabbit, and sheep manures, which are especially high in nitrogen, will burn plant roots and interfere with germination just like any synthetic high-nitrogen fertilizer. These soluble nutrients have the same damaging effect on the soil ecosystem as well. For tips on safely working with fresh manures in your garden, see "Using Fresh Manure" on page 121.

Manure that is stored in a liquid slurry system (as is usually the case with swine manure) is generally less of a danger as far as burning plant roots. You can apply it directly to the garden. It's best to

NUTRIENT, ORGANIC MATTER, AND MOISTURE CONTENT OF MANURES

Kind of Animal Manure	Nitrogen	Phosphate	Potash	Organic Matter	Moisture
Chicken	1.1	0.8	0.5	25–45	55–75
Cow	0.6	0.2	0.5	17	83
Duck	0.6	1.4	0.5	25–45	55–75
Horse	0.7	0.3	0.6	22–26	74–78
Pig	0.5	0.3	0.5	14	86
Rabbit	2.4	1.4	0.6	33	43
Sheep	0.7	0.3	0.9	32–34	66–68
Steer	0.7	0.3	0.4	17	83

SOURCE: Reprinted from *The Rodale Book of Composting*, edited by Deborah L. Martin and Grace Gershuny. Emmaus, Pa.: Rodale Press, 1992.

NOTE: Numbers indicate percentages.

spray it on or inject it directly into the soil (preferably just before turning in a green manure) and then immediately mix it in. Liquid manures are difficult to compost, and this method ensures that very few nutrients will be lost.

Uncomposted dry manures are easy to use in the garden and are available commercially (see "Using Fresh Manure" on page 121 for some tips on working with fresh manures in your garden). Uncomposted dried manures are available commercially under several brand names. You can find manure from all manner of beasts, including zoo and circus animals. One commercial compost maker in Georgia uses cricket manure from a nearby bait farm. Human and pet feces should be handled with extreme care, however. Here are descriptions of the major characteristics of the more common barnyard droppings:

Cattle manure. Cow manure is moister and less concentrated than that of other animals. Because of their complex digestive systems, ruminants like cows, sheep, and goats produce manure that's especially rich in beneficial microorganisms.

Horse manure. Horse manure tends to be "hot," meaning it has a high nitrogen and low moisture content. That's why it is traditionally used in making hotbeds for early vegetables. If manure comes from heavily bedded animals, combine it with other types of manure or high-analysis organic wastes to balance the carbon:nitrogen ratio.

Poultry manure. Because it is so high in soluble nitrates, poultry manure should always be composted or incorporated with a high-carbon mulch or cover crop the season before planting a food crop. If you raise your own birds, be sure to use plenty of bedding, especially under roosting areas. Use a respirator if you clean out an old poultry house, since dry poultry manure can carry spores of a human respiratory disease.

Rabbit manure. Rabbit manure may contain even more nitrogen than some poultry manure, so the same cautions apply. However, because it is drier, it decomposes more readily. If you raise rabbits, consider growing earthworms directly under their cages to turn those valuable droppings into even more valuable castings.

Sheep manure. Sheep manure is very similar to horse manure, except that sheep are rarely pampered with as much dry bedding as horses are. Goat manure is comparable.

Swine manure. Pigs produce a fairly concentrated manure, but commercial hog farmers generally store it as a liquid slurry. Mix it with horse manure that contains lots of bedding material, or apply it with a bulky mulch or cover crop.

SOURCES OF SPECIFIC NUTRIENTS

If your soil is lacking in a particular nutrient, such as potassium, calcium, or sulfur, you may want to add a fertilizer high in that nutrient to supply what is needed. There are a wide range of organic materials that you can choose from to supply whatever nutrient is lacking.

Nitrogen Sources

Broadcast these materials on your garden soil or apply them in spots for a nitrogen boost when plants are deficient. Many high-nitrogen materials are of animal origin and may attract dogs and other animals. Avoid this problem by composting them in enclosed bins or thoroughly incorporating them with soil.

USING FRESH MANURE

If you have access to a good source of fresh manure and can't compost it first, follow these guidelines for maximizing its value and minimizing its hazards:

• Avoid adding raw manure to leguminous crops. The soluble nitrates will suppress nitrogen fixation.

• Spread fresh manure before seeding a nonleguminous green manure crop.

• Work raw manure into the soil when incorporating crop residues or a cover crop.

• Wait at least two weeks after applying raw manure to plant corn, squash, and cabbage-family crops.

• Avoid planting leafy greens, potatoes, or carrots in the same season that you spread raw manure.

• Never spread raw manure just before a heavy rain. Avoid spreading it on land adjoining surface water or uphill from a well.

• Sprinkle rock phosphate over the manure to minimize nitrogen loss and improve the biological availability of the phosphorus. (If you keep animals, this is a good thing to do whenever you add fresh bedding.)

• Avoid spreading manure on snow or frozen ground. Store it in a protected pile or containing structure until spring.

Alfalfa meal. This material is actually ground-up alfalfa hay. It may be sold in granular or pelletized form. Alfalfa meal contains about 5 percent nitrogen, plus a significant amount of potassium. It also contains a plant growth stimulant called triacontanol.

Blood meal. Also known as dried blood, this material is sometimes mixed with other materials to make it easier to spread. It contains 13 percent nitrogen. Blood meal is sometimes used to repel animal pests.

Cottonseed meal. This material is the waste left after pressing cottonseed oil. It contains about 6 percent nitrogen and significant amounts of phosphorus. It is commonly used for acid-loving plants such as blueberries and azaleas. Cotton is among the most heavily sprayed crops in the world, and pesticides are concentrated in the seeds. Compost cottonseed meal before using it in your garden.

Feather meal. Feather meal is basically ground-up feathers but may also contain some meat scraps. It contains about 11 percent nitrogen. Feathers are usually steam-treated to help break them down more readily.

Fish emulsion. This material consists of filtered and stabilized fish solubles, which are by-products of the fish protein concentrates used for animal feeds. It contains 4 to 5 percent nitrogen. Fish emulsion is used for foliar fertilization, in irrigation systems, and as a root drench for transplants. Most commercial fish emulsions are processed with sulfuric or phosphoric acid to make them more sprayable and inhibit decomposition in the container. A spray-dried product that is not acid-treated and can be reconstituted in water is becoming more widely available.

Fish meal. Fish meal is composed of ground and dried fish parts, in some cases whole fish, which are products of the fish processing industry. It contains around 5 percent nitrogen and significant amounts of phosphorus and potassium.

Guano. Guano is bat or bird excrement that has generally been deposited over a long period of time and has dried and aged. It contains up to 15 percent nitrogen, 10 percent phosphorus, and significant amounts of calcium.

Hoof-and-horn meal. This material is a by-product of beef slaughterhouses. It contains about 12 percent nitrogen and significant amounts of phosphorus. Hoof and horn meal can vary in quality from a fine, pleasant-smelling product to a sticky, smelly one.

Leather meal. Leather meal is a tannery by-product consisting of ground leather scraps and leather wastes. It contains about 10 percent nitrogen and often has unacceptably high levels of chromium, a heavy metal. Manufacturers claim that the chromium is present in a very stable form that is not available to plants; however, by adding it to your soil you can be asking for problems if soil chemistry changes ever cause the chromium to become more soluble.

Nitrate of soda (Chilean nitrate). This is a highly soluble natural fertilizer, mined from salt deposits in South America. It contains 16 percent nitrogen, but also 18 percent sodium, which is harmful to soil organisms. It is not recommended for home gardeners, although it may be used sparingly as a compost booster.

Seafood meal. Seafood meal is composed of crab, lobster, and shrimp wastes, which are by-products of the seafood processing industry. It contains about 4 percent nitrogen and significant amounts of phosphorus, as well as chitin, a material that both is beneficial as a soil texturizer and stimulates organisms that inhibit harmful soil nematodes.

Soybean meal. This by-product of soybean oil production is generally sold as animal feed. It contains about 7 percent nitrogen and significant amounts of potassium. Soybean meal helps stimulate soil microbial activity.

Tankage, meat meal, and paunch manure. These slaughterhouse by-products are not generally available to home gardeners in raw form, but they are frequently used in commercially blended fertilizer products.

Urine (human). This material is free, easy to collect, and generally safe to use (make sure you only use urine from healthy people). It contains about 1 percent nitrogen. It can be diluted as a foliar fertilizer for an extra boost when plants are deficient.

Phosphorus Sources

Phosphorus, because it is so chemically reactive and forms insoluble compounds, is a difficult nutrient to provide in a highly available form through natural sources. The best way to supply phosphorus to deficient soils is by incorporating phosphorus-rich materials such as those listed below into your compost. Green manure is another good way to add phosphorus to your soil. (See "Growing Green Manures" on page 50 for details on growing and using green manures.)

Bonemeal. Finely ground bones, generally steamed, are a by-product of animal slaughterhouses. Bonemeal contains 10 to 12 percent phosphorus, a small amount of nitrogen, and about 24 percent calcium. It is the best source of readily available phosphorus, useful for transplanting and as an early season starter when soil microbes are too sluggish to release much phosphorus from organic matter.

Colloidal phosphate. This material is actually a clay washed out from between layers of rock phosphate as the phosphate is mined. It contains 16 to 20 percent phosphorus, of which about 2 percent is readily available, and about 19 percent calcium. It has a lower total phosphate content than rock phosphate, but in a more available form.

Rock phosphate. Rock phosphate is finely ground phosphate mined from many locations, including Florida, Idaho, and North Carolina. It contains 32 percent total phosphorus and 33 percent calcium. The phosphorus becomes more readily available in acid conditions.

(continued on page 132)

SELECTING ORGANIC FERTILIZERS

Organic Amendment	Primary Benefit	Average Analysis
Alfalfa meal	Organic matter	5-1-2
Apple pomace	Organic matter	0.2-0-0.2
Aragonite	Calcium	96% calcium carbonate
Bat guano (ancient)	Nitrogen	2-8-0
Bat guano (fresh)	Nitrogen	10-3-1
BioActivator	Organic matter	1 billion beneficial bacterial spores per gram
Blood meal	Nitrogen	10-0-0
Bluegrass hay	Organic matter	1.8-0.6-1.8
Bonemeal (steamed)	Phosphate	1-11-0; 20% total phosphate; 24% calcium
Borax	Trace minerals	10% boron
Calcitic limestone	Balancer; calcium	65–80% calcium carbonate; 3–15% magnesium carbonate
Cattle manure (dry)	Organic matter	2-2.3-2.4
Coffee grounds	Nitrogen	2-0.3-0.2
Colloidal phosphate	Phosphate	0-2-2
Compost (dry commercial)	Organic matter	1-1-1

*Use these suggested application rates based on your soil's fertility, as indicated by soil test results and your personal observations.

Average Application Rate (per 1,000 sq. ft.)*			Comments
Low	Medium	Adequate	
50 lb.	35 lb.	25 lb.	Contains triaconatol (a natural fatty acid growth stimulant) plus trace minerals
250 lb.	150 lb.	100 lb.	Contains trace minerals
100 lb.	50 lb.	25 lb.	Can replace limestone
25 lb.	15 lb.	10 lb.	Contains calcium
30 lb.	20 lb.	10 lb.	Contains calcium
4 oz.	3 oz.	2 oz.	Beneficial bacteria to inoculate composts and green manure crops
30 lb.	20 lb.	10 lb.	—
250 lb.	150 lb.	100 lb.	—
30 lb.	20 lb.	10 lb.	—
5 oz.	4 oz.	3 oz.	—
100 lb.	50 lb.	25 lb.	—
200 lb.	150 lb.	100 lb.	Should be composted or applied in the fall
—	—	—	Acid-forming; needs limestone supplement; to apply, incorporate in compost
60 lb.	25 lb.	10 lb.	—
200 lb.	100 lb.	50 lb.	—

(continued)

SELECTING ORGANIC FERTILIZERS—
CONTINUED

Organic Amendment	Primary Benefit	Average Analysis
Compost (homemade)	Organic matter	0.5-0.5-0.5 to 4-4-4; 25% organic matter
Compost (mushroom)	Organic matter	—
Corn stover (dry)	Organic matter	1.2-0.4-1.6
Corn stover (green)	Organic matter	0.3-0.1-0.3
Cottonseed meal	Nitrogen	6-2-1
Cowpeas (dry)	Organic matter	3.1-0.6-2.3
Cowpeas (green)	Organic matter	0.4-0.1-0.4
Crab meal	Nitrogen	4-3-0.5
Dolomitic limestone	Balancer; calcium; magnesium	51% calcium carbonate; 40% magnesium carbonate
Eggshells	Calcium	1.2-0.4-0.1
Epsom salts	Balancer; magnesium	10% magnesium; 13% sulfur
Feather meal	Nitrogen	11-0-0
Fescue hay	Organic matter	2.1-0.7-2.4
Fish emulsion	Nitrogen	4-1-1; 5% sulfur
Fish meal	Nitrogen	5-3-3

*Use these suggested application rates based on your soil's fertility, as indicated by soil test results and your personal observations.

| Average Application Rate (per 1,000 sq. ft.)* | | | Comments |
Low	Medium	Adequate	
2,000 lb.	1,000 lb.	400 lb.	—
350 lb.	250 lb.	50 lb.	Ask supplier whether material contains pesticide residues
250 lb.	150 lb.	100 lb.	—
1,000 lb.	600 lb.	400 lb.	High in sugars when tilled or dug in while still green
35 lb.	25 lb.	10 lb.	May contain pesticide residues
200 lb.	150 lb.	100 lb.	—
800 lb.	600 lb.	400 lb.	—
150 lb.	100 lb.	50 lb.	Also useful to help control harmful nematodes
100 lb.	50 lb.	25 lb.	—
100 lb.	50 lb.	25 lb.	Contains calcium plus trace minerals
5 lb.	3 lb.	1 lb.	—
30 lb.	20 lb.	10 lb.	—
200 lb.	150 lb.	100 lb.	—
2 oz.	1 oz.	1 oz.	—
30 lb.	20 lb.	10 lb.	—

(continued)

SELECTING ORGANIC FERTILIZERS—
CONTINUED

Organic Amendment	Primary Benefit	Average Analysis
Flowers of sulfur	Balancer	99.5% sulfur
Granite meal	Potash	4% total potash; contains 67% silicas and 19 trace minerals
Grass clippings (green)	Organic matter	0.5-0.2-0.5
Greensand	Potash	7% total potash plus 32 trace minerals
Gypsum	Balancer; calcium	22% calcium; 17% sulfur
Hairy vetch	Organic matter	2.8-0.8-2.3
Hoof-and-horn meal	Nitrogen	12-2-0
Horse manure	Organic matter	1.7-0.7-1.8
Humates	Organic matter	Humic acids of variable composition
Kelp meal	Potash; trace minerals	1.5-0.5-2.5
Lespedeza hay	Organic matter	2.4-0.8-2.3
Oak leaves	Organic matter	0.8-9.4-0.1
Orchard grass hay	Organic matter	2.3-0.7-2.8
Oyster shells	Calcium	33.5% calcium
Peat moss	Organic matter	pH range 3.0-4.5
Poultry manure (dry)	Organic matter	4-4-2

*Use these suggested application rates based on your soil's fertility, as indicated by soil test results and your personal observations.

Average Application Rate (per 1,000 sq. ft.)*			
Low	Medium	Adequate	Comments
10 lb.	5 lb.	2 lb.	—
100 lb.	50 lb.	25 lb.	—
500 lb.	300 lb.	200 lb.	—
100 lb.	50 lb.	25 lb.	—
40 lb.	20 lb.	5 lb.	Do not apply if pH is below 5.8
200 lb.	150 lb.	100 lb.	—
30 lb.	20 lb.	10 lb.	—
200 lb.	150 lb.	100 lb.	—
50 lb.	30 lb.	15 lb.	—
20 lb.	10 lb.	5 lb.	—
200 lb.	150 lb.	100 lb.	—
250 lb.	150 lb.	100 lb.	—
200 lb.	150 lb.	100 lb.	—
100 lb.	50 lb.	25 lb.	—
—	—	25 lb.	Use around acid-loving plants; apply as needed
100 lb.	50 lb.	25 lb.	Should be composted or applied in fall

(continued)

SELECTING ORGANIC FERTILIZERS—
CONTINUED

Organic Amendment	Primary Benefit	Average Analysis
Red clover hay	Organic matter	2.8-0.6-2.3
Rock phosphate	Phosphate	0-3-0; 32% total phosphate; 32% calcium; contains 11 trace minerals
Sawdust	Organic matter	0.2-0-0.2
Sheep manure (dry)	Organic matter	4-1.4-3.5
Soybean meal	Nitrogen	7-0.5-2.3
Sul-Po-Mag	Potash; magnesium	0-0-22; 11% magnesium; 22% sulfur
Sweet clover hay	Organic matter	2.2-0.6-2.2
Swine manure (dry)	Organic matter	2-1.8-1.8
Timothy hay	Organic matter	1.8-0.7-2.8
Wheat bran	Organic matter	2.6-2.9-1.6
Wheat straw	Organic matter	0.7-0.2-1.2
White clover (green)	Organic matter	0.5-0.2-0.3
Wood ashes (leached)	Potash	0-1.2-2
Wood ashes (unleached)	Potash	0-1.5-8
Worm castings	Organic matter	0.5-0.5-0.3

SOURCE: Reprinted by permission of the Necessary Trading Company. Copyright © 1985, 1991. All rights reserved. Necessary Trading Company, One Nature's Way, New Castle, VA 24127.

*Use these suggested application rates based on your soil's fertility, as indicated by soil test results and your personal observations.

Average Application Rate (per 1,000 sq. ft.)*			Comments
Low	Medium	Adequate	
200 lb.	150 lb.	100 lb.	—
60 lb.	25 lb.	10 lb.	—
250 lb.	150 lb.	100 lb.	Be sure sawdust is well-rotted before incorporating
100 lb.	50 lb.	25 lb.	—
50 lb.	25 lb.	10 lb.	—
10 lb.	7 lb.	5 lb.	Do not use if applying dolomitic limestone; substitute greensand or other potassium source
200 lb.	150 lb.	100 lb.	—
200 lb.	150 lb.	100 lb.	Should be composted or applied in fall
200 lb.	150 lb.	100 lb.	—
200 lb.	150 lb.	100 lb.	—
250 lb.	150 lb.	100 lb.	—
800 lb.	600 lb.	400 lb.	—
20 lb.	10 lb.	5 lb.	—
10 lb.	5 lb.	3 lb.	—
250 lb.	100 lb.	50 lb.	50% organic matter plus 11 trace minerals

MINED SOIL AMENDMENTS

Natural mined materials such as rock phosphate and greensand are kind to soil organisms, but they are nonrenewable resources. The phosphate mining industry, especially, is an environmentally destructive one. There is also some concern, particularly in Europe, about peat depletion, with calls for prohibiting the use of peat moss in organic production. The best strategy for reducing your reliance on mined products is to recycle organic sources of essential nutrients through compost, mulch, and green manure. In potting mixes, substitute leaf mold and well-rotted sawdust for peat.

Soap phosphate (Organophos). This by-product of the soap industry is used in some commercially blended fertilizers. It contains 15 to 20 percent phosphorus.

Potassium Sources

Potassium can be readily supplied through compost and by mulching with materials rich in this element. Highly soluble potassium sources are recommended only for soils diagnosed through soil or tissue testing as deficient. Follow lab recommendations when using potassium amendments. An oversupply of potassium can cause problems with soil balance and pH. It can also cause "luxury consumption" (or overconsumption) of potassium by plants, which can interfere with the plants' uptake of other essential nutrients.

Granite meal. This material is a fine rock powder from granite quarries. It contains up to 5 percent total potassium and other minerals in a very slowly available form. Granite meal is useful for long-term soil building.

Greensand. Greensand is a mined mineral deposit from ancient seabeds. It contains about 7 percent total potassium and other minerals in a slowly available form. Greensand helps loosen clay soils and stimulates biological activity.

Kelp meal. Dried and ground seaweed of the species *Ascophyllum nodosum* is harvested from the North Atlantic Ocean. It contains about 2.5 percent potassium, some nitrogen, a large number of micronutrients, some vitamins, and amino acids. Kelp meal stimulates soil biological activity and improves soil structure.

Langbeinite (Sulfate of Potash-Magnesia, or Sul-Po-Mag). Langbeinite ore is a mined mineral, although many commercially available sources are industrial by-products. It contains 22 percent potassium, 22 percent sulfur, and 11 percent magnesium in a highly soluble form. Use with caution due to its high solubility.

Potassium sulfate. This naturally occurring mined mineral is also manufactured synthetically. It contains 50 percent available potassium, making it a highly soluble source of potassium. It is not recommended for direct use by home gardeners because it is so concentrated. Potassium sulfate is often used in commercially blended products.

Wood ashes. These residues from wood fires contain about 8 percent potassium, as well as calcium and micronutrients in a highly available form. Overuse can result in serious mineral imbalances.

Calcium Sources

Most calcium sources are benign to soil organisms. Use calcium amendments only if soil test results indicate a need for additional calcium.

Aragonite. This mineral substance is precipitated by sunlight passing through ocean water and mined from the ocean floor near Bermuda. It contains 96 percent calcium carbonate.

Eggshells. Ground-up eggshells are a poultry industry by-product. They contain calcium, trace minerals, and a small amount of nitrogen (see the illustration below).

Gypsum. Gypsum is a mined calcium sulfate (gray in color) or an industrial by-product (white in color). It contains about 23 per-

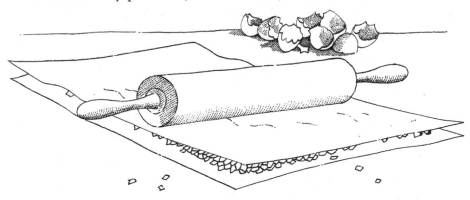

Eggshells add extra calcium to fertilizer mixes or to the compost pile. You may be able to buy crushed shells commercially, or you can make your own by sandwiching eggshells between two sheets of waxed paper and rolling over them with a rolling pin.

HOW MUCH NUTRIENT DO YOU NEED?

You don't need a Ph.D. (or a pHD) to figure out how much fertilizer or amendment you need to add to correct a soil imbalance or to meet the nutrient requirements of your plants. All you need to know is how much of any specific nutrient you need, provided as part of your soil test results. If your soil-testing laboratory only gives results in terms of "low," "medium," and "high," ask the lab for the corresponding figures. Then calculate how much of a given material will supply that amount of nutrient, based on the material's percent analysis in the table on page 108 or as listed on its label.

Here's an example to help you with the method:

1. Your soil test tells you that potassium is low. Low potassium levels require an addition of 50 to 100 pounds per acre, depending on the type of crop being grown and the soil texture. You need to add 80 pounds of potassium per acre.

2. Divide 80 (the number of pounds of potassium needed per acre) by 40 (because there are approximately 40 units of 1,000 square feet per acre) to get 2 (the number of pounds of potassium needed per 1,000 square feet of garden).

3. Now figure out how much potassium you'll be providing in your compost. Let's say you have enough compost to spread about 100 pounds for every 1,000 square feet of garden. You estimate its NPK analysis at 1-1-1. You'll be getting half of your potassium needs from the compost.

4. If you've been saving wood ashes, and your soil pH is low, you may decide to use them to supply potassium. The table tells you they contain about 8 percent potassium.

5. Calculate the amount of wood ashes you'll need by dividing the number of pounds of potassium you need by the percent composition of your chosen amendment. In this example, you need 1 pound of potassium, and your ashes contain 8 percent potassium. Divide 1 (the pounds of potassium needed) by 0.08 (the percentage of potassium in the wood ashes) to get 12.5 (the amount of wood ashes you need).

6. To bring the potassium level of your soil up to an adequate level, add 12.5 pounds of wood ashes in addition to 100 pounds of compost for each 1,000 square feet of garden.

cent available calcium and 18 percent sulfur. Gypsum is valuable for adding calcium and sulfur without affecting soil pH. It also helps loosen clay soils.

Limestone. Limestone is a quarried, finely ground rock powder. Dolomitic limestone contains about 50 percent calcium carbonate and 40 percent magnesium carbonate. Calcitic limestone contains about 70 percent calcium carbonate and 15 percent magnesium carbonate. It is used to increase soil pH.

Oyster shells. A by-product of the seafood industry, oyster shells must be finely ground to be useful as a soil amendment. They contain 31 to 36 percent calcium plus trace minerals.

Magnesium, Sulfur, and Micronutrient Sources

Apply magnesium separately only if a soil test has diagnosed a deficiency problem. Sulfur deficiency is rarely a problem, especially if you add enough organic matter, but sulfur-rich fertilizers are sometimes used for their acidifying properties.

Most of the materials described in the preceding sections are also rich in micronutrients, as are most organic materials you might include in a compost pile. The amendments listed below either contain an especially rich balance of micronutrients or are helpful for correcting specific deficiencies that have been identified through soil or tissue testing. Never apply single-element micronutrients, such as boron or zinc, without instructions from a lab—a small error can drastically upset balances.

Borax. Borax is a mined mineral (hydrated sodium borate) containing about 10 percent boron. It is also used as a cleaning agent, water softener, and wood preservative. Use borax only where boron deficiencies have been determined by soil or tissue testing.

Chelates. These materials are synthetic compounds of metallic nutrients (generally micronutrients, but also magnesium and calcium) bound up in a complex organic molecule. They are easily absorbed by plants, especially if applied to the leaves.

Epsom salts. Epsom salts are mined, processed magnesium sulfate. They contain 10 percent magnesium and 13 percent sulfur. Use them only in accordance with soil test recommendations, preferably as a foliar spray, to minimize spot toxicity from spills.

Flowers of sulfur. This material is actually elemental sulfur, which may be mined or recovered as an industrial waste product. It contains 92 percent sulfur. Use it in place of aluminum sulfate to lower soil pH.

Kelp extract. Kelp extract is a liquid or dry soluble concentrate extracted from *Ascophyllum nodosum* seaweed. It contains a large selection of micronutrients and potassium, as well as plant growth hormones. Kelp extract is useful as a growth stimulant.

MANAGING

YOUR

SOIL

PUTTING IT ALL TOGETHER

The first five chapters of this book have given you a thorough grounding in the basics of how the soil ecosystem works and what you, as its caretaker, can do to keep it in good health. In order to begin applying this new information, it's helpful to sort it all out into a comprehensive soil-care system.

Each of the sections that follow represents one essential step of a program for building and maintaining healthy soil without synthetic fertilizers. Each step affects all the others, and all of them are necessary for success. Follow these steps, and you will have an unfailing formula for productive, living soil.

PLAN AHEAD

One of the first steps to successful soil care is good planning. Integrate soil-improvement chores into your overall yard and garden planning process. When it's too cold or too hot to garden, make plans for the growing season. Sit down with your garden journal and soil test results, and identify problems you may need to address. Was there enough compost to go around? Will you need to lime this year? Did you find clumps of undecomposed sod in your new bed at the end of the season?

If you're just starting in a new place, outline the basics first, such as general garden layout and bed design, soil drainage and

139

Learn about the living soil.

Feed the soil.

Use the right tools.

Improve the soil
with green manures.

Buy fertilizers and amendments wisely.

Healthy soil means a happy gardener. Give the hardworking microorganisms beneath your feet plenty of organic matter; tinker with your soil chemistry, if needed; and practice good gardening techniques. It's all connected.

other qualities, and types of crops or plantings you intend to put in. Think about your long-term plan: Do you hope to add more permanent beds? Put in more fruit trees? Landscape around a new addition?

Now is the time to research sources of tools and soil amendments and compare prices. Inventory the supplies you already have, and make a list of what you'll need, along with a wish list of products you'd really love to try. Many of these items are only available through mail order ("Soil-Care Supplies" on page 260 includes mail-order sources). Check into new sources of organic matter in your neighborhood, and make plans to improve or expand your composting system.

Figure out a rotation plan for the vegetable garden, and order seeds for green manures along with your vegetable and flower seeds. Mix up a batch of potting soil to start seedlings or repot houseplants. Just getting your hands into some soil can be the most inspirational thing imaginable.

Contact your nearest organic farmers' organization to find out about conferences, workshops, and other educational events it may offer (see "Organic Certification" on page 261 for addresses of ones in your area). They usually welcome hom gardeners and may even have resource people who can help you with specific problems. Sharing stories with other gardeners will always teach you something new and interesting. Cooperative Extension Service offices sometimes offer workshops on subjects such as home composting. Learning new tricks and ideas about caring for soil and plants is a lifelong voyage of discovery and satisfaction. Each year, you renew your understanding of the living earth and your connection to it.

GET TO KNOW YOUR SOIL

To take good care of your soil, you must understand its natural tendencies and observe how it changes as you work with it. Tour your garden at least once a week: Examine general plant health, notice where weeds are taking hold, and check out drainage and other soil conditions. Make note of any changes, and try to figure out why they occurred.

Keep a garden journal to record your observations. Include information about weather, fertility improvement, cultural problems, and other noteworthy garden events. Keep soil test results in it. Over time, it will become the cornerstone of your soil-improvement system and your overall garden-management bible.

If you're acquiring new property or expanding your garden area to undeveloped land, observe and record its slope, drainage patterns, and existing vegetation. Note any obvious problems, such as erosion, standing water, thin or sickly plant coverage, steep slopes, or salt crust.

Contact the local office of the Soil Conservation Service to get information about your soil type and its limitations and best uses. Identify the predominant weed species, and find out if they are indicators of a particular condition. See if you can notice any symptoms of nutrient deficiencies (see "Nutrient Deficiency Symptoms" on page 91 to learn about clues to these problems).

How does the soil feel under your feet—is it soft and springy, or does it feel more like walking on a sidewalk? Dig up a handful of soil and evaluate its texture—does sand, silt, or clay predominate? How hard was it to dig? Finally, if you're feeling ambitious, dig down a foot or so and see if there's any sign of hardpan.

A few times a season, take a trowel or shovel out to your garden for a closer look. Examine soil moisture and structure—are there crumbly particles with lots of pore spaces, or does it seem dense and heavy? Can you poke your finger in easily? How far down must you dig to detect moisture?

Examine plant roots—do they look deep and vigorous? Dig up a clover or other leguminous plant and check for round nodules on the roots (a healthy leguminous plant will have lots of round nodules). Look at the organic fraction of your soil. How much undecomposed plant debris do you see? Do you still recognize residues of last season's garden? Observe any signs of soil-dwelling animals, especially earthworms, and make note of conditions that seem to attract them.

All of these clues can help you learn about the physical characteristics of your garden soil and identify problem areas. Continually observing and recording these kinds of details will give you the information you need about the success of your soil management practices or about changes you might want to make in the future. For more information on judging the physical qualities of soil, see Chapter 1. To find details on identifying and solving soil problems, see Chapter 7.

Learn about Your Living Soil

In many respects, the biological health of your soil is just as important as its physical characteristics. Soil is a complex fabric of living organisms—that's why we say, "Feed the soil, not the plant." Everything you do for your soil is ultimately aimed at replenishing and building soil humus. Humus is a product of soil biological activity, and the only way to create more of it is to cater to the needs of soil organisms: bacteria and fungi, earthworms and springtails, plant roots and prairie dogs.

The soil community is an interconnected web. Producers create carbohydrates and proteins from simple nutrient elements, usually through photosynthesis. Consumers, from simple protozoans to humans, depend on the food created by green plants. Decomposers bring the basic chemical nutrients full circle, from consumers back to producers. Decomposers, which are primarily bacteria and fungi, are found almost exclusively in the soil. Microbial decomposers account for 60 to 80 percent of the total soil metabolism. Without these decomposers, life would grind to a halt as we suffocated in our own wastes.

Microorganisms and other members of the soil community, like earthworms, thrive in a soil that is in good physical condition—loose, crumbly, well-aerated, and moisture-retentive but well-drained—the same conditions that most plants prefer. You can keep your soil in good shape and supply the organisms with the organic matter they need by adding compost or raising green manure crops. And regular assessments of your soil's chemistry will help you maintain the proper conditions of fertility and pH, so both the soil organisms and your plants will thrive. To find out more about the thriving ecosystem of soil organisms, see Chapter 2. For more information on worms in the compost pile and other compost organisms, see Chapter 4.

Feed the Soil with Compost

Composting provides a crucial link in your soil's food web, recycling organic wastes into vital humus. Compost is part of the answer to just about any soil-improvement need, from drainage to nutrient deficiencies. You may be able to buy it in a bag, but it's easy (and much cheaper) to make your own.

No matter what your situation, there is a composting system that will work for you. You can compost anywhere, under just about any conditions. Compost indoors by making a worm box or barrel. Set up a drum composter in a garage or shed. Buy a prefabricated compost bin for your yard, or make one using inexpensive or salvaged materials. Double- and triple-bin systems allow you to turn your compost by transferring materials from one bin to the next; you can do the same thing with a movable enclosure. Refer to Chapter 4 for complete details on starting and maintaining a thriving, productive compost pile. Or see "Compost-Based Fertilizers" on page 106 for information on buying comercially packaged compost.

Compost is the ultimate garden elixir because it is so versatile. Use it to improve soil structure, drainage, and aeration; to stimulate soil organisms; and to provide plant nutrients. No need to worry about spills or overdoses—use as much as you have, anytime you have it.

Apply compost in early spring to get vegetables and flowers started right, in summer to perk up heavy feeders, and in fall to prepare lawns for dormancy. Work it into the soil before planting, or lay it under the mulch around your trees. When using it in germinating mixes, be extra careful that it is thoroughly decomposed. Give all your plants an extra boost with compost tea, either watered into the ground or sprayed on the leaves. Whatever your soil is like, more compost can only help it. For ideas on using compost in specific areas of your garden, see Chapters 8 through 12.

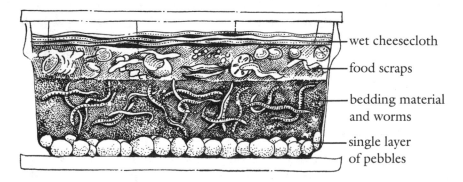

wet cheesecloth

food scraps

bedding material and worms

single layer of pebbles

An indoor worm bin is a great way for apartment dwellers or cold-climate gardeners to recycle their kitchen garbage. Nutrient-rich worm castings give a boost to plants.

You can never have too much compost. Work it into the soil before planting, sidedress during the growing season, scatter it on the lawn, and spread it around trees.

BUILD SOIL HUMUS

Along with applying compost, planting cover crops and green manures and working them into the soil are effective ways of feeding soil organisms and building humus. These practices benefit your garden in other ways, too, by suppressing weeds, protecting from erosion, interfering with plant pests and diseases, and bringing up nutrients from the subsoil. Best of all, you'll be building fertility at a very low cost, without having to haul and spread anything.

Cover crops are meant primarily to protect the soil, while green manures are meant to feed it. Choose legumes to contribute the most nitrogen to the soil. Fast-growing grains, cabbage-family crops, or buckwheat will protect bare soil and smother weeds. Use perennials or biennials, like clover or alfalfa, where you can grow them for more than one season before tilling them in. Plant cold-hardy crops to hold soil over the winter. Experiment with new species and with combinations like rye and vetch to find just the qualities you need. Even weeds can be valuable soil food—just be sure to work them in before they set seed!

Green manures are especially useful when preparing new ground for vegetables, flower beds, and orchards. If possible, start at least a year before you intend to plant. Work green manures into rotation plans for your vegetable garden. You can even plant low-growing white Dutch clover between your beds as "living mulch," and mow occasionally to keep it contained.

Perennials, lawns, trees, and shrubs can't be rotated with green manures, and most vegetable gardens need organic matter replenished faster than is possible by relying on green manures alone. Your number one choice for organic matter is compost, which is mostly

A green manure adds organic matter and nutrients. Legume-and-grass combinations, which have fibrous, matted root systems, are excellent for increasing organic matter and nitrogen, phosphorus, and potassium nutrition of crops that follow.

humus and is alive with biological activity. If you have a plentiful supply, you need look no farther.

Mulch is another key source of soil food, especially for permanent plantings. Mulch protects from erosion, keeps moisture in, smothers weeds, moderates temperature, and feeds soil organisms. Many common materials make excellent mulch: grass clippings, straw, hay, sawdust, wood chips, leaves, newspapers, and cardboard. If you have access to a shredder, the possibilities are endless. Be careful not to import weed seeds into your garden, and make sure you have plentiful available nitrogen to balance high-carbon mulches like sawdust and wood chips.

All of these techniques will help you increase the level of humus in your garden soil. And by adding humus, you can improve soil properties like structure and drainage, encourage the growth and health of soil organisms, and balance soil nutrients and pH. Along with growing green manures and cover crops and mulching, you'll learn about other techniques of building soil humus in Chapter 3. For details on composting, see Chapter 4.

MONITOR SOIL FERTILITY

While your ultimate goal is to create a naturally balanced and fertile soil, there are times when your garden may need a boost. Use purchased fertilizers and soil amendments to supplement, not to replace, a fertility-building program based on adding compost and organic matter. Base your choices on a good understanding of your soil and crop requirements, as well as the quality and cost of products available.

Soil testing helps complete the picture of your soil's health status. Many gardeners forgo soil testing altogether, choosing to depend on their own observations. But for other gardeners, soil testing is a valuable aid, and in cases of suspected deficiency, soil tests can either confirm or disprove your beliefs.

Decide how you will go about monitoring soil chemical balances—with a home soil test kit, the local Cooperative Extension office, or a private soil-testing laboratory—and get into a routine. You may decide to do only basic pH and nutrient analysis or to pay for more-sophisticated tests that show organic matter or micronutrients.

To enable you to compare results more accurately, always take your samples at the same time of year. Most important, note how test results correspond with your own observations of fertility levels. For instance, you should notice the number of earthworms increasing as your organic matter levels have risen.

If you do need to add nutrients to your soil, the material of choice is usually compost. But if you don't have enough compost to go around, or if your soil is lacking in a specific nutrient, you may have to use a commercial fertilizer or amendment. Learn to read the labels on commercially packaged products. Many bagged "organic" fertilizers are blends of rock powders, dried organic wastes, and other natural ingredients that are rich in various plant nutrients. They are formulated to be used like synthetic commercial fertilizers, although they tend to be lower in immediately available nutrients. They generally supply much higher total nutrient content in a slow-release form, along with many micronutrients and some organic matter.

Be sure to find out what all the ingredients are. Avoid those that pose a risk of toxic contamination, such as leather dust or cottonseed meal. You can create formulas similar to those of the bagged—at a lower cost—by mixing commercially available organic wastes, such as bonemeal, blood meal, hoof-and-horn meal, and alfalfa meal, with rock powders, such as greensand, granite dust, and rock phosphate.

If a soil test tells you that your soil is low in a particular mineral nutrient, you can add rock powders to your compost, or else you can spread them when you add organic matter to the soil. If your soil tends to be acid, plan on liming regularly, and pay attention to mineral balances.

Regular doses of seaweed, either as kelp meal or as a foliar spray, ensure good micronutrient supplies for soil and crops. If plants are showing definite signs of nutrient deficiencies, use high-analysis organic wastes as a side-dressing, or make up a tea using manure, compost, or fish emulsion or a similar concoction to water or spray directly on the plants.

Keeping your soil fertility at a balanced level will encourage your plants to grow well and help the soil organisms to thrive. It is one of the most important aspects of maintaining a healthy, productive soil. Chapter 5 explains in detail how to evaluate your soil's fertility and deal with nutrient deficiencies.

Use the Right Tools

Building humus through composting and organic matter management is essential to improving soil tilth, but the tools you use to work your soil can also make a big difference. The ideal is to keep soil disturbance at a minimum, putting biological agents to work doing as many of your mixing, tunneling, and aerating jobs as possible. Use permanent beds, perennial plantings, and deep mulches to reduce the need to dig, till, or cultivate.

Good hand tools are the best investment you can make for successful gardening. If you have a small yard and are reasonably energetic, you shouldn't need anything else. Power tools such as tillers and shredders can be extremely useful, but tillers are often overused, and this misuse can damage soil structure.

One of the functions of cultivation is to introduce more air into the soil, but be careful to avoid tools that pulverize topsoil. When you destroy soil structure, you disrupt earthworms and microbes and make the soil more vulnerable to being blown around. This is another reason why rotary tillers make poor cultivating tools. Rotary tillers can also cause a hardpan by the force of the blades continually beating at the same depth.

Cultivation is a good way to keep weeds down. A sharp, light cultivating hoe allows you to slice off weed seedlings just below the surface with little effort. Wheel hoes are a valuable tool for larger gardens. Once the soil has warmed up, mulch as much as possible to keep weeds in check. Using a combination of proper cultivation techniques and mulching can help you keep weed problems to a minimum.

To learn more about tools and techniques for working the soil without harming the soil community, see Chapter 2. Chapter 3 discusses methods for incorporating green manures and other humus-building materials. Turn to Chapters 8 through 12 to learn soil-working techniques for specific areas like vegetable gardens, flower beds, tree and shrub plantings, lawns, and container plantings.

OVERCOMING PROBLEM SOILS

Few things are as satisfying as reclaiming a "hopeless" plot of land, though it may take a lot of time and effort. Building organic matter and humus is a good start. Most of the problems covered in this chapter can be at least partially overcome by adding humus and encouraging biological activity in the soil. Plenty of compost and organic mulch are essential to heal soils that have been damaged by erosion, neglect, or pollution.

Soil problems often have more than one cause. As with most problems, the key to correction lies in understanding what's causing the trouble. Review Chapter 1 for guidance on how to evaluate your own soil conditions. When in doubt, explain your soil conditions to your local Cooperative Extension agent, and ask for his or her advice before you try any drastic measures like installing drainage tiles or bringing in new topsoil.

DRAINAGE PROBLEMS

Too much water, and thus too little air, suppresses biological activity and literally bogs down the soil ecosystem. Plants that aren't specially adapted to wet feet will suffer in poorly drained soil, and many of them will die. But soils that drain too fast can also present problems: Water and nutrients are leached through the soil, and plants fail to grow and thrive.

Any soil can suffer from drainage difficulties. They are caused by a number of factors, ranging from a high water table to hard-

150

packed soil. Drainage problems come in all degrees—some are relatively simple to correct, but a few border on the hopeless. Poor drainage can make matters worse if your soil also has other difficulties, such as acidity or heavy metal contamination.

Be familiar with your soil's structure and characteristics before you begin a program to correct poor drainage. If you're evaluating property to buy or rent and gardening is a high priority for you, pay careful attention to the property's drainage.

TOO MUCH WATER

If your soil is wet most of the time because the underground water table is relatively close to the surface, as may be the case if you live in a low-lying river valley or if springs are seeping into your best garden site, there isn't much you can do to eliminate the cause of the problem. Runoff from buildings can also be hard to avoid. In such cases, you have to create lower places for water to drain to, channel water away from the house, or find ways to lift plant roots out of the quagmire.

If your drainage problems are severe, consider changing your gardening plans instead of your drainage. Grow garden vegetables and herbs in containers to solve the problem. Include a garden of tolerant perennials or a bog garden. You may discover a whole new world of possibilities if you accept the challenge.

Raising the Roots

The simplest and most satisfying remedy to poor-drainage problems is building raised beds. A few weekends of work will be needed to establish the beds, but maintaining them is often easier than maintaining other types of beds. Use a thick mulch of straw, wood chips, or leaves between the beds. The mulch minimizes the need to cultivate in the paths, and it allows you to get out into your garden after a rain without experiencing that sinking (or squishing) feeling.

But sometimes raised beds aren't a feasible project. Maybe the poorly drained area isn't the garden—you'd just like to have a dry patch of lawn for summer picnics. And sometimes raised beds alone won't make enough of a difference, especially if your climate is rainy. Don't despair—in the sections below, there are a few more tricks you can try.

Channeling Excess Water

We have a long history of reclaiming swamplands for agriculture or development, and although the practice of widespread wetlands elimination is rightly criticized, the techniques can be useful for a small yard or garden. But consider these options a last resort: They require time, money, and professional advice. Careful planning is a must, and government permits may be necessary. Be sure to get help from a professional excavating contractor before you begin any drainage project.

Perforated drainage pipes or drain tiles. Drainage pipes or hollow ceramic tiles can be installed to funnel excess water to a catchment area. The catchment area may be a roadside ditch, street gutter, stream, or pond. You can make a simple dry well from a 55-gallon drum with both ends removed. Bury the drum and fill it with stones. Be sure the top of the drum is below the lowest point of the drainage pipes.

Place pipes 4 to 6 inches below the soil surface, sloping at a grade of 3 to 6 inches per 100 feet, toward the catchment area. A

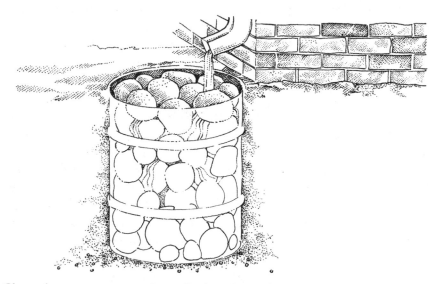

Channel excess water to a dry well where it can drain away. Cut both ends off of a 55-gallon barrel. Then, dig a hole large enough so that the barrel will sit in it below the drainage pipe or soil level. Insert the barrel, and fill it with stones. Then cover the top of the barrel with soil. A dry well can serve as a catchment area for subsurface drainage pipes or as a drainage area to handle excess runoff from house gutters, as shown here.

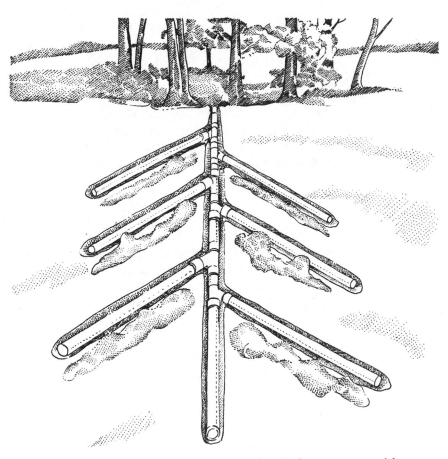

Plan the layout of perforated drainpipes in a herringbone pattern, with branches 20 feet apart. Slope the pipes toward the catchment area at a grade of 3 to 6 inches per 100 feet.

herringbone pattern, with branches about 20 feet apart, works well. Line the trenches with sand or gravel, and backfill with coarse gravel before covering with sand or topsoil. Water the site well so that it settles. Add more topsoil, if needed.

Drainage ditches. The same method used by highway engineers to keep water from collecting on roadways can be used in your garden. But keep in mind that drainage ditches can be unsightly and even dangerous: They destroy your lawn and create a hazardous obstacle to moving around the yard.

Your local Soil Conservation Service office can help you design drainage projects, including ponds. If necessary, they can recommend a consultant or contractor qualified to do the work you need. Depending on how large your property is, what adjoins it, and where the drainage water will empty, you may need to get permits from local zoning boards.

The basic principle is to divert the water that is flowing downhill toward your site so that it flows around your site instead of across it. Sometimes all you need is a small ditch at the highest end of your plot to lead water off to a grassy lower area. Such a ditch may be only 6 to 8 inches deep. To prevent erosion, line it with stones or gravel, or grade it off in a gradual slope and seed it with grass.

Ponds. If you have the room to dig a pond, you'll get many benefits beyond drying out your garden site. Even a small pond, strategically placed, can enhance the aesthetics, biological diversity, and microclimate of your yard at the same time. A pond can be stocked with fish of some kind, which can provide a tasty fringe benefit to your drainage project. Ponds also provide a measure of fire protection for rural homes. Of course, ponds do require a fair amount of effort and expense to make and maintain. And in households with small children, a pond can represent a serious danger.

Before you decide to dig a pond, ask yourself these questions:

• Will it be fed by surface runoff or an underground spring? Make sure you have a reliable source of water before you begin.

• Is your soil impermeable enough to hold water? Coarse-textured soils need a layer of clay or a plastic liner. Medium-textured soils may need compression to prevent seepage.

• How much earth will need to be excavated? By hand or by machine? The size of your pond may well be limited by the budget you have for the project.

• Where will the runoff go? Be sure you're not just transferring your problem to another part of your property or even to a neighbor.

Your local Cooperative Extension Service or Soil Conservation Service can advise you about pond planning issues, including permits needed.

HARDPAN

Another common reason for poor drainage is the existence of hardpan—a layer of compressed soil or clay that exists 6 inches to a foot or more beneath the soil surface. The problems associated with hardpan go beyond poor drainage. Plant roots can't penetrate such a layer. Denied access to subsoil nutrients, they grow sideways, competing with each other.

If your garden spade slides easily into your soil, then seems to hit a barrier at a certain depth, you probably have a hardpan problem. Sometimes these compacted layers occur naturally, particularly in regions with heavy rainfall, such as the Southeast. Check with your local Soil Conservation Service about whether your area is prone to hardpans. If this is the case, whatever you do to remedy the situation may be only temporary, and hardpan will re-form due to inherent chemical and physical soil qualities. Often, a hardpan has been unintentionally created, especially by heavy machinery traffic or repeated plowing. Excessive use of rotary tillers, besides damaging soil structure, can create compaction at the tine depth.

Breaking Up Hardpan

The most direct way of correcting hardpan is mechanically. Farmers use chisel plows, pulled through the field with a powerful tractor, to shatter hardpan. If you have a large area to work with and are just starting to develop your site, it may be worthwhile to find someone who can chisel-plow it for you.

Double digging raised beds will accomplish the same purpose

PREVENTING HARDPAN

You can prevent most hardpan problems from occurring by observing a few simple rules:

• Avoid working your soil when it's too wet. Squeeze a handful of soil: If it crumbles, it's dry enough to work. If it makes a soggy, sticky ball, stay out of the garden.

• Avoid walking on planted areas as much as possible.

• Keep vehicle traffic—bikes, all-terrain vehicles (ATVs), and snowmobiles—off lawns and fields, unless you have specifically set aside areas for such traffic.

• Avoid practices that cause compaction, such as frequent plowing or rotary tilling.

• Build and maintain soil humus. A healthy, biologically active soil encourages high populations of earthworms, whose tunnels provide air and water passages through the soil. Also, the chemical properties of humus alleviate chemical imbalances that can lead to hardpan formation.

in a small garden; for details on this technique, see "Double Digging" on page 158. Or you can use a device called a U-bar. A U-bar works something like a chisel plow but on a small scale. The tines are made of sturdy rods bolted to the frame. You use the U-bar by pushing the tines into the soil and rocking them back and forth. Doing this over the entire garden once or twice a season will break up any hardpan within reach of the tool, as well as generally improving air and water penetration. It's not as strenuous a task as digging, because you aren't actually moving soil around.

If you notice hardpan as you dig deeply (when planting trees and shrubs, for instance), use a garden fork or U-bar to break it up beyond the radius of your planting hole. Do the same around established trees and perennials if you suspect hardpan.

Work the soil with a sturdy U-bar once or twice a season. Push the U-bar into the soil with your foot, and rock the tines back and forth to break up hardpan and improve aeration.

Natural Hardpan Helpers

The best long-term measure for overcoming and avoiding hardpan problems is to put biological agents to work for you. Many deep-rooted plants such as alfalfa, sweet clover, comfrey, dandelion, and daikon radish are capable of breaching hardpans and can be grown as a green manure expressly for that purpose. Earthworms are the ultimate soil excavators—whatever you do to attract and keep them in your soil will pay off in many more ways than just eliminating hardpan problems. Using a thick layer of mulch and adding green manure to your soil will create the ideal soil conditions for these helpful creatures. (See "Growing Green Manures" on page 50 for more information, planting green manures for soil improvement.)

HEAVY-TEXTURED SOIL

Soil that has a high clay content and too little organic matter can be extremely difficult to work with. It waterlogs easily when wet, and when it dries out, it can resemble concrete.

Lighten up heavy soils by adding large amounts of sand, peat, or compost, or any combination of these. Remember that peat will acidify the soil—a boon for alkaline soils. But if your soil is already acid, monitor your pH and include lime, if necessary. Mulching is vital for heavy soil. Besides adding organic matter, the mulch prevents clay soil from being exposed to the baking effects of the sun.

Soil Texturizers

Materials such as greensand and other mineral-rich rock powders also have a reputation as soil texturizers, in part because an abundance of balanced micronutrients stimulates microbial activity and humus formation. A number of products on the market are touted as cures for heavy soils. Humates are mineral deposits of humic acids mined in North Dakota, Texas, New Mexico, and Idaho, often as by-products of lignite or soft-coal mining. Adding humic acids can improve soil texture and nutrient availability in soils that are low in organic matter, but it can never substitute for increasing humus content by building organic matter. Commercial soil conditioners (such as Roots), which contain enzymes, microbial cultures, and other biochemical growth stimulants, may sometimes be effective in the short term on very poor soils.

DOUBLE DIGGING

If your garden is filled with well-drained soil that has a loose, light texture, consider yourself blessed—double digging isn't necessary. But if you have heavy, poorly drained soil, double digging is a must. No doubt about it—double digging is hard work. But the benefits can far outweigh the effort, and you generally only have to do it once.

The technique entails removing a layer of soil down to one spade's depth, then loosening the layer of soil below that with a garden fork. When replacing the top layer, you generally add compost and other organic amendments.

Here's how to double dig a bed:

1. Measure off the bed. Dig a trench 1 foot wide by 1 foot deep at one end of the bed, piling the soil in a wheelbarrow or on a groundcloth.

2. Loosen the subsoil (the soil in the bottom of the trench) by inserting a garden fork and wiggling it back and forth at regular intervals along the length of the trench. Don't remove or invert the soil as you do this. To get some goodies down into the lower root zone, add a little compost at this time.

3. Dig another trench adjoining the first one, tossing the soil from the second trench into the first trench as you go. If you are digging up sod, shake out as much soil as possible from each chunk, and pile it separately to decompose, rather than taking the chance of having it regrow in your bed. Layer in compost and other organic materials and mix well.

4. Repeat Steps 2 and 3 for the rest of the bed. When you get to the last trench, fill it in with the topsoil you saved from the first trench.

The surface of your bed will now be 3 to 4 inches higher than when you started, due mainly to the newly loosened soil. Leave it the way it is and just start planting, or support the edges with stones or landscape timbers to make it look neat and reduce erosion. Periodic aerating with a garden fork is a good idea, especially if your soil is naturally heavy-textured. Otherwise, treat your new permanent bed just like any other garden space—and enjoy the improved health and vigor of your plants.

Sometimes heavy-textured soils have high magnesium levels. In these soils, the particles bind together too tightly, closing off air passages. If a soil test points to an excess of magnesium, improve the condition by adding calcium in the form of gypsum (calcium sulfate).

EXCESSIVE DRAINAGE

If your problems are of the opposite nature—light-textured, sandy soils over gravel parent material or subsoil—they can be just as

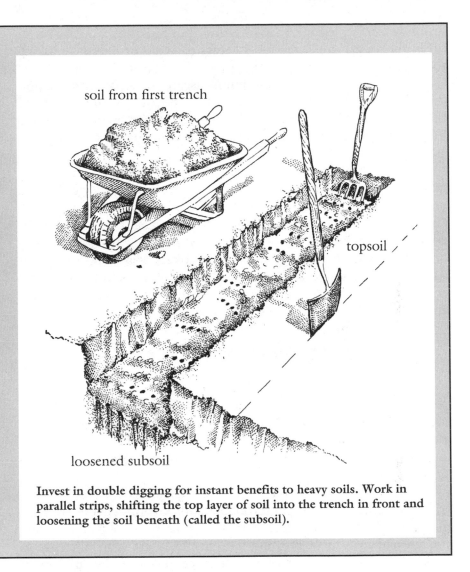

soil from first trench

topsoil

loosened subsoil

Invest in double digging for instant benefits to heavy soils. Work in parallel strips, shifting the top layer of soil into the trench in front and loosening the soil beneath (called the subsoil).

frustrating. This type of soil leads to a lack of moisture and nutrients. Organic matter and humus break down too rapidly, and minerals are quickly washed away. Coarse texture also means a low cation exchange capacity, so nutrient reserves are generally low to begin with. For more information on cation exchange capacity, see "Cations Simplified" on page 99.

The first solution that occurs to you will most likely be to add water or irrigate. But this approach is not without its pitfalls. Irrigation can be expensive, and it can cause other problems, such as groundwater depletion and salinization (salt buildup). You are better off in the long run if you look for ways to avoid or minimize having to irrigate.

If your soil drains too fast, humus is still the all-around champion soil moisture holder. Because of its porous, spongy texture, humus can hold several times its weight in water. Add as much humus in the form of finished compost to your soil in spring and fall as you can.

Think about improving these "droughty" soils by using methods that reverse the techniques needed to improve drainage. Instead of raised beds, try sunken beds. Choose a low spot for the garden and create waterways to direct water through it. Put other moisture-conserving techniques to work, too. Mulch heavily. Plant windbreaks to break the force of the wind and keep soil from drying out so quickly. Cultivate and rotary-till as little as possible to avoid exposing moist soil to the drying air. Plant drought-tolerant species and cultivars, rather than moisture lovers.

DEALING WITH SLOPES

Depending on how steeply your land slopes and what other problems your soil has, gardening on a slope can be either frustrating or maintenance-free. The trick is to keep water runoff under control and avoid erosion. You can create a garden that is beautiful and productive without calling in the bulldozers. Try a combination of the following techniques.

Planting groundcovers. Planting a groundcover is sometimes the best solution for steep, erodable soil. Groundcovers are fast-growing perennials and shrubs that tend to sprawl or creep along the ground instead of growing upright. They are generally easy to grow and require little or no maintenance. There are groundcovers adapted to just about any soil condition and exposure, from full sun to shade. Many species, such as periwinkle (*Vinca minor*), creeping junipers (*Juniperus* cultivars), and thymes (*Thymus* spp.), can enhance the beauty of your sloping landscape as well.

Tilling on the contour. Till gently sloping land on the contours, perpendicular to the direction of the slope, forming slight ridges that act as mini-terraces to keep water from rushing downhill with your topsoil. Alternate tilled beds with equal strips of grass or a perennial groundcover to help slow down the progress of running water.

Minimizing soil disturbance. In agriculture, the minimum tillage method is used to plant annual crops with the least possible soil disturbance. In the garden, you can use your own methods of minimum tillage. Try a continuous mulch of straw, leaves, newspapers, or cardboard. Expose the soil only enough to put out transplants or to allow the seeds you plant to come up. Or plant a living mulch, such as white Dutch clover, and till it in only where you are going to plant your crop. In the North, plant cover crops of summer grains like oats or millet, which die over winter and can be left in place in the spring without competing with crops you plant.

Building terraces. Farmers in many Third World countries have built terraced gardens for centuries. These terraces are still productive, and they create some of the most beautiful landscapes imaginable. Terracing, illustrated on page 162, requires a lot of work, not only in the building stages but in regular maintenance. But with careful design and intensive management, you can enjoy a high level of productivity from a small area of terraced soil.

WHAT IS PERMACULTURE?

Permaculture—a term coined by ecologist Bill Mollison—is a combination of the words *permanent* and *agriculture*. He defines it as "the conscious design and maintenance of agriculturally productive ecosystems that have the diversity, stability, and resilience of natural ecosystems." Loosely translated, permaculture involves creating agricultural environments that not only are productive but also resemble natural ecosystems. Like natural environments, permaculture systems contain many different forms of life, and they are able to remain stable and adaptable over time. The principles of permaculture are based on close observations of how natural systems work, and they try to imitate that process in constructing food-producing systems.

Permaculturists around the world work at finding native plant species, adapted to various climate and soil conditions, that are useful for food, fuel, or fodder. In the United States, much of this effort is directed at helping gardeners create edible landscapes, in which plants are selected for culinary or medicinal as well as aesthetic qualities.

Soil building and conservation are central to permaculture, which strives to avoid disturbing the soil by promoting perennial polyculture (perennial plantings of mixed species). For example, if you have a few dwarf fruit trees on a slope, you might interplant them with perennial flowers such as yarrow (*Achillea* spp.) and coneflowers (*Echinacea purpurea*). Besides being beautiful, the flowers have medicinal qualities, and they harbor beneficial insects that help control orchard pests.

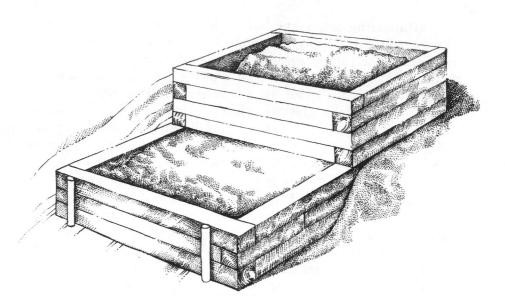

Turn a slope into a productive garden by constructing terraces. Create your terraces by digging stepped beds directly into the slope. Move the soil from the back of each bed to fill in the front of the beds.

NO TOPSOIL

Coping with a site that is virtually devoid of topsoil, whether due to erosion or removal of soil, is one of the ultimate gardening challenges. You can't be as patient as nature, slowly re-creating topsoil over hundreds of years. Purchased topsoil may offer instant gratification for a small area, but it's an expensive solution for a whole yard.

Your goal is to build humus as quickly as possible. If you have access to large amounts of compost, such as from a municipal composting facility, get all you can. Build a compost pile of your own, and make as much of your own compost as possible. See Chapter 4 for guidance on composting methods and advice on gathering raw materials.

If your site is newly graded and bare, get something growing on it right away. Assume that practically no nutrients are available, and look for organic fertilizers that can supply the necessary plant nutrients until you can build up soil fertility levels. Plant a legume species, such as clover, either by itself or as part of a lawn mixture, to build fertility. Refer to Chapter 10 for more on establishing and fertilizing a lawn.

SOIL CHEMISTRY IMBALANCES

The cause of soil fertility problems is often a lack or excess of chemical nutrients. Imbalances can result from natural factors, such as rainfall, or from abusive practices, such as overfertilization. Chapters 1 and 3 have more information on soil chemistry.

ACID SOIL

Acid soil is a fact of life in many areas, especially where rainfall levels are high. Water percolating through the soil dissolves mineral nutrients and leaches them away to the subsoil or waterways. Any place where drainage is poor is likely to be more acid, since base nutrients dissolve in standing water. Areas where evergreen forests predominate also tend to have acidic soil because conifer needles release acids as they decompose. (Acid rain, although it has a marked impact on lakes and can harm foliage, has not been shown to be a factor in soil acidity.)

If you live in one of the areas shown on the map below and no lime or other neutralizing amendments have been applied to your soil in a long time, chances are your soil has a low pH. The presence

Some areas of the country tend to have acid soils; these are indicated by the shading on the map above. Acid soils often exist where evergreen forests predominate.

ACID-TOLERANT PLANTS

If your soil is on the acid side, consider choosing plants that actually prefer acid conditions rather than trying to amend the soil to fit the needs of other plants. Below you'll find a list of some plants that tolerate or thrive in acid soil. Before you choose any of these plants for your garden, keep in mind that not all of them grow equally well in all climates. Check with a garden reference book or your local Cooperative Extension Service if you're not sure whether a particular plant will thrive in your climate.

Acid-Tolerant

Grasses and Green Manures
Bent grass
Fescue
Poverty grass

Trees and Shrubs
Abies spp. (firs)
Carya illinoiensis (pecan)
Cedrus spp. (cedars)
Kalmia latifolia
   (mountain laurel)
Myrica spp. (bayberries)
Picea spp. (spruces)
Pinus spp. (pines)
Quercus spp. (oaks)
Rhododendron spp.
   (azaleas and rhododendrons)
Taxus spp. (yews)

Flowers
Asclepias tuberosa (butterfly weed)
Calluna spp. (heathers)
Chrysanthemum spp. (chrysanthemums)
Convallaria majalis (lily-of-the-valley)
Erica spp. (heaths)
Lilium spp. (lilies)

Linum spp. (flaxes)
Lobelia cardinalis (cardinal flower)
Lupinus spp. (lupines)
Tagetes spp. (marigolds)

Vegetables
Chicory
Dandelion
Endive
Fennel
Peanuts
Potatoes
Radishes
Rhubarb
Shallots
Sorrel
Sweet potatoes
Watermelons

Fruits
Blackberries
Blueberries
Cranberries
Huckleberries
Raspberries

of acid-tolerant plants such as wild strawberries is a good indicator of this problem (see "Indicator Weeds and Soil Conditions" on page 16 for a list of other indicator species). For a precise determination, get your soil tested.

Acid soil syndrome is a term referring to the wide range of problems related to low pH. Acid soil may suffer from:

• Deficiency of cation or base nutrients, such as calcium, magnesium, and potassium.

Somewhat Acid-Tolerant

Grasses and Green Manures
Alsike clover
Barley
Buckwheat
Corn
Cowpeas
Kentucky bluegrass
Millet
Oats
Red clover
Rye
Vetches
Wheat

Trees and Shrubs
Cornus spp. (dogwoods)
Euonymus spp. (euonymus)
Fothergilla spp. (fothergillas)
Gardenia spp. (gardenias)
Gaultheria procumbens (wintergreen)
Malus spp. (crab apples)
Rosa rugosa (rugosa rose)

Flowers
Gypsophila elegans
  (annyal baby's-breath)
Hemerocallis spp. (daylilies)
Liatris spp. (gayfeathers)
Nicotiana spp. (flowering tobacco)
Platycodon grandiflorus spp. (balloon flower)
Primula spp. (primroses)
Sinningia speciosa (gloxinia)
Viola × *wittrockiana* (pansy)

Vegetables
Beans
Brussels sprouts
Carrots
Collards
Cucumbers
Eggplant
Garlic
Kale
Kohlrabi
Mustard
Parlsey
Peas
Peppers
Pumpkins
Squash
Sweet corn
Tomatoes
Turnips

Fruits
Apples
Bananas
Gooseberries
Grapes
Strawberries

- Reduced availability of nutrients such as phosphorus and nitrogen in forms that are accessible to plants.
- Increased solubility of iron, manganese, and especially aluminum to undesirable levels that can interfere with plant growth.
- Reduced bacterial activity, especially of nitrogen-fixing rhizobia on legume roots.
- Slower release of nutrients from organic matter.
- Reduced soil nutrient storage capacity.

THE MARVEL OF HUMUS

Building organic matter and improving soil biological activity is essential to moderating both extremes of pH. One of the many marvelous qualities of humus is its capacity to serve as a buffer, neutralizing both acids and bases. Applying large amounts of compost and mulching are the best strategies for healing and maintaining soils suffering from either too low or too high a pH.

What all this adds up to is the consequences of impoverished soil: poor germination, slow growth and maturation, and disease problems.

Correcting Acidity

Fortunately, soil acidity is one of the easiest problems to fix. Liming materials, which raise soil pH through the addition of base nutrients, are cheap and widely available. You can use most laboratory or home-test pH readings to determine soil acidity with relative confidence.

Be careful about which liming material you choose. Base your choice on which minerals are most deficient in your soil, not how much you need to raise your pH. Using dolomitic lime, which con-

LIMING MATERIALS

Most plants will thrive at a pH of 6.5 to 6.8. If your soil's pH is too low, you'll need to add liming materials to raise it to the ideal level. Be sure to keep in mind what nutrients your soil is deficient in, and avoid adding nutrients that abound in your soil. How much of which material to add depends on whether your soil texture is heavy (clayey), medium (neither excessively sandy nor clayey), or light (sandy). Use the table below to guide your rate of application.

Material	Primary Nutrient(s)	Application Rate (lbs. per 100 sq. ft.)
Calcitic lime or aragonite	Calcium	Heavy soil: 9.0 Medium soil: 6.5 Light soil: 2.5
Dolomitic lime	Calcium, magnesium	Heavy soil: 7.75 Medium soil: 6.0 Light soil: 2.0

tains magnesium, for example, can cause problems if soil magnesium levels are already high in relation to calcium. A more complete soil analysis that shows mineral balances is helpful.

The ideal level for soil pH is 6.5 to 6.8. Most plants will thrive at this level. Use the following table to estimate how much of which liming material to use. Avoid slaked or hydrated limes; they are highly caustic and harmful to soil organisms. Wood ashes will raise the pH considerably; however, to avoid overloading the soil with potassium, do not add more than 2 pounds of wood ashes per 100 square feet of soil in a given year.

Keep in mind that ground rock powders are slow to act and need time for bacterial action to release their nutrients; you won't gain the full benefit from an application for a year or more. While you are waiting for the soil-balancing action to happen, choose plants that are more tolerant of acid conditions.

ALKALINE AND SALINE SOILS

Soils that are too alkaline are usually found in dry to arid regions. If a high pH is accompanied by a high level of soluble sodium in a soil, it is referred to as a sodic soil. Alkaline soils are also

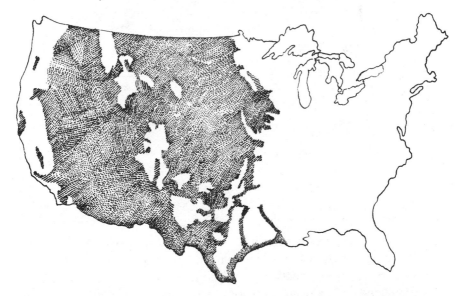

Dry to arid regions of the country are often areas of alkaline soil; these are indicated by the shading on the map above. Nutrients can become unavailable to plant roots in alkaline conditions.

ALKALINE-TOLERANT PLANTS

Many plants tolerate or thrive in soils that are on the alkaline side. If your soil has a high pH, consider growing some of the plants listed below. (Before you choose any of these plants for your garden, keep in mind that not all of them grow equally well in all climates. Check with a garden reference book or your local Cooperative Extension Service if you're not sure whether a particular plant will thrive in your climate.)

Grasses and Green Manures
Alfalfa
Barley
Bermuda grass
Cotton
Rye
Sorghum
Sweet clover

Trees and Shrubs
Acer saccharum subsp. *nigrum* (black maple)
Catalpa spp. (catalpas)
Celtis spp. (hackberries)
Ceratonia siliqua (carob)
Crataegus spp. (hawthorns)
Euonymus spp. (euonymus)
Gleditsia triacanthos (honey locust)
Gymnocladus dioica (Kentucky coffee tree)
Platanus spp. (sycamores)
Quercus macrocarpa (bur oak)
Robinia pseudoacacia (black locust)
Ulmus americana (American elm)

Flowers
Dianthus caryophyllus (florist's carnation)
Geum spp. (avens)
Gyposphila paniculata (baby's-breath)
Iris spp. (irises)

Lathyrus odoratus (sweet pea)
Phlox spp. (phlox)
Reseda odorata (mignonette)
Tropaeolum majus (garden nasturtium)

Vegetables
Asparagus
Beets
Broccoli
Cabbage
Cauliflower
Celery
Chinese cabbage
Leeks
Lettuce
Muskmelons
Okra
Onions
Parsnips
Salsify
Spinach
Sugar beets
Swiss chard
Watercress

Fruits
Avocados
Date palms
Olives
Persian limes

more prone to problems of salinity or salt buildup, usually resulting from irrigation or use of fertilizers with a high salt content or a combination of these two practices. Soil salinity is not a new problem — several ancient civilizations are thought to have crumbled as a result of soil salinization after centuries of irrigation.

At high pH, elements tend to form compounds that may be

more or less soluble than those formed in a more-neutral-pH environment—the more soluble an element, the more readily a plant root will be able to absorb it. (Refer to Chapter 5 for more about chemical interactions in the soil.) Many nutrients, paticularly micronutrients and phosphorus, become less available to plant roots when the soil is high in pH and/or salt. Some minerals, including sodium and selenium, become more available to plants in alkaline soil and may reach toxic levels. Salt causes most plant roots to dry out because water flows from their cells into the saltier soil solution, seeking equilibrium. Finally, soil structure is chemically degraded by high sodium levels, and soil organic matter can be chemically destroyed under alkaline conditions. If, no matter what you do, plants that need a lower pH just won't grow for you, your only choice may be to work with alkaline- and salt-tolerant plants and leave the blueberries for others to grow.

Correcting Alkalinity

Soil alkalinity is an easier situation to diagnose than to remedy. As is true for acidity, indicator plants and pH testing are reliable means of detecting alkalinity problems.

Correcting a high pH isn't quite as simple as neutralizing acidity, although there are some acidifying materials that can be used. Elemental sulfur and gypsum (calcium sulfate) are both effective means of lowering pH and converting sodium to a less soluble form. Apply sulfur at a rate of 2 to 3 pounds per 100 square feet for each unit of decrease in pH desired. Or, if your soil is high in sodium, apply gypsum at a rate of 4 to 6 pounds per 100 square feet for each unit of decrease in pH desired. For example, if your pH level is 8.2, you will need to add 30 pounds of sulfur or 60 pounds of gypsum per 1,000 square feet to decrease the pH level to 7.0. It's important to mix these materials into the surface and keep the soil moist for them to work. If you have to apply large quantites of these amendments, it is a good idea to split the application and apply each half several months apart to get a more gradual reduction in the pH. Otherwise, soil organisms may have a hard time adjusting to the drastic change in pH.

For a more gradual change in pH, you can also add large amounts of peat or other acidifying organic materials, such as compost made from pine needles or sawdust. This will help texturize the soil in addition to lowering pH. Cottonseed meal is sometimes used

SALT TOLERANCES OF PLANTS

Salt from road and sidewalk de-icing or from natural soil-forming processes can be toxic to some plants, causing leaf browning, poor growth, or even death. Fortunately, if you live in an area with saline soil, you can still grow many wonderful plants. Below you'll find lists of plants that are easily damaged by salt, along with plants that are moderately to highly salt-tolerant. (Before you choose any of these plants for your garden, keep in mind that not all of them grow equally well in all climates. Check with a garden reference book or your local Cooperative Extension Service if you're not sure whether a particular plant will thrive in your climate.)

Salt-Sensitive Plants

Grasses and Green Manures
Alsike clover
Field beans
Ladino clover
Meadow foxtail
Red clover
White Dutch clover
Trees and Shrubs
Fraxinus pensylvanica (green ash)
Liriodendron tulipifera (tulip tree)
Picea abies (Norway spruce)
Pinus strobus (Eastern white pine)
Rosa spp. (roses)
Spiraea spp. (spireas)
Tsuga canadensis (Canada hemlock)
Flowers
Cosmos spp. (cosmos)

Vegetables
Beans
Cabbage
Carrots
Celery
Onions
Peppers
Radishes
Fruits
Apples
Lemons
Oranges
Peaches
Pears
Plums

as a natural soil acidifier; however, unless you compost it first or know where it came from, you may risk introducing toxic levels of pesticides into your soil (see "Cottonseed Meal" on page 121 for more information on this material).

Eliminating Salts

Salinity is easily observed as a white crust on the soil surface—similar to the deposit you find on clay flowerpots. Salt concentration can be measured by a test for electrical conductivity, commonly used

Salt-Tolerant Plants

Grasses and Green Manures
Alfalfa
Barley
Bermudagrass
Birdsfoot trefoil
Fava bean
Oats
Rape
Rye
Sudan grass
Sweet clover

Trees and Shrubs
Betula pendula (European white birch)
Cercis spp. (redbuds)
Clethra spp. (summersweet)
Forsythia × *intermedia* (border forsythia)
Gleditsia triacanthos (honey locust)
Juniperus chinensis var. *chinensis* 'Pfitzerana'
   (Pfitzer juniper)
Juniperus horizontalis (creeping juniper)
Ligustrum spp. (privets)
Lonicera spp. (honeysuckles)
Weigela spp. (weigelas)

Flowers
Achillea tomentosa (woolly yarrow)
Alcea rosea (hollyhock)
Aquilegia spp. (columbines)
Aster spp. (asters)
Chrysanthemum spp. (chrysanthemums)
Coreopsis spp. (coreopsis)
Delphinium spp. (delphiniums)

Dianthus spp. (pinks)
Digitalis spp. (foxgloves)
Gaillardia spp. (blanket flowers)
Helianthus spp. (sunflowers)
Hibiscus moscheutos (rose mallow)
Hosta spp. (hostas)
Limonium spp. (statice)
Monarda didyma (bee balm)
Papaver orientale (oriental poppy)
Petunia × *hybrida*
   (garden petunia)
Phlox spp. (phlox)
Portulaca grandiflora (rose moss)
Sedum spp. (sedums)
Yucca spp. (yuccas)

Vegetables
Beets
Broccoli
Kale
Lettuce
Spinach
Sugar beets
Tomatoes

Fruits
Coconuts
Dates
Figs
Grapes
Olives

for commercial greenhouse and potting soils (where high salt content can also be a problem).

The only way to eliminate salt buildup is through leaching—literally washing the salts away by drenching the soil with clean, salt-free water. Leaching is only feasible if fresh water is plentiful and cheap—which is often not the case in areas where salinity occurs—and if there is no danger of washing the dissolved salts back into the water table. Also, soils high in sodium must be leached in the presence of an added source of soluble calcium, such as gypsum, or the leaching process will actually worsen the situation.

If your soil has a tendency toward salinity, use strategies that reduce surface evaporation. Sometimes salinization happens when the water table is high, so that water is constantly drawn up to evaporate at the surface. In such cases, improving drainage is a necessary step (see "Drainage Problems" on page 150 for techniques to improve drainage problems). Irrigate often but lightly. Mulching to reduce evaporation is critical. Be sure to avoid salty fertilizers, such as langbeinite (Sul-Po-Mag); fortunately, such fertilizers are rarely needed on salty soils.

SEVERE NUTRIENT IMBALANCES

Even an otherwise healthy, fertile soil may suffer from an extreme oversupply of a particular nutrient, causing other critical nutrients to be bound up (unavailable to plant roots). This means that two or more nutrients interact chemically to make compounds that are very insoluble. So, for example, even though there may be lots of phosphorus in your soil, too much calcium will turn it into insoluble calcium phosphate, which your plants can't take up.

Bound-up nutrients can occur naturally, as in certain muck and peat soils, which have an extremely high content of organic matter. The problem can also happen as a result of overfertilization or misapplication of fertilizer materials, especially micronutrients. Gardeners who are overenthusiastic users of wood ashes can seriously overload their soil with potassium and calcium. This excess binds up magnesium in the soil, making it unavailable to plant roots and creating a magnesium deficiency even when that element is in good supply.

Correcting Imbalances

If you suspect a nutrient imbalance, soil testing in combination with plant tissue analysis is the only way to confirm your hunch. (See "Testing Your Soil" on page 93 for more details on taking a soil test.) In some cases, an imbalance can be readily corrected by adding more of the bound-up nutrient. In a severe case of overapplication of potassium, such as with wood ashes, leaching with fresh water can help the situation.

Foliar application is the most effective means of providing micronutrients, since the soil imbalance will not affect their absorption. If magnesium is deficient due to oversupply of potassium, spraying plants with magnesium sulfate (Epsom salts) is the best short-term remedy. Zinc and manganese must be foliar-applied to plants growing on certain muck soils, due to the soil chemistry in those situations. Foliar feeding is also a valuable strategy for growing many crops in soil whose pH is otherwise unsuitable—for example, blueberries can be successfully grown in neutral or even alkaline soil if they are given foliar-applied iron.

CONTAMINATED SOILS

In today's polluted world, reclamation of poisoned soils is a major issue. Whether soil contamination is caused by waste dumps, abandoned mines, pesticide residues, peeling paint, or air pollution, you can use a number of methods to reduce the danger to soil organisms and plants—and to your own health. (See "Precautions and Remedies" on page 175 for more specific information on these methods.) In some cases, simply having a better understanding of the real risks can help you cope more intelligently with them.

DETECTING CONTAMINATION

It isn't always simple to detect and diagnose contamination problems. The best clue to a potential problem is the history of your land. Find out how your piece of property and the land nearby were used. Investigate the types of industries that were and are in the vicinity. Orchards, for example, may suffer persistent arsenic, lead, mercury, and copper contamination. Pesticides containing these elements were common before World War II and were often used in orchards. You may be surprised by what you find out about your soil. One orchard in New York State was found to have such high levels of arsenic, lead, and DDT that the soil was legally classified as hazardous waste!

Mining operations, even if abandoned, may contribute heavy metals to surrounding soil and water for decades. Electrical-appliance manufacturers are responsible for PCB pollution, and smelters can emit nickel, cadmium, mercury, and other metals into the air at unsafe levels.

Lead is among the most widespread soil contaminants, not only from automobile exhaust in urban gardens but also from flakes of lead-based paint that have fallen to the ground around any old,

WELCOME TO TAINTED ACRES

Land that was previously used for chemical-intensive agriculture can still contain toxic residues, depending on what materials were used and how recently they were used. The most helpful source of information about pesticides that might have been applied to your soil is the county Cooperative Extension office. The extension office can tell you which chemicals have commonly been used on what types of farms in your area. They can also tell you how long—theoretically speaking—these chemicals might be expected to persist in your soil. Disturbing evidence suggests that even pesticides considered highly degradable, such as the now-illegal EDB (ethylene dibromide), may actually be held so tightly in between soil particles that laboratory testing fails to detect them, so they are assumed to have broken down. Furthermore, some pesticides, such as those related to parathion, degrade into compounds that are more toxic and more persistent (retaining their chemical form for a longer period of time) than the original chemical.

wooden structure in the past 200 years. The list of potential sources of lead contamination goes on and on.

If you have reason to suspect the presence of toxic contaminants in your soil, you should have a special test done—routine soil testing will not give you this information. Contact your Cooperative Extension Service or state environmental regulatory agency to find out how to take a soil sample, where to send it, and how much the special soil test will cost. Knowing what element or compound you are looking for will save significant expense. Industrial contaminants such as PCBs and dioxin, which are hazards in minuscule concentrations, may require more sophisticated scientific sleuthing; arrange testing only when you have reason to suspect contamination. If you find that your soil is polluted, check into citizen activist groups in your state to track down suspected polluters.

Soil contaminants fall into two broad chemical categories: inorganic substances and hazardous organic compounds. Inorganic substances include heavy metals and nometallic compounds like fluorine. Hazardous organic compounds are usually synthetic products derived from petroleum, such as pesticides and plastic resins.

INORGANIC CONTAMINATION

Increasing industrial use of various inorganic compounds— including heavy metals as well as nonmetallic elements—has led to

LEAD IN THE GARDEN

Lead is the most common heavy metal contaminant in soil, and it's especially dangerous for children under the age of six and pregnant women. Soil with over 1,000 parts per million (ppm) of lead is considered to be high-lead soil; 500 to 1,000 ppm is considered moderate; and anything under 500 ppm is low. Lead is an exception to the recommendation of keeping metallic elements in place. This metal is so immobile (think of the expression "lead feet") that removal of the top inch or so of soil in a small area will effectively get rid of the problem. Your local office of the Cooperative Extension Service can advise you on how to safely remove and dispose of lead-contaminated soil.

high concentrations of these substances in the environment. They may find their way into soil as part of synthetic pesticides or through air pollution, improper waste disposal, or application of sewage sludge. Although many of these elements are needed by plants and animals in trace amounts, concentrated levels of them can be toxic. Some pose a threat to your family's health, and others may accumulate in your soil and harm soil organisms or damage plants. Long-term risks and effects on soil ecosystems are largely unknown.

The most common soil-contaminating elements include arsenic, boron, cadmium, copper, fluorine, lead, manganese, mercury, nickel, and zinc. "Sources of Soil Contamination" on page 176 provides information on the source of these elements, their normal concentration in soil and plants, and other important characteristics.

Precautions and Remedies

Once your soil is contaminated with any metallic element, the issue becomes keeping the metal where it is and not allowing it to enter the food chain. Direct contact with the soil is the main health hazard of heavy metal contamination. When children play in soil that contains flakes of lead paint, they can both inhale the lead as dust and absorb it through their skin. Lead-contaminated soil causes serious health problems in some neighborhoods.

Contaminated soil is also a major concern for vegetable gardeners. Plants that absorb metallic elements through their roots will generally suffer symptoms of poisoning, such as stunted growth and yellowing. Plants contaminated with cadmium, however, are usually symptom-free and appear healthy. If you suspect contamination, do

SOURCES OF SOIL CONTAMINATION

Soil contamination can come from a wide array of sources. If your soil is contaminated, figuring out the source of the pollutant is an important step to developing an effective treatment program. Below you'll find a listing of the most common contaminants, along with their average natural concentrations in the soil and in plants.

| Element | Major Sources | Concentration (ppm) | | Comments |
		In Soil	In Plants	
Arsenic	Pesticides, air pollution	0.1–40	0.1–5	Behaves like phosphorus in the soil
Boron	Gasoline, irrigation water	2–100	30–75	Spot toxicity may occur; leaches easily
Cadmium	Smelting, sewage sludge, plating, batteries, fertilizer impurities	0.1–7	0.2–0.8	Leaves may take up toxic amounts without visible signs.
Copper	Industrial dusts, mine effluents, sewage sludge, fungicides	2–100	4–15	Less available near neutral pH with good drainage
Fluorine	Fertilizers, pesticides, air pollution	30–300	2–20	Localized problem; some plants sensitive to excess
Lead	Leaded gasoline, smelting, fertilizers, pesticides	2–200	0.1–10	Food contamination mainly from air pollution; immobile
Manganese	Mine seepage, fly ash, fertilizers	100–4,000	15–100	Less available near neutral pH with good drainage
Mercury	Fungicides, air pollution (from evaporation of metallic form)	—	—	Not readily absorbed by plants; water pollution is the main concern

(continued)

SOURCES OF SOIL CONTAMINATION— CONTINUED

| Element | Major Sources | Concentration (ppm) | | Comments |
		In Soil	In Plants	
Nickel	Fertilizers, smelting, gasoline combustion	10–1,000	1	Less available near neutral pH with good drainage
Zinc	Sewage effluents, industrial waste, fertilizers, pesticides	10–300	15–200	Less available near neutral pH with good drainage

SOURCE: Reprinted with the permission of The Macmillan Company from *Nature and Properties of Soils*, 8th edition by Nyle C. Brady. Copyright © 1974 by Nyle C. Brady.

not eat root and leaf vegetables grown in your soil. They may have particles of contaminated soil or airborne contaminants on them. Eating fruit and seed crops is less dangerous.

If you get your soil tested and find out that it is contaminated, you will want to take steps to deal with the problem. One way to remedy a contamination problem is to reduce the solubility of the contaminants. Metals are immobilized in the soil in two primary ways:

1. In a process called chelation, a metal is latched onto by a large, complex biochemical molecule (such as those that constitute humus) and thus prevented from entering the soil solution. For this reason, compost and humus formation are the keys to reducing the biological availability of most soil contaminants.

2. Keeping pH levels close to neutral and making sure drainage is adequate virtually assures chemical immobilization. Also, since phosphorus has an affinity for most metal contaminants, adding extra-rich phosphate sources can help tie up the metals. However, in the case of arsenic, adding phosphorus enhances plant uptake of the contaminant. To reduce arsenic availability, add zinc and iron instead.

Remember that heavy metals don't go away—they can become a time bomb, awaiting soil conditions (such as depletion of humus) that might cause them to be released into the food chain. Although we can live with the heavy metals that are present now, we must continue to exert social and political pressure to prevent the future release of toxic materials into our environment.

Nonmetal inorganic compounds, such as boron and fluorine, are more reactive and harder to immobilize in soil than metallic compounds. Try leaching them out by flushing the soil with large quantities of water.

PESTICIDE CONTAMINATION

The behavior of pesticides and other synthetic organic compounds in soils is complex and variable. Soil texture, drainage, aeration, chemistry, climate, and biological activity all affect the action of pesticides. If there is a good likelihood that your soil has had pesticides—including insecticides, herbicides, fungicides, fumigants, or other biocides—applied to or dumped on it, try to find the answers to these important questions:

- Which pesticides were applied?
- How recently were they applied?
- How quickly do they degrade in soil?
- How much of a health threat do they pose?

The previous landowner is the most likely person to know the answers to these questions. Otherwise, you could try asking neighbors who may know how the land was treated in the past. You may not be lucky enough to get specific answers to the first two questions, but you can usually find out what general types of herbicides were used on the property and have your soil tested for contaminants from those groups. If you don't have any idea what possible contaminants might be present, you can have your soil tested for a wide range of different suspects, but these more-extensive tests will most likely end up costing you more money.

Pesticide Concerns

Health concerns about pesticide residues are mostly an issue of direct contact with soil. If your soil contains significant residues of toxic organic compounds, observe the same precautions as for heavy metal contamination (see "Precautions and Remedies" on page 175).

Effects of pesticides on soil organisms are poorly researched. Fungicides, which kill all kinds of fungi, can severely interfere with organic matter processing. Beneficial nitrogen-fixing organisms, such as the *Rhizobium* bacteria that live on the roots of legumes like peas and beans, are generally sensitive to environmental poisons of all kinds. Often, chemicals kill the beneficial organisms that prey upon soil pests or pathogens, leaving them to thrive unchecked. Some chemicals kill all-important earthworms, and the chemicals that don't kill them may still accumulate in their bodies and be passed along to birds and other worm-eating animals. Such a transfer of chemicals can lead to unfortunate consequences higher on the food chain because as the chemicals are passed along they become more and more concentrated and therefore more and more toxic.

Gone but Not Forgotten

Toxic materials applied to or dumped on soils may encounter several possible fates. If they are organic, they may break down into simpler, usually harmless, compounds. If they are heavy metals or

PERSISTENCE OF PESTICIDES

Some pesticides are more persistent than others, meaning that they take longer to break down into simpler chemical forms that are no longer toxic. If you suspect that a specific pesticide has been used on your land in the past, check the table below to find out approximately how long that pesticide generally remains in the soil.

Pesticide	Time Remaining in Soil
Arsenic	Indefinite
Benzoic acid herbicides (such as amiben and dicamba)	2–12 months
Carbamate herbicides (such as barban and CIPC)	2–8 weeks
Carbamate insecticides (such as sevin and carbaryl)	1–8 weeks
Chlorinated hydrocarbon insecticides (such as DDT, chlordane, and dieldrin)	2–5 years
Organophosphate insecticides (such as malathion and diazinon)	1–12 weeks
Phenoxy herbicides (such as 2,4-D and 2,4,5-T)	1–5 months
Triazine herbicides (such as atrazine and simazine)	1–2 years
Urea herbicides (such as monuron and diuron)	2–10 months

LIVING WITH CONTAMINATED SOIL

If your soil has noticeable levels of lead or another persistent (long-lasting) toxin, follow a few simple precautions:

• Grow food crops as far as possible from heavily trafficked roads to reduce airborne pollution. Plant a windbreak or erect a fence or other type of barrier.

• Avoid planting food crops close to structures, such as older houses, sheds, and barns, that may have been painted with lead-based paint.

• Make sure that children wash their hands after playing in the soil, and keep play areas protected with mulch to minimize soil exposure.

• Mulch and use cover crops to keep dust levels down and organic matter levels up.

• Keep soil well-limed so that its pH is between 6.5 and 6.8.

• Avoid growing root or leaf crops in heavily contaminated soil. Where lead levels are moderate to low, it is adequate to peel roots and discard outer leaves of leaf crops. Wash all vegetables carefully. Broccoli, cauliflower, kale, and collards have all been shown to take up very little lead from the soil.

• Grow food plants in containers filled with fresh, uncontaminated soil.

• If lead levels are high, topsoil should be removed entirely and properly disposed of. Consult your Cooperative Extension Service office or state environmental agency before attempting to do this.

inorganic compounds, such as organochlorines, they will be more persistent, meaning that they may retain their chemical form for a long time. If they are degradable compounds, which are mainly degraded by microbial activity, they will degrade faster if soil is biologically active. If they are herbicides that have been used consistently on the same soil, they may be degraded more quickly because they have enriched the soil with microbes that consider them to be tasty. If, however, a combination of pesticides has been applied, one of the chemicals may have killed the soil microbes that would have helped to degrade one of the other chemicals.

Persistent compounds can be prevented from entering the food system by locking them up in humus molecules. In that case, what you have is a "toxic sink," or a biochemical jail full of undesirable characters. The way you keep them locked up is to keep high levels of stable humus in your soil. In fact, research is showing that some pesticides and herbicides previously believed to have "gone away" may still exist in the soil, bound up too tightly to be detected by laboratory analysis. This is one situation where high humus levels may be cause for concern. If soil conditions change to favor the decom-

FUTURE SOLUTIONS FOR CONTAMINATED SOIL

Some work has been done on seeding soil with pesticide-degrading microbe cultures, and there is even a fungus that shows promise in transforming toxic selenium buildups in soil into a gas that evaporates harmlessly. Genetic engineers are looking into taking genes from microbes that consume specific pesticides and patching them into more suitable soil bacteria. Many scientists believe that such strategies are of questionable value, since conditions that favor establishment of a given strain of microbes are unpredictable. It is more productive to stimulate indigenous species of pesticide-degrading microbes by adding organic matter and balanced trace minerals, and cultivating and tilling to increase soil aeration.

position of the stable humus, its toxic prisoners will be freed to wreak environmental havoc. (See Chapter 3 for a discussion of humus and the factors affecting its decomposition.)

Some pesticides do undergo chemical degradation, most notably in the presence of sunlight. Others, such as fumigants like methyl bromide, readily leave the soil in a gaseous state or leach quickly in rainwater. While this may be good news for the gardener whose soil was contaminated, it may have a detrimental effect on people downwind or downstream. Some reports show that working activated charcoal into the soil can help degrade pesticide residues. For advice on how to speed degradation of specific soil contaminants, consult your Cooperative Extension Service office.

Although short-term methods can be effective in dealing with chemicals, we need to take action that will prevent soil-contamination problems in the long term as well. One of the best long-term methods to combat the problems related to soil contamination is educating yourself and others about the benefits of organic farming and gardening as well as the ill effects of gardening with chemicals. Inform yourself about the chemicals used to produce items you buy, and look for "cleaner" substitutes. (A few mail-order sources for such products are listed in "Environmentally Friendly Products" on page 261.) Educate your neighbors and colleagues about organically grown food and other alternatives that avoid the need for toxic chemicals. Another long-term method is taking political action to prevent the use of chemicals by others, from home gardeners to large businesses. Support public policies that impose heavy penalties on polluters. Every little bit you contribute now can have an enormous impact on the future of the soil—and the planet.

CHAPTER 8

SOIL NEEDS OF VEGETABLES

$\mathbf{I}$t stands to reason that you should provide good nourishment for any plant you expect to nourish you and your family. And let's face it—growing vegetables is a lot of work. Your efforts will pay off much better if your soil has everything that it—and your crop—needs.

GETTING A GOOD START

If you have followed the suggestions for building healthy soil, your vegetable crops should do just fine. In general, vegetables require about 2 pounds of nitrogen, 1 pound of phosphorus, and 3 pounds of potassium per 1,000 square feet each year, along with a balanced complement of micronutrients. Because you are extracting some of these nutrients from the soil whenever you harvest produce, you must put something back. Just how much you need to put back depends on a number of factors. Most of the biomass (the total volume of living material) that you remove from your garden comes from air and water. Only a small amount of material is removed from the soil to produce that biomass. Some nutrients get recycled into the garden in the inedible portions of your crops—leaves, stalks, or roots that you till under or compost after harvest.

Most vegetables do well in the proverbial "rich, moist, well-drained soil" with a pH level in the 6.2 to 6.8 range. Some crops, however, are more fussy than others about their needs for water, drainage, soil pH, or specific nutrients. "Soil Needs of Vegetables" on page 193 lists commonly grown vegetables and indicates how demanding they are regarding soil quality.

KNOW YOUR VEGETABLES

To help you understand what kinds of soil conditions and nutrients your vegetables need, consider the structure and growth habit of the plants in your garden and how you use them. To help you understand what kinds of soil conditions and nutrients your vegetables need, you have to spend some time getting to know your plants. The following sections will help you to examine the root structure and growth habit of your vegetables, as well as consider how you use the grown plants. When you know all of these things

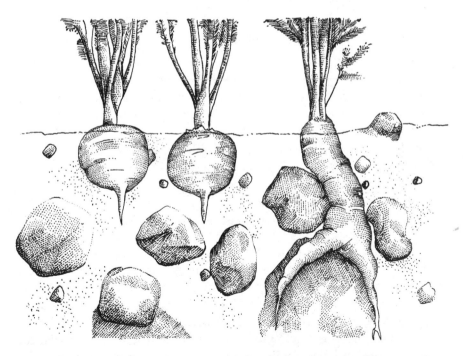

If your soil is rocky or soggy but you hanker for carrots, try a short-rooted cultivar like 'Kundulus'. This cultivar does not grow as deeply, so it won't split in rocky soil like the long-rooted cultivar shown on the right.

about your vegetables, you'll have an easier time providing them with the conditions they need to reach their peak in nutrients and flavor.

Root Structure

The size and shape of a plant's roots and its arrangement of root hairs can give you some hints about the plant's soil needs. Is the plant shallow- or deep-rooted? Shallow-rooted crops, such as lettuce, onions, peas, and spinach, do poorly without a continuous source of soil moisture. Also, shallow-rooted crops often tolerate soggier conditions than deep-rooted ones, like asparagus, beans, carrots, and tomatoes. (The ability to tolerate "wet feet," however, usually depends more on a plant's ability to resist disease than on its root structure.) Are the roots thick and fibrous, having many little root hairs, or are they relatively smooth? Plants with lots of root hairs, such as grasses, are likely to be better at nutrient scavenging, especially for phosphorus, than those with smooth roots.

Growth Habit

After you've looked at the roots, take a look at the rest of the plant. Its growth habit can supply more information on its plant needs. Is your crop a fast, vigorous grower that matures rapidly, or a slow-growing, long-season crop? Rapid growers, like corn and spinach, need lots of available nitrogen in comparison to slow growers like onions and parsnips. Bushy plants that produce massive yields, such as potatoes, are greedier feeders than compact, comparatively low-yielding plants like peppers.

Edible Portion

Now let's take a look at the vegetable's edible portion—the part of the plant that is most important to any vegetable grower. Do you want to encourage maximum production of roots, leaves, flowers, or fruit? When you want lots of lush, leafy growth to put in your salad bowl, plenty of available nitrogen is crucial. Phosphorus is essential for root development and sugar formation, so large, sweet carrots and beets will require a good supply of it. Plentiful potassium is needed to mature seeds and fill starch-storage organs like potatoes.

Nutritional Content

Understanding the nutritional content of your vegetables can give you good clues to their fertilizer needs. If a vegetable is particularly high in some nutrient, the plants will probably benefit from supplemental feedings of that nutrient. Broccoli, for example, is a good source of dietary calcium, so you can guess that adequate soil calcium levels are important for growing broccoli. Similarly, beans and peas, which are high in phosphorus, need plentiful soil phosphorus levels.

Related Crops

Knowing what plants are related to each other is a good way to learn about the characteristics and preferences of vegetables that you like to grow (and eat!). Related plants in a family are likely to have traits in common. For example, beets, Swiss chard, and spinach are all members of the goosefoot family, Chenopodiaceae, which evolved along seashores. As you might expect, these vegetables are among the most tolerant of saline soil conditions. Some vegetable families, such as Umbelliferae, include plants with a wide range of soil and climate preferences, so you can't always draw conclusions from this information.

Many of the plants you grow in your garden are related to each other. Here are the major families you'll meet.

Chenopodiaceae. Known as the goosefoot family for the characteristic leaf shape, this family includes the ubiquitous lamb's-quarters—a weed to some, a delicacy to others.

Compositae. The characteristic flower of this family is actually a composite of many tiny disk flowers surrounded by showy ray flowers. Edibles in this family include lettuce and sunflowers. Marigolds and zinnias are Compositae-family ornamentals.

Cruciferae. This large family includes plants cultivated for their tangy leaves, such as cress, mustard, and bok choy; others grown for their edible flower heads, such as broccoli and cauliflower; and even a plant grown for the oil content of its seeds—rapeseed.

Cucurbitaceae. This family is characterized by a vining, fast-growing habit and a love of heat. Cucumbers and gourds are in this family.

Gramineae. This family has more members than any other, but it is usually represented in the home vegetable garden only by corn (if you don't count the grassy weeds that are part of this family!).

Labiatae. Members of this family are easily identified by a stem that is square in cross-section. Many herbs, such as sage and oregano, are Labiatae members.

Leguminosae. Another extremely important and widely adapted family, Leguminosae is characterized by its often trifoliate (three-lobed) leaf structure and pealike flowers. Its other all-important quality is its symbiotic relationship with members of the *Rhizobium* genus of bacteria, which transform atmospheric nitrogen into a form usable by plants. Because the bacteria make nitrogen absorption easy for leguminous plants, the plants often generate nitrogen surpluses to return to the soil in a form usable by other plants.

Liliaceae. Many bulbs, such as garlic, leeks, onions, and shallots, are members of this family. It also includes some of our favorite bulb-forming flowers, such as daffodils and ornamental lilies.

Solanaceae. While this family claims some of our favorite edibles, like tomatoes and peppers, it also includes some of the most poisonous plants known, such as the aptly named deadly nightshade.

Umbelliferae. The name of this family comes from its umbrella-like flower heads. Many flowers and medicinal herbs, such as celery, caraway, and dill (illustrated on the opposite page), are umbels.

To find more information on the needs of related vegetable crops, see "Soil Needs by Family" on page 189.

FERTILIZING VEGETABLES

It's easy to get carried away trying to fine-tune fertility, but the truth is that most common garden vegetables do well in basic, well-drained soil, enriched with compost and other organic materials. The results of research aimed at determining the demands of a particular crop may vary depending on climate, native soil fertility, and the cultivar that is grown. Oftentimes, fertilizer tables are oriented toward maximum yields without considering nutritional quality or pest resistance. Excessive nitrogen recommendations, for instance, may indeed lead to impressive growth—often at the cost of making the crop more susceptible to attack by insects and disease.

When deciding how to fertilize your crop, you also need to consider how effectively a plant is able to utilize relatively unavailable nutrients from rock minerals. Lettuce and squash, for example, demand a ready supply of soluble nutrients. Legumes, on the other

celery   caraway   dill   parsley   carrot

The umbels (umbrella-like flower heads) of dill, parsley, caraway, celery, and carrot are the clue that they're all members of the family Umbelliferae.

hand, in addition to being able to use atmospheric nitrogen, can often make good use of phosphorus in mineral form.

If you garden intensively—trying to maximize every square inch of bed space and planning succession crops for the full growing season—chances are that common fertilizer recommendations, including those in this book, will not provide adequate crop nutrition. Fertilizer recommendations are based on responses of crops planted in single rows at standard spacing, which is much less productive and much less demanding of nutrients per square foot of garden.

The best general-purpose fertilizer for vegetables is compost.

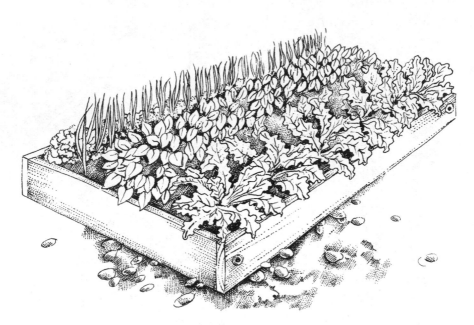

In intensive planting, plants are grown close together, allowing you to grow more plants per square foot of garden space. Keep in mind that intensive planting requires more nutrients than row spacing.

Once you have established good soil humus levels and mineral balances, yearly applications of about 1 pound per square foot of garden will maintain organic matter levels and replenish nutrients removed with your produce. You can spread compost either in the fall, working it in when you seed a cover crop or prepare your garden for winter, or in the spring, when you make the soil ready for new seeds and seedlings.

ADDING FERTILIZER

Additional fertilization with supplemental materials may be necessary if you are growing a lot of heavy feeder crops, such as corn and potatoes; if your soil nutrient levels test a bit low; or if you just don't have enough compost. Refer to the discussion of fertilizer materials under "Fertilizer or Amendment?" on page 101 to help you decide which materials to apply.

Supplemental fertilizers can be used to stimulate good root development for an early season start. Northern gardeners who are trying to get a jump on the season sometimes find it necessary to treat early crops with nitrogen and phosphorus, since soil microbes

SOIL NEEDS BY FAMILY

This table includes the major families of garden vegetables. Other families may be represented in the vegetable patch, including Polygonaceae, which includes buckwheat, rhubarb, and sorrel; Convolvulaceae, the morning-glory family, which provides us with yams and sweet potatoes; and Malvaceae, the mallow family, to which okra belongs.

Family: Chenopodiaceae

Members: Beets, spinach, sugar beets, Swiss chard, and lamb's-quarters (which are weeds to some and delicacies to others)

Likes: Prefer cooler weather; need rich soil; do better in alkaline than acidic conditions; adequate calcium and nitrogen essential

Dislikes: Avoid too much soluble nitrogen because they can concentrate it as unhealthful nitrates, especially under cold, low-light conditions

Family: Compositae

Members: Chamomile, chicory, dandelions, endive, globe artichokes, Jerusalem artichokes, lettuce, salsify, and sunflowers

Likes: Adapted to wide variety of climate and soil conditions; varying cultural needs

Family: Cruciferae

Members: Broccoli, brussels sprouts, cabbages, cauliflower, kale, kohlrabi, bok choy and other Oriental greens, radishes, rapeseed, rutabagas, turnips, mustards, and cresses

Likes: Prefer cool growing conditions; require good soil moisture and plentiful available nutrients

Dislikes: Avoid acidic conditions; will be set back by deficiencies of calcium and boron

Family: Cucurbitaceae

Members: Cucumbers, gourds, melons, pumpkins, and winter and summer squash

Likes: Need ample available nutrients to thrive; tolerate fresh or partially composted manure well; need good drainage and reasonable pH levels

Dislikes: Don't tolerate magnesium deficiency well

(continued)

SOIL NEEDS BY FAMILY—CONTINUED

Family: Gramineae

Members: Corn, oats, rice, wheat, and other cereal crops

Likes: Need adequate nitrogen early in growth

Dislikes: If nitrogen is excessive, grains can suffer from lodging—a condition in which seed heads get too heavy for the stalks

Family: Labiatae

Members: Many culinary and medicinal herbs, such as basil, catnip, oregano, rosemary, sage, savory, thyme, and the various mints

Likes: Generally tolerant of poor soils and cold weather; basil demands plenty of nitrogen and warmth

Dislikes: Avoid excess nitrogen to increase aromatic-oil content

Family: Leguminosae

Members: Green, dry, bush, and pole beans; peas; fava beans; peanuts; and soybeans, as well as fodder and soil-improving crops, including alfalfa, clovers, and vetch

Likes: Prefer neutral soil and need adequate calcium, phosphorus, and potassium; varying requirements for climate and drainage; nitrogen-fixing process requires boron and molybdenum

Dislikes: Excess boron detrimental to beans and peas

Family: Liliaceae

Members: Asparagus, garlic, leeks, onions, and shallots

Likes: Most don't mind cold. Need a steady supply of moisture and good drainage; require good phosphorus, potassium, and sulfur levels

Dislikes: Apply seaweed extract to boost supply of micronutrients

Family: Solanaceae

Members: Eggplant, peppers, potatoes, tobacco, tomatillo, and tomatoes

Likes: Greedy potassium consumers; can stand somewhat acidic conditions

(continued)

SOIL NEEDS BY FAMILY—CONTINUED

Dislikes: Tropical in origin and frost-sensitive; the potato—a mountain plant—can tolerate more cold than the others; excess nitrogen suppresses flowering and fruit set in favor of rampant vegetative growth; sensitive to magnesium deficiency

Family: Umbelliferae

Members: Caraway, coriander, dill, parsley, carrots, celery, celeriac, fennel, and parsnips

Likes: Generally tolerate poor soil and cold weather; root crops need good phosphorus and potassium supplies

Dislikes: Good drainage essential for most, except for celery, which originated in swamps

are too sluggish under cold, wet conditions to release many nutrients. Spread a 1-inch band of rock phosphate or bonemeal in the seed furrow to give a boost to crops, such as potatoes, that demand high phosphorus.

Fertilizers can also be used as a mid-season side-dressing. Apply a band of fertilizer material alongside the growing plant, preferably just before cultivating or mulching. Side-dressing is helpful during critical development stages, such as fruit blossom-set, or when drought or cold stress are harming a crop by reducing nutrient release from soil organic matter. It can also help to stimulate regrowth of leafy crops, such as Swiss chard or basil.

When plants are in nutrient-related trouble, water-based and foliar nutrient applications have the advantage of being very fast-acting. Foliar application is also a good way to spread micronutrients when a soil test has turned up some deficiency. Apply various combinations of fish emulsion, seaweed, compost tea, and other more exotic substances, such as herbal preparations, with a garden sprayer or through irrigation water. This kind of feeding accomplishes many of the same nutrient-boosting goals as a mid-season side-dressing. Many gardeners routinely spray seaweed extract at regular intervals. It can improve resistance to disease and stimulate growth, as well as providing balanced micronutrients in a readily available form.

Apply compost or supplemental fertilizers alongside the growing plants as a side-dressing during the growing season, at blossom set, or during periods of cold weather or drought. You can also side-dress leafy crops to stimulate regrowth.

Use the "Soil Needs of Vegetables" table on the opposite page to help decide how much (if any) additional fertilization your vegetables may need. It is also a useful guide for planning crop rotations.

CROP ROTATION:
THE WHY AND HOW

Crop rotation has long been recognized as a valuable farm practice. It makes sense anywhere that annual crops, such as most vegetables, are grown. Crop rotation is simply changing what is grown in a given spot from season to season. This is usually done with some plan in mind, to maximize the beneficial interactions of one kind of plant following another. But even if all you do is move your tomatoes to a different place in the garden, it will help.

SOIL NEEDS OF VEGETABLES

To get the best out of your vegetable plants, you need to give them the most appropriate soil conditions. Below you'll find a guide to the most common crops, along with their nutrient and moisture needs. (After the common name in each entry, you'll find the name of the botanical family to which the plant or plants belong. Use this information when you are planning crop rotations, to identify the relationships between your different crops.)

Key: 1 = Light feeder
2 = Needs high nitrogen
3 = Needs high phosphorus and potassium
4 = Tolerates more acid conditions
5 = Tolerates more alkaline conditions
6 = Needs pH near neutral
7 = Needs good drainage; can't stand wet feet
8 = Needs lots of water; tolerates heavy soil
9 = Needs lots of water, but can't stand wet feet

Plant	Requirements	Comments
Asparagus (Liliaceae)	2, 3, 5, 7	Deep-rooted perennial
Beans (Leguminosae)	1, 6, 7	Manganese, zinc, and iron essential; use proper inoculant for nitrogen fixation
Beets (Chenopodiaceae)	2, 3, 5, 7	Needs micronutrients, especially boron; avoid raw manure
Broccoli, brussels sprouts, cabbage, cauliflower, Oriental greens (Cruciferae)	2, 3, 6, 8	Needs calcium, sulfur, and boron
Carrot, parsnip (Umbelliferae)	1, 4, 7	Avoid excess nitrogen; needs deep soil
Celery (Umbelliferae)	2, 3, 4, 8	High boron demand; needs plenty of humus
Corn (Gramineae)	2, 3, 4, 7	Side-dress when knee-high; needs zinc
Cucumbers (Cucurbitaceae)	2, 3, 4, 9	Needs lots of humus; magnesium important

(continued)

SOIL NEEDS OF VEGETABLES—
CONTINUED

Plant	Requirements	Comments
Eggplant (Solanaceae)	2, 3, 4, 7	Plants grow poorly in cool, wet soil
Garlic, shallots (Liliaceae)	1, 3, 4, 7	Needs micronutrients and sulfur
Kale, collards, mustard (Cruciferae)	2, 3, 4, 8	*See* Broccoli
Lettuce, endive, chicory (Compositae)	2, 3, 6, 9	Calcium, manganese, and copper important
Melon (Cucurbitaceae)	2, 3, 5, 9	*See* Cucumber
Onion, leek (Liliaceae)	1, 3, 6, 9	Needs high humus; has high sulfur and micronutrient needs
Pea (Leguminosae)	1, 4, 7	Use proper inoculant; needs manganese
Pepper (Solanaceae)	1, 4, 7	Needs sulfur and magnesium; avoid excess nitrogen
Potato (Solanaceae)	2, 3, 4, 7	Avoid raw manure; more acidic conditions prevent scab
Spinach, Swiss chard (Chenopodiaceae)	2, 3, 5, 7	Has high micronutrient need
Squash (Cucurbitaceae)	1, 3, 4, 7	*See* Cucumber
Sweet potato (Convolvulaceae)	1, 3, 4, 7	Drainage is crucial; tolerates poor soil
Tomato (Solanaceae)	3, 4, 7	Avoid excess nitrogen
Turnip, radish, rutabaga (Cruciferae)	1, 4, 7	Avoid excess nitrogen. *See also* Broccoli

Crop rotation means a healthier garden, better use of soil nutrients, and improved soil. Here's how those benefits happen.

Interrupting the cycles of diseases, insects, and weeds. Disease pathogens can build up to disastrous levels if the same species, or even members of the same family, are grown on one site year after year. Many insect and nematode pests are relatively immobile, even in small gardens where cucumber beetles have no problem finding the new squash patch. To cleanse the soil of tough weeds like couchgrass, use smother crops, such as buckwheat, in rotation plans.

Planning for complementary nutrient requirements. To avoid exhausting soil reserves of any given nutrient, rotate nutrient-demanding crops with those that have lesser needs. For example, follow beans and peas, which require little soil nitrogen, with corn, a heavy feeder.

Building organic matter. By including green manures and cover crops in a rotation, you protect soil from erosion and improve organic matter levels. See "Growing Green Manures" on page 50 for more information on cover crops and green manures.

Improving soil structure. Alternating shallow-rooted and deep-rooted crops takes advantage of their differing abilities to extract soil nutrients from different levels in the soil. Deep-rooted crops create aeration channels that loosen heavy soils, benefiting crops that follow. Their deep roots can also extract nutrients from the subsoil that are not available to shallow-rooted crops.

Other benefits also result from rotating your garden crops. Some research shows that certain crops, such as grasses, increase earthworm activity, while others, such as onions, have a growth-stimulating effect on crops that follow them.

PLANNING ROTATIONS

The first two factors to take into account when developing your own rotation plan are how much space you have and what vegetables you really like. In order to plan rotations, you need to keep records of what grows where each season in the garden. Notes about which soil amendments you used and any noteworthy observations such as pest or disease problems are also part of a complete rotation plan.

The next step in planning your crop rotation is dividing your vegetable plot. Count the number of categories of crops you have, then divide your plot into that many segments. (The segments should be roughly equal in size.) Then make adjustments as you go along, in order to more closely tailor the plan to your preferences. Below are some guidelines to help you plan your rotation.

Consider plants' feeding habits. Alternate heavy feeders with light feeders and soil-improving crops. To find out what kind of "feeder" a particular crop is, see "How's the Appetite?" below.

Keep families together. Group plants in the same family together, especially those that are attacked by the same pests and diseases. But avoid planting a crop where a crop from the same family grew in the previous season, or pests may build up to damaging levels.

Choose complementary companions. Group crops according to their space and cultural requirements. For example, leafy greens, squash, and corn have similar nutritional needs, and their growth habits make them good neighbors.

Pick a primary crop for planning purposes. If you like a diverse, intensively planted bed, choose one dominant crop type for each area. For example, you may want to plant onions or herbs as companion plants with your cabbages—but if most of your bed is cabbages, just consider it a cabbage bed for rotation purposes. I like to plant spinach and lettuce next to pea vines for shade, and I treat that segment of the garden like a row of peas in my garden planning charts.

HOW'S THE APPETITE?

Here are some guidelines to use in planning crop rotations and determining nutrient needs.

Heavy feeders: Asparagus, beets, broccoli, brussels sprouts, cabbage, cauliflower, celery, collards, corn, kale, kohlrabi, lettuce, parsley, potatoes, rhubarb, spinach, squash (summer and winter), tomatoes

Light feeders: Carrots, garlic, leeks, mustard, onions, parnsips, peppers, radishes, rutabagas, shallots, Swiss chard, turnips

Soil improvers: Broad beans, lima beans, peanuts, peas, shell beans, snap beans, soybeans

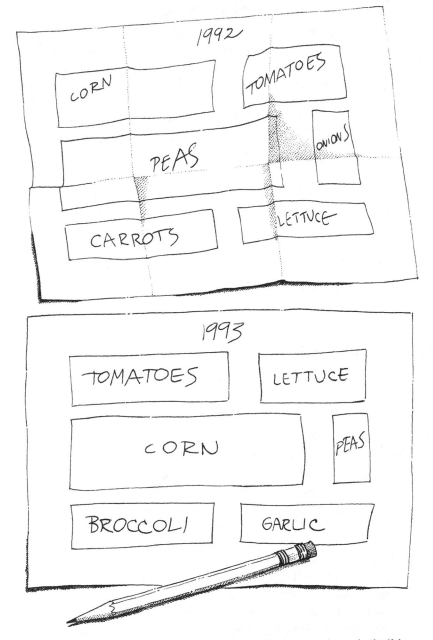

Crop rotation interrupts the cycles of diseases, insects, and weeds; builds organic matter; and improves soil structure. Plan your rotations to alternate shallow-rooted crops with deep-rooted crops and heavy feeders with light feeders to avoid exhausting soil nutrients.

When Not to Rotate

Sometimes rotations aren't practical. You may find that certain kinds of crops just like a particular area of your garden. It may make sense to always plant the peas along the fence that you already have. In such cases, look for other ways to replace the functions that rotation serves. If you use plenty of compost and are careful about supplying nutrients, you can avoid soil depletion. Mulching is a good way to build organic matter and prevent diseases carried by soil particles that splash onto leaves. Use cover crops to increase the diversity of plant interactions in your soil. Try companion planting or interplanting green manures between rows of vegetables.

SEASONAL SOIL CARE FOR VEGETABLES

Use the following calendar to plan your vegetable garden's soil-care program throughout the year. Refer to the appropriate chapters for more details about the practices listed.

SPRING

Till or dig in winter cover crops as soon as the soil is workable, at least 2 to 3 weeks before planting seeds. If you don't have any spring crops planned for a particular site, plant a summer green manure there. If you've mulched any beds for the winter, push the mulch off to the sides of the bed to allow soil to warm up. Or, if the mulch is light, till or dig it in along with a layer of well-decomposed compost or other organic fertilizer, if needed. This is also a good time to apply supplemental nitrogen and potassium to any beds that need these nutrients. Turn any compost piles that have been sitting over winter, and set up a new compost bin or site.

Before you start your spring planting, prepare seedbeds by raking out stones and clods. Plant your crops following your rotation plan, and apply mulch after plants have developed several sets of leaves.

SUMMER

During the summer, regularly inspect your plants for signs of nutrient deficiency or other problems; side-dress and/or foliar-feed as needed. Tend your compost piles. In late summer, plant your fall crops, following your rotation plan.

FALL

At the end of the growing season, clean up the garden. Remove diseased plant material, woody stalks, and any other debris that will break down more quickly if composted. If you don't plan to use a cover crop or mulch, leave some plant debris on the surface to prevent erosion. Otherwise, lightly till or dig in remaining plant debris. Build compost piles with garden debris, leaves, and yard trimmings.

Fall is a great time to take soil samples. Send them to a laboratory or follow instructions with your home test kit. Add and incorporate finished or partially decomposed compost, and fertilize beds with phosphorus and lime as indicated by soil test results.

If you are planning a new garden or expanding the old, dig or turn under sod now. Plant all beds with a winter cover crop or apply a layer of mulch to protect soil and add organic matter.

WINTER

During the winter, add mulch anytime the soil is bare. Waiting until the ground freezes can be helpful because grubs, cutworms, and other pests will be exposed to lethal freezing temperatures. Continue adding kitchen scraps to your compost piles. Use your time indoors to plan next season's crop rotations and to order soil-improving materials and tools.

CHAPTER 9

SOIL NEEDS OF FLOWERS

Your best chance for success in the flower garden is to use plants adapted to your particular climate and soil conditions. Most perennials are undemanding, perfectly happy in ordinary garden soil. They'll do even better with judicious use of fertilizer and mulch. If your soil tends to the extreme, you can still find a wide variety of colorful plants for any conditions, from bone-dry to heavy clay to wet and boggy. Matching the plant to the site is much easier than reconstructing the garden.

START RIGHT WITH PERENNIALS

If you're planning to put in a new perennial bed, taking the time to properly prepare your soil will pay off with healthier plants and fewer disease problems over the long run. Unless you are growing plants especially adapted to bogs and wetlands—an increasingly popular alternative for gardens in wet spots—your first considerations in starting a new perennial bed are drainage and aeration.

ORGANIC MATTER IS THE KEY

If you're blessed with rich sandy loam with a pH between 6.5 and 6.8, there isn't much you need to do to ensure healthy flowers. Work in ½ inch or so of compost in spring or fall, and keep perennials well-mulched with 3 to 4 inches of clean organic matter. Provide sufficient water and, for more demanding plants, occasional feedings of compost tea, fish emulsion, and seaweed extract, and you can't go wrong.

Most perennials would rather have soil that is too sandy than too heavy, but water drains fast through light, sandy soils, carrying nutrients with it. This kind of soil either requires frequent watering or limits your options to plants that can tolerate drought. To increase water-holding capacity and nutrient reserves of sandy soils, build organic matter with compost and mulch.

Poor circulation of air and water in heavy or waterlogged soils is a recipe for disease—a much bigger issue for most flowers than nutrient availability. Friable, porous soil that permits unimpeded root growth is needed in order for roots to efficiently use soil nutrients. If your soil has drainage or texture problems, try the following methods to improve it. (See "Drainage Problems" on page 150 for full details on these and other remedies.)

• Create double-dug raised beds, and renovate at regular intervals with a garden fork.

• Mix in large quantities of sand, peat moss, or leaf mold. Monitor pH and add lime, if needed, to balance the acid qualities of peat moss.

• Build organic matter and humus and stimulate soil biological activity by digging in lots of compost or laying it under thick layers of organic mulch. If possible, prepare new bed sites the year before with a deep-rooted legume cover crop. See "Growing Green Manures" on page 50 for details on cover crops and green manures.

BALANCING THE BED

Give your perennials the best possible start by enriching their new home with a good layer of compost, well-incorporated throughout the bed so roots are encouraged to branch out. Work in some kelp meal, about 1 pound per 100 square feet of bed, to provide a balanced micronutrient source. It's a good idea to test your soil before planting perennials. If you will be putting in heavy feeders or you have depleted soil nutrient levels, work in a moderate application of a blended organic fertilizer with an NPK equivalent of 5-10-5. (For information on NPK analyses, see "Choosing the Right Fertilizer" on page 104.) Use slow-release rock powders to replenish mineral reserves and adjust pH.

A DIET FOR FLOWERS

Of the "big three" plant nutrients—nitrogen, phosphorus, and potassium—the latter two are especially important for most flowering plants. These nutrients play a critical role in almost every aspect of the development of flowering plants—from root growth to seed formation.

Phosphorus is key to inducing flowering. It's crucial for root formation and growth and the development of plant reproductive organs. Bonemeal, an excellent source of this important nutrient, is the mainstay of any organic perennial maintenance program. Bulbs are also voracious consumers of calcium, which is also supplied in bonemeal. Don't worry too much about overfertilizing, since excess phosphorus will stay tied up in the soil and not leach down into the groundwater.

Potassium plays an important role in plant structure and seed formation. This nutrient is often deficient in humid climates, which receive more than 30 inches of precipitation a year, and in soils washed by frequent or heavy rainfall. Potassium leaches easily, especially from sandy, light-textured soils. In such soils, use a potassium-rich organic mulch, such as straw or weed-free hay, and add a potassium-rich supplement, such as kelp meal or greensand, to your compost pile.

COLOR AND FRAGRANCE

Flower color, intensity, and aroma are all influenced to some degree by soil nutrition. Sulfur and micronutrients, especially iron, are critical for the subtle biochemical processes that result in the delicate hues and sensual smells that draw us to cultivate flowers.

Different soil characteristics affect plant color and fragrance in different ways. The metallic elements that make paint colors vivid have the same effect on flower colors when they are present in the soil. The balanced micronutrients in seaweed, when applied as fertilizer, have been shown to intensify flower colors. Soil acidity and alkalinity has an effect on the colors of some flowers as well. For example, bigleaf hydrangea (*Hydrangea macrophylla*) has blue blossoms when grown in acid soils and pink ones when grown in more alkaline soils. As a general rule, though, for the brightest, most beautiful flowers, just make sure that your soil is healthy, biologically active, and well-amended with compost and other organic fertilizers.

All plants need some nitrogen, but overfertilization with this element encourages plants to remain in their leaf-producing, vegetative stage rather than getting down to the business of blossoming. Excess nitrogen also makes plants more susceptible to disease and pest attack, and it can shorten the life of perennials.

HOW TO FEED FLOWERS

Many established perennials need feeding from time to time, even if you start with excellent soil. If your plants are growing slowly or if soil test results point to low nutrient levels, supplemental fertilizer may be necessary. Feed most plants annually; those with heavy nutrient demands need additional boosts another two or three times over the season. You can feed perennials through side-dressing, by watering with compost tea, or by foliar fertilization. Remember to avoid overfeeding: Too much nitrogen will give you more leaves, not more flowers. And overfed perennials can outgrow their allotted space too quickly.

Side-dress perennials with compost, rock powders, bonemeal, or blended organic fertilizers. Your choice depends on what you have available and what your own preferences are. (Refer to "Fertilizer or Amendment?" on page 101 for information about

For a nutrient boost, water perennials with compost tea. Bundle finished compost in a cheesecloth square and soak in water overnight. Dilute the liquid with water until it is the color of weak tea, and then use it to water or spray on your plants.

these materials.) If mulch is already in place, pull it back and work the material into the soil around the base of the plant; be gentle to avoid damaging roots. If the soil is dry, water after fertilizing, then replace the mulch.

Make nutrient-rich compost tea by the barrel or by the watering can. Use it to perk up drought- or cold-stressed plants, or to stimulate blossoming. Compost tea has also been shown to prevent certain plant disease problems. (See "Brewing Compost Tea" on page 203 for an illustration of how to make compost tea.) You can also make enriched watering solutions by adding fish emulsion and seaweed extract to irrigation water.

Foliar-feed your flowering plants in early morning or evening or on an overcast day. Spray leaves with a solution of fish emulsion or seaweed extract, prepared according to instructions on the product label. Make sure all leaf surfaces are covered with mist. Stop using the fish emulsion after mid-season to avoid stimulating lush growth that won't be cold-hardy. Avoid foliar feeding when your plants have fungal disease problems, such as mildew. The dampness encourages fungal growth.

When transplanting, whether you are using purchased plants or dividing your own, sprinkle a little bonemeal in the hole around the root zone to provide an extra boost of phosphorus right where it is needed. To minimize transplant shock, water in your new plants well with a seaweed solution.

Give new transplants a quick dose of phosphorus by sprinkling a little bonemeal in the hole around the root zone.

ESPECIALLY FOR ANNUALS

Annual flowers, which live out their entire life cycle in a single season, have many of the same needs as perennials. Information in this chapter for perennial flowers applies equally to annuals. Here are a few more tips on planning soil care with annuals in mind:

• Annuals are generally shallow-rooted. They need good soil moisture and readily available nutrients.

• Annual flowers can be interplanted in the vegetable garden as companion plants and as homes for beneficial insects. Consider them light feeders when planning crop rotations, because very few nutrients are removed in harvest.

• Promote vigor and prolong the blooming season of annuals with regular foliar feeding of seaweed three to four times a season.

• Stimulate pansies into reblooming by applying a side-dressing of compost or balanced organic fertilizer.

IMPROVING AN ESTABLISHED PLANTING

Short of digging up an existing bed and starting over, what can you do to rescue perennials planted in poor soil? That depends on the nature of the problem and how extreme it is. If plants are struggling along in conditions to which they are unsuited, it's often best to remove them and select others that can tolerate your particular situation. If drainage is the main problem, though, you may be able to salvage the planting by digging drainage trenches. (See "Drainage Problems" on page 150 for more solutions to poorly drained soil.)

You can improve nutrient availability and even soil structure—within reason—without uprooting the bed and starting over. The magic of compost, as usual, is a big part of the solution. Because you can't place fertilizer materials directly where the roots are growing, soil organisms are your only means of moving around immobile nutrients like phosphorus to make them available to plants. Generous applications of compost will stimulate increased biological activity, as well as replenishing nutrients. It may take some time and patience, but as the soil microorganisms go to work for you, even deep-rooted perennials will begin to thrive along with them. Compost can also help fend off plant diseases because it both improves overall health and vigor and contains natural antibiotics.

MULCH MATTERS

Mulch is another good way to add organic matter and humus to established perennial beds. Besides helping build soil, mulch protects your garden from drying out or overheating in summer and from freezing and frost heaving in winter. It smothers out most weeds and can be decorative, too, adding color and texture to your landscape. Be sure to avoid nonorganic mulches, such as plastic or gravel, if your aim is richer soil. Whatever advantages nonorganic mulches may have, improving soil fertility isn't among them.

Use common sense when you mulch—there *is* such a thing as overdoing it! Dumping a heavy load on the heads of your plants may save you time, but you're asking for trouble: Soggy mulch close to stems and crowns of your perennials can induce rot. Be sure to keep the mulch a few inches away from the base of the plant. If you apply mulch too early in the spring, your soil will remain cold and biologically sluggish. Wait until the soil has warmed before mulching. Deep mulches can harbor destructive rodents, slugs, and snails, so keep your mulch light, renewing it frequently, if these pests are a problem in your garden.

Practical and Attractive Mulches

Mulch is not only practical in your flower garden, it can make a statement, too. Use inexpensive mulches, such as straw, as a bottom layer, and top them with a more visually appealing—and more expensive—choice such as shredded bark. Other materials besides those described below also make fine mulch, so be creative. Depending on where you live, there may be valuable food-processing wastes available; anything that is fairly light and dry, such as peanut hulls or grain chaff, is suitable. Coarse mulches like bark and shredded brush are generally best for more permanent plantings. If you use them where you have to do a lot of transplanting, such as on annual beds, the wood pieces tend to work into the soil, making it difficult to get good soil-root contact for young plants.

Bark. Various kinds of bark mulch products are sold at garden supply stores. Choose smaller-size pieces to build soil organic matter more rapidly or coarser ones for mulch that will last longer.

Buckwheat hulls. This material is an excellent soil conditioner but is very light and fluffy. It is hard to keep in place in windy locations; top it with something heavier.

Cocoa bean hulls. This attractive mulch decomposes fairly quickly. Unless you live near a chocolate factory, it can be expensive to buy. For a few weeks after application, your garden will smell like bitter chocolate.

Grass clippings. Allow grass clippings to dry before spreading them so they won't mat into anaerobic clumps. A thin layer of grass clippings is more beneficial as a mulch sublayer, to give an extra shot of nitrogen. Grass clippings left on the lawn will improve the soil there.

Hay. Hay is easy to find, visually pleasant, and a terrific soil builder. But it can cause trouble in the flower garden: If the hay was cut after seed heads matured, you'll be seeding grass and weeds as you spread it. Hay can be difficult to spread around. You'll need to pull it apart by hand, which can create a lot of nose-annoying dust.

Pine needles are practical as well as attractive. Use them as a mulch for acid-lovers like azaleas, rhododendrons, and camellias.

Dust from moldy hay is harmful to breathe. Wear a face mask when applying it.

Leaves. Easy to get in the fall, leaves offer excellent winter protection and soil improvement. Certain species, such as oak, decompose very slowly and acidify soil. Shred leaves with a lawn mower or power shredder to reduce problems of matting.

Newspaper. Some people use newspaper as their basic weed-suppressing material, camouflaged with something more appealing. In the amounts used for mulch, there's no evidence that the heavy metal content of the inks, even of color magazines, will pose a problem.

Pine needles. This material, illustrated on page 207, is attractive to look at, and it suppresses weeds well. Pine needles increase soil acidity, a plus for acid lovers like rhododendrons and camellias.

Sawdust. Attractive and easy to handle, sawdust serves as a good soil conditioner as it decomposes. Fresh sawdust may tie up soil nitrogen; compost it first or apply it with a good nitrogen source such as blood meal or alfalfa meal to counteract this problem.

Shredded brush. Shrub trimmings, prunings, and other plant materials are excellent all-purpose mulches. You can collect them from your own yard or from local highway departments, but be sure it didn't come from an herbicide-sprayed area. Woodier brush may tie up nitrogen; add a high-nitrogen supplement such as blood meal with the mulch.

Straw. Not only is weed-free straw attractive, but it is an excellent soil conditioner as well. Shredding the straw makes it easier to apply around established plantings.

ADDING AMENDMENTS

If your soil needs supplemental minerals, place them around your plants and lightly scratch them into the surface before laying your mulch material. You can even practice a type of composting, layering partially rotted or raw food wastes or even manure under the mulch. (Only try this modified "sheet composting" around well-established plants. New seedings or transplants can be damaged by some of the decomposition products.) If you have enough compost to put on a 3- to 4-inch layer, you can use it for mulch. If your compost supply is limited, sprinkle it around before you put down a top layer of mulch.

KNOW YOUR PLANTS' NEEDS

Consult a reliable reference book when choosing plants for a flower garden. Look for plants suited to your conditions. Some plants are widely adaptable and need only good garden soil and reasonable care. Others are known to be highly demanding of nutrients or finicky about drainage. Your local nursery is a good source for plants that do best in your general area, and knowledgeable staff can help you make selections suited to your site.

FLOWERS WITH SPECIAL NEEDS

Many common garden flowers are adaptable, but some have special needs. Use the following lists to help you make the most of your flower garden through the seasons.

Light feeders. These plants like a lean soil, though they do well in most ordinary garden soils. Avoid excess nitrogen.

Achillea spp. (yarrows)
Asclepias tuberosa (butterfly weed)
Calendula spp. (calendulas)
Callistephus chinensis (China aster)
Clematis spp. (clematis)
Coleus × *hybridus* (coleus)
Hemerocallis spp. (daylilies)
Hosta spp. (hostas)
Impatiens spp. (impatiens)
Papaver orientale (oriental poppy)
Petunia × *hybrida* (garden petunia)
Tagetes spp. (marigolds)
Tropaeolum majus (garden nasturtium)
Viola × *wittrockiana* (pansy)
Zinnia elegans (zinnia)

Heavy feeders. These nutrient-hungry plants do best with extra applications of organic fertilizers. Side-dress in early spring with a high-phosphorus organic fertilizer with an NPK equivalent of 5-10-5, and reapply in mid-season. (See "Choosing the Right

Fertilizer" on page 104 for more information on NPK analyses.) In place of an early spring application, fertilize peonies after blooming.

Antirrhinum majus (snapdragon)
Astilbe spp. (astilbes)
Chrysanthemum spp. (chrysanthemums)
Chrysanthemum × *superbum* (Shasta daisy)
Dahlia spp. (dahlias)
Delphinium spp. (delphiniums)
Dicentra spp. (bleeding hearts)
Gysophila spp. (baby's-breaths)
Hyacinthus orientalis (hyacinth)
Paeonia spp. (peonies)

Heavy phosphorus feeders. These plants appreciate an extra dose of phosphorus for better bloom and growth, but their nitrogen and potassium needs are average.

Alcea rosea (hollyhock)
Gladiolus × *hortulanus* (gladiolus)
Verbena spp. (verbenas)

Some flowers bloom best when soil is on the lean side. Nasturtiums are light feeders and bloom well in poor soils, though they also do well in most ordinary garden soils.

P/K boost. These plants aren't heavy feeders, but they do benefit from extra phosphorus (P) and/or potassium (K) at blossom time. Apply the nutrients when the flowers are in bud. (Plant name is followed by the nutrient it craves.)

Dianthus spp. (pinks): P
Lilium spp. (lilies): P and K
Narcissus spp. (daffodils): P and K
Phlox spp. (phlox): K

SEASONAL SOIL CARE FOR FLOWERS

The best time to fertilize varies from plant to plant and from region to region. Learning the particular needs of plants in your garden is a skill you will build over the seasons of close observation. The basic timetable can be summarized as follows.

SPRING

In spring, work in compost and other soil amendments when preparing new beds. This is also the time to side-dress established plants that are heavy feeders with compost, bonemeal, or blended organic fertilizers as appropriate. (Wait until fall to fertilize bulbs and most perennials.) Apply mulch after soil has warmed up and plants are well-leafed-out.

SUMMER

During the summer, foliar-feed or water your plants with compost tea as needed. Give all flowering plants a boost with some extra phosphorus when buds are forming. Test your soil in time to plan for fall fertilization.

FALL

This is the time for the regular annual feeding for most perennials. Be conservative, and avoid sources of soluble nitrogen, which can encourage plants to produce succulent new growth that will be damaged by cold temperatures. Correct any soil deficiencies detected by your summer soil test. Apply bonemeal to your bulb plantings to prepare them for fall and early spring growth. If necessary, mulch all flower beds for winter protection.

CHAPTER 10

SOIL NEEDS OF LAWNS

Caring for lawns without the use of chemicals has become a popular idea in recent years, with suburban landscapers and lawn care specialists scrambling to present this option to their customers. This approach is mainly due to people who want to protect their families from exposure to toxic pesticides: According to a 1980 report by the National Academy of Sciences, lawns receive the heaviest pesticide applications of any land area in the United States. Contamination of groundwater with nitrate fertilizers and pesticides is another consequence of indiscriminate lawn-chemical use. Now the word is out that organic lawn care is also cheaper and, in the long run, requires less work to maintain — and can result in lawns that are every bit as lush and beautiful as those in a slick chemical-company ad.

As is true for every other part of your garden, good soil care is fundamental to achieving and maintaining a healthy lawn. Organically managed lawns grow more slowly, so they need less mowing. Also, because their roots are deeper, they are better able to withstand drought and take in nutrients. If lawn care is really a chore that you dread, think about ways to reduce the area of lawn you have. Determine which areas of your yard don't really have to be grass-carpeted, and plant them with wildflowers, perennials, and low-maintenance groundcovers instead.

Planting a New Lawn

The best time of year to start a lawn depends on where you live. In the North, or anywhere you intend to plant cool-season grasses, fall is the time to do it. In the South or where you intend to plant warm-season grasses, plant new lawns in spring and early summer.

Think of planting a new lawn as putting in a new perennial planting—when you do it the right way from the beginning, the effort pays off for years. The best time to undertake major soil-improving tasks is before you plant your lawn. Although many soil problems can be corrected after a lawn is established, whatever you can do to get a new planting off to a good start will more than repay your effort.

Your first priority is good drainage. If your soil is heavy clay, you'll need to improve air and water penetration. To do so, add an amendment such as sand, peat moss, rotted sawdust, or compost before you sow your grass seed. Ideally, your lawn should slope very gradually, to encourage water to drain off. Fill in any depressions where water might collect. Be sure there are proper drainage pathways for runoff from your roof and gutter. In some cases, you may need to install buried drainage tiles or some other system to carry away excess water. (Consult "Drainage Problems" on page 150 for more ideas about improving drainage.)

It is best to have your soil tested the season before establishing your new lawn. However, if you don't have time to do so a season before, make sure you have the test done as early as possible, and don't plant your lawn until you receive the results. Top your prepared but unplanted seedbed with a ½-inch layer of compost or a compost-based organic lawn fertilizer to get those soil organisms working. Place any necessary mineral soil amendments like lime and

A Healthy Diversity

A diversity of grass species with a good dose of legumes thrown in is good insurance against pests, disease, and unpredictable weather-related stresses. A fast-growing annual in the mix, such as annual ryegrass, will help protect tender emerging shoots of slower-growing species. Clover adds an extra boost of nitrogen for its companion grasses, reducing the amount you have to provide through fertilizer.

rock phosphate right in the root zone, where they will do your grass the most good. Use a rake to work it lightly into the very top of the soil as you do the final smoothing before broadcasting your seed.

It pays to do a little research on the best grass species to plant in your area. More attention is being paid these days to breeding for pest and disease resistance. Your local Cooperative Extension Service office often has current information on suitable cultivars.

After seeding, pack the soil down by rolling it with a lawn roller or tamping gently with the head of your rake. Water well, and protect the new planting with a light scattering of mulch to prevent erosion and conserve moisture. If you just have a small area of lawn, try using a wide piece of floating row cover, which will speed germination by raising the soil temperature. It's important not to let the soil dry out in this critical early stage, even if you have to hand-water it. Avoid mowing or even walking on the new lawn until it's been up and growing for a few weeks and is at least 2 inches tall.

RENOVATING OLD SOD

Replanting a lawn from scratch is a drastic procedure. You'll need to rotary-till the whole area thoroughly to break up old sod so that it decomposes quickly, then painstakingly rake out clumps and follow the process described for seeding a new lawn. If you don't want to rake out the clumps, apply a high-nitrogen fertilizer like blood meal or alfalfa meal before tilling to help the clumps decompose. Then give the clumps of old lawn a couple of weeks to break down before you plant.

To save your back and budget, consider spot therapy rather than a major overhaul. You can usually revive a neglected or abused lawn by overseeding. To reduce stress and stimulate grass to regrow as quickly as possible, overseed during a cool, moist time of year—a couple of weeks before your first fall frost in the North or early spring in the South. Here's how to do it:

1. Mow the selected area on a very low blade setting.

2. Rake vigorously to scratch up the surface. For larger areas, use a rotary tiller with the tines set very shallowly to just skim the surface. Go as quickly as you can without losing control of the machine.

3. Rake off any patches where the sod gets a little too chewed up by the tiller. Fill in any holes or low spots with good topsoil.

4. Broadcast lime or other soil amendments as recommended by your soil test results. (Refer to "Testing Your Soil" on page 93 for more information on soil tests.)

5. Broadcast seed at one-and-one-half times the recommended rate for new seedings.

6. Add a topdressing of compost, ½ inch or thicker.

7. Go over the area with a lawn roller to get good contact between the soil, seed, and compost, and then water thoroughly. Wait until the new patch of lawn is at least 2 inches high before mowing.

If your lawn is past salvaging with spot fixes, use a rotary tiller to break up old sod, then rake out clumps and reseed.

SOIL BUILDING AND LAWN MAINTENANCE

When you manage your lawn from the perspective of soil health, you can begin to make sense out of some contradictory and confusing sets of advice. For example, conventional wisdom advises you to remove grass clippings to prevent thatch buildup; however, leaving clippings on your lawn can actually keep it healthier and reduce the need to fertilize it if you take care of your microscopic soil workers. Managing a healthy, chemical-free lawn grown on healthy soil takes less time and effort than the out-of-balance chemically dependent lawn and soil.

CUT BACK ON MOWING CHORES

Mowing too close too often creates extra stress for your lawn, opening the way to pests and disease. You can in good conscience cut back on that every-three-days routine, erring on the side of shagginess for better health. (If you like, you can clip it a bit shorter when preparing it for dormancy, though.) Another advantage of organic lawn care is that grass grows more slowly when it is not overfertilized with synthetic nitrogen.

Then there's the task of raking up the clippings and composting them—don't bother! If your soil is healthy, the microorganisms in it will make clippings disappear in a short time, helping to feed the growing grass in the process. A mulching lawn mower, which shreds the clippings and spreads them out to rot faster, can be a worthwhile investment. If your soil biological activity is sluggish, causing thatch to build up, removing the clippings may be necessary. This situation, however, is also an indication that it's time to take care of those soil organisms: Feed them and get some air into the soil, and they will perk up and help keep thatch under control.

GIVE YOUR LAWN A BREATH OF FRESH AIR

If your soil is heavy-textured or gets a lot of traffic, regular aerating can work wonders. Compacted soil leads to thatch and disease problems even if it has all the nutrients it needs. A lack of air leads to the proliferation of anaerobic soil organisms, which give off alcohols

For aeration and thatch removal, use an inexpensive core cultivator to poke holes in the soil.

and other waste products that are toxic to plant roots. Several special aerating tools are available, ranging from power aerators that you either rent or hire someone to use to inexpensive hand devices that you use by walking along and shoving them into the ground. Simply poking holes in the turf works fine for most cases. Use a sturdy pitchfork or spading fork, and drive it 4 to 6 inches deep at regular intervals, rocking it slightly each time.

FERTILIZE FOR GOOD GROWTH

Another technique that helps keep soil organisms happy is top-dressing—spreading soil amendments in a thin layer over the whole lawn. Most commercial organic fertilizers and rock powders will work well in a regular lawn spreader. To use homemade compost as a topdressing in a spreader, screen it well first. Of course, you can just go out with a bucket and scatter it by hand, too. Depending on your soil needs (whether from a soil test or your own observations), you can also use other organic materials, such as rotted sawdust, for topdressing. The main idea is to stimulate the soil organisms by providing them with some extra nourishment. A yearly topdressing is

Screen homemade compost with a box sieve, then apply with a lawn spreader for a topdressing. Spread a thin layer over the entire lawn.

plenty for maintenance, but if you're healing an abused lawn, try several doses a year. Consult "Fertilizer Timing," on page 220 for the best schedule.

WATERING THE RIGHT WAY

Excessive or improper watering is often the culprit in cases of disease invasion, since fungal diseases thrive in moist conditions. If soil organic matter levels are reasonable and drought-tolerant grass species or cultivars are used, watering is rarely necessary in many parts of the country. It is especially important to avoid watering too early in the spring. This encourages roots to stay shallow, rather than growing deep in search of water. Shallow roots make it necessary to water more often and also detract from overall turf vigor.

Water thoroughly and only when it is absolutely necessary. Frequent light watering will likewise keep roots from going deep and is only called for when establishing new seedings. When you do have to water, adjust the rate of water application so the water has enough time to soak into the soil. Level, sandy soil can absorb about 1 inch per hour, but clay soil can only soak up one-tenth as much.

LAWN NUTRITION

If you don't care about having the greenest lawn in town and you leave grass clippings where they fall, you hardly need to think about fertilizing. If your soil is basically healthy, lightly top-dressing with compost once every few years may be all you need to do. After all, perennial grass sod is the ideal crop for building soil organic matter, especially if you don't remove the grass clippings.

Nitrogen is crucial for active growth stages, such as early in the

NITROGEN NEEDS OF GRASSES

Use this table to find the pounds of actual nitrogen per 1,000 square feet per year that your type of grass needs. Both low- and high-maintenance doses are given. See "Fertilizer Timing" on page 220 for a schedule of when to fertilize your lawn. If you don't know what kinds of grasses are growing in your lawn, check with your local Cooperative Extension office for help in identifying them.

Species	Nitrogen (lbs. per 1,000 sq. ft.)	
	Low	High
Bahiagrass (*Paspalum notatum*)	2	4
Bentgrass (*Agrostis* spp.)	2	4
Bermudagrass (*Cynodon dactylon*)	1	4
Bluegrass, Kentucky (*Poa pratensis*)	2	3
Buffalograss (*Buchloe dactyloides*)	1	2
Carpetgrass (*Axonopus compressus*)	2	3
Centipedegrass (*Eremochloa ophiuroides*)	2	4
Fescue, fine (*Festuca* spp.)	1	2
Fescue, tall (*Festuca arundinacea*)	1	2
Ryegrass, perennial (*Lolium perenne*)	2	3
St. Augustinegrass (*Stenotaphrum secundatum*)	2	4
Zoysiagrass (*Zoysia* spp.)	2	3

SOURCE: Reprinted with permission from *The Chemical-Free Lawn* by Warren Schultz (Rodale Press, 1989).

FERTILIZER TIMING

When and how often you fertilize depends on where you live, what kind of grass you grow, and what you want for your lawn. Here is a general calendar, offering medium- and low-maintenance schedules. Actual doses depend on the grass species you grow. To determine what the fertilizer dose for your grass species should be, consult "Nitrogen Needs of Grasses" on page 219. If you only have a minimum of time to spend working on your lawn, the low-maintenance schedule is probably best for you. But if you're willing to invest a little more time for better results, the smaller but more frequent fertilizer applications in the medium-maintenance schedule will produce a more lush and vigorous lawn.

Humid Northeast

Low maintenance: Full low dose in September, October, or after grass stops active growth.

Medium maintenance: One-half of high dose in September or October and one-half in May or June after first rampant growth slows.

Humid South

Summer Grasses

Low maintenance: One-half of low dose in June and one-half in August.

Medium maintenance: One-quarter of high dose every month, May through August.

Winter Grasses

Full low dose in September or October.

season and when you want a new seeding to get off to a good start. Phosphorus is needed early to get roots growing vigorously, but it is also important later in the season to get them ready for dormancy. Potassium strengthens grass stalks and makes them more resistant to disease, stress, and traffic. It also helps grass plants build starch reserves in roots for the winter.

The best time to fertilize is when the grass is entering its period of dormancy—the fall in the North and the spring in the South. Many organic fertilizer manufacturers produce special blends for lawns—check with your local distributor for the range of products available. Natural commercial lawn fertilizers are available with an NPK analysis of around 5-3-4, applied at a rate of about 20 pounds per 1,000 square feet. (See "Choosing the Right Fertilizer" on page

Great Plains

Low maintenance: Full low dose in September.

Medium maintenance: One-half of high dose in September and one-half in November or one-half of high dose in September, one-quarter in November, and one-quarter in May.

Dry Southwest

Summer Grasses

Cool-season grasses, irrigated: One-half of high dose in October or November and one-half in May or June.

Warm-season grasses, irrigated: One-quarter of high dose every month, May through August.

Warm-season grasses, nonirrigated: One-half of low dose in April or May and one-half in August.

Winter Grasses

Cool-season grasses: Full low dose in October or November.

Humid Northwest

Low maintenance: Full low dose in October, November, or after grass stops growing actively.

Medium maintenance: One-half of high dose in October or November and one-half in May or June after first rampant growth slows.

SOURCE: Reprinted with permission from *The Chemical-Free Lawn* by Warren Schultz (Rodale Press, 1989).

104 for more information on NPK analyses.) Unlike chemical fertilizers, a single yearly application of these products is enough. Their nutrients will be released at a gradual rate as plants need them, and they are less likely to be washed away.

Calcium, magnesium, and sulfur also play a major role in grass nutrition. Many commercial lawn fertilizers are formulated with extra sulfur, which also enhances disease resistance. Essential micronutrients that may sometimes be deficient in lawns include iron and manganese; you should also watch for zinc and copper problems on highly alkaline soils. (See "Nutrient Deficiency Symptoms" on page 91 for symptoms to look for and the deficiencies they may indicate.) Before using any micronutrient fertilizers, have your soil tested to confirm the problem, and use the correct application rate for the product recommended. Provide extra micronutrients by foliar feeding, spraying 1 pint of seaweed concentrate per 1,000 square feet, or add a few pounds of kelp meal when you top-dress. Seaweed has been shown to offer a variety of stress-reducing and growth-enhancing effects.

In humid climates, where precipitation is more than 30 inches a year, apply lime every few years to keep soil pH between 6.5 and 6.8. Most grass species prefer this slightly acid level, although some will tolerate greater acidity or alkalinity. Adding lime is an easy and effective way to raise the pH of an acid soil. Adjust highly alkaline or saline soils with sulfur or gypsum. (See "Correcting Alkalinity" on page 169 for more information about this process.)

THE UNHEALTHY LAWN

Organic vegetable gardeners know that their keen eye is a big part of the organic method. Organic lawn care depends just as much on your sharp eye and intuitive approach. The following sections describe some of the danger signals to watch for.

THATCH AND DETHATCH

All lawns have some thatch—a layer of dead stems and other plant debris that's kind of like mulch. Get on your knees and spread apart the blades of grass to find thatch; it's the layer of fine tan straw that lays on the soil surface. Anything under ½ inch is healthy; when you notice more than 1 inch of undecomposed thatch, it's time to take immediate action.

Ordinarily, clippings and other organic debris are quickly decomposed by earthworms and other soil organisms. Thatch buildup is generally a sign that this biological activity has been suppressed. Lawns that have been heavily dosed with soluble fertilizers and weed- and pest-control chemicals are likely candidates for thatch buildup.

To avoid thatch problems, mow your grass a little less often and not too closely, and hold back on unnecessary nitrogen fertilizer. If you already have thick thatch, dislodge it by vigorously raking with a stiff wire rake. Collect the raked-out thatch and add it to the compost pile. Special hand and power tools are also available for thatch removal; some of them cut holes through the turf to aerate the soil—a necessary process for preventing further thatch problems. Top-dress after dethatching with about ½ inch of good compost. You may have to repeat this process for several seasons if the soil has been badly abused.

NUTRIENT DEFICIENCIES

Symptoms like yellowing leaf blades, dying back of leaf tops, and brown spots can indicate any number of problems. Many lawn pests and diseases cause symptoms that resemble those of nutrient deficiencies. How can you tell the difference?

Nutrient deficiencies tend to be more evenly distributed over the lawn, while pests and diseases usually appear in irregular patches. Check the table "Nutrient Deficiency Symptoms" on page 91 to see if there might be a particular nutrient problem. If you suspect a nutrient deficiency, the best course is to have your soil tested before taking corrective action. You may get immediate results from a good topdressing of ½ inch or more of compost or an organic lawn fertilizer or from a foliar feeding with fish emulsion and seaweed extract.

hardpan

Picture-perfect lawns are more prone to problems than those with a weedy patch here and there. Dandelions help break up hardpans and bring up nutrients from the subsoil.

WEED INVASION

Uniform lawns, composed of just a single grass species, are really ecologically unhealthy. A single-species monoculture is more prone to problems with disease, insects, and the vagaries of climate than a mixed-species spread.

A healthy lawn may have a weedy patch here and there, but unless the grass is getting crowded out, this is no cause for concern. A laissez-faire policy toward weeds is much better than chemical warfare. Taller mowing heights and adequate fertilization discourage crabgrass, which likes poor soil and needs light to grow. The few weeds that are really unsightly—curly-leaf dock, for instance—can be dug out by hand.

Dandelions are actually beneficial to lawns, helping to break up hardpans and bring up nutrients from the subsoil. Moss is an indicator of acid, infertile soil that is too shaded for the grass species there. Nutsedges are a sign of poor drainage and compacted soil. Plantains also indicate compaction—you might notice them growing mostly along heavily trafficked areas and driveway edges. (Refer to "Indicator Weeds and Soil Conditions" on page 16 for more information on indicator weeds.)

PESTS AND DISEASES

Overfertilizing and using chemicals can kill off natural disease-suppressing organisms. Naturally healthy soil with good drainage and air penetration is the key to preventing lawn problems. To help control pests and diseases without resorting to chemicals, begin by selecting resistant grass cultivars that are well-adapted to your climate and soil. Proper watering and mowing regimes, top-dressing with compost, and regular aerating are also important strategies.

SOIL NEEDS
OF TREES
AND SHRUBS

CHAPTER 11

Before you invest in permanent plantings, you'll need to do some homework. Planting trees is an investment, not only in money, but in the future. You'll want species that thrive in your location and that serve your needs. Because trees have such large root systems, it's best to match the species to the existing conditions, rather than modify your soil to suit the plants. Don't despair if your planting site is poorly drained, sandy, or even undermined by hardpan—all kinds of trees are available for all kinds of sites. The time you spend thinking about your needs and the plant's needs will pay off in the long run.

THE RIGHT PLANT
FOR THE RIGHT PLACE

Even if a gorgeous exotic specimen seems to be thriving in a neighbor's yard, it doesn't mean the same plant will do well for you. Before you decide on a particular tree or shrub, evaluate your planting site carefully. Is your site protected or does it bear the brunt of winter or summer winds? What's the soil like in and around the planting spot? Will water drain downhill and settle there? Consider how much sun or shade will fall on the new tree or shrub—and think about where the new plant will cast its shadow.

225

Will the mature tree interfere with overhead wires?

Is the site exposed to strong winds
or is it protected?

Is there a slope
that will drain
water to the
tree site?

What is the soil like?

A new tree is a member of the family for years to come. Choose a site
carefully, considering the weather conditions, soil characteristics, and water
availability. Consider the tree's mature height, and make sure that it won't
interfere with overhead utility wires.

LEADING QUESTIONS

A new tree is a member of your gardening family that will be around for a long time. Most home grounds can support only a few large trees. Think about selection and site before you invest. Here are some questions to consider:

• **Do you want a deciduous or evergreen tree?** It's not just a question of autumn leaf raking: Some evergreens, like magnolias, shed leaves year-round. Some deciduous trees, like ginkgos, drop their leaves all at once. Evergreen trees provide shade and shelter year-round; deciduous trees shed their leaves and let the sun through in winter.

• **What's the purpose of the tree?** Trees can provide privacy, shade, or fruit, or they can function as a windbreak or noise absorber.

• **What size and shape of tree will best serve your purposes?** A columnar type works well for screening or hedge but not for shade.

• **Is the tree sturdy?** This may sound like a silly question, but some trees are prone to weak or brittle wood and storm damage. Leguminous trees, such as locusts or catalpas, tend to be weak-wooded. Ask your nursery owner for advice.

• **Will the tree drop litter?** Plant trees that bear berries and fruit where birds and children will enjoy them, not where foot traffic will track them into the house. Avoid planting a fruiting tree near walkways or driveways.

• **Is the tree notorious for self-seeding, invasive roots, or suckering?** Do a little research on the tree you're considering, and avoid choosing one that is prone to any of these problems.

Learn as much as you can about the particular species in which you are interested. Consider color, size, shape, and other design elements for your landscaping needs. Cold or heat tolerance, productivity (in the case of fruit bearers), disease resistance, common pest problems, pruning requirements, and water needs are all qualities you need to know when selecting trees and shrubs. Choose plants that are well-suited to your climate and personal preferences.

Take a minute to look up from the planting site—straight up! Are there utility wires anywhere overhead that the growing tree will interfere with? Remember to think about the full-grown size and shape of the plant you have in mind. Is it a sprawler that will interfere with other nearby plants? Will it outgrow its site beside the driveway or front walk, requiring regular pruning to keep it in bounds? It is much easier (and cheaper) to avoid these problems than to deal with them a few years later!

SOIL CONCERNS

Selecting a tree or shrub for your site means matching up soil needs and preferences, too. Your local Cooperative Extension Service office is a good source of information. They can tell you if alkalinity, salinity, or other soil problems are a factor in your area, and they can recommend trees and shrubs suited to your conditions. "Resources" on page 259 lists other organizations that can help you find plant species and cultivars adapted to your soil conditions. If you are developing a new site for landscaping, refer to "Drainage Problems" on page 150 for details on how to improve drainage. Adding fertilizers and mulch to provide extra nutrients or amending the pH in the immediate vicinity may save an existing tree or shrub that is naturally unsuited to your site.

Well-suited trees and shrubs are more vigorous and less troubled by pests and disease than species that struggle along in conditions they don't like. Consider the following basic conditions when making your selection.

Soil pH. Many plants tolerate acid soil, and others can grow in alkaline soil. Some, like blueberries, rhododendrons, and camellias, really need acid soil to thrive, while others do poorly if pH is not close to neutral.

Nutrient needs. Is your selected tree or shrub usually satisfied with limited nutrient supplements, or does it demand a diet high in nutrients? Will your soil be able to feed it? Certain flowering shrubs, such as roses and camellias, and most fruiting plants have heavier nutrient needs than do hedges and shade trees.

Drainage. Shallow-rooted species, such as cedars and red maples, are better adapted to poorly drained sites than are deep-rooted ones like walnuts.

Good Choices for Problem Soils

Trees grow just about everywhere in the wild, on practically any kind of soil. Once you identify the conditions available on your site, you can look for species that are adapted to those conditions. A soil test of the general area can help determine any serious nutrient deficiencies or pH problems. Sample the soil as close as possible to the spots where you expect to plant.

Saline soil occurs naturally in some areas of the United States, primarily the West and Southwest. It's also a consideration in the

North, where streets are routinely salted for snow and ice. If you're planning a row of shrubs near the road in the North or if your site has saline soil, consider salt-tolerant species like those listed in "Salt Tolerances of Plants" on page 170.

Take advantage of natural adaptations to problem soils, and choose your new plantings wisely. The following are agreeable plants for less-than-perfect soils.

Trees and shrubs adapted to wet areas. If you have a wet or poorly drained area, consider planting one or more of the following:

Acer negundo (box elder)
Clethra alnifolia (sweet pepperbush)
Cornus alba 'Sibirica' (Siberian dogwood)
Cornus sericea (red-osier dogwood)
Cupressus spp. (cypresses)
Fothergilla gardenii (dwarf fothergilla)
Gaylussacia brachycera (box huckleberry)
Ilex glabra (inkberry)
Leiophyllum buxifolium (box sand myrtle)
Mahonia spp. (mahonias)
Myrica cerifera (wax myrtle)
Rosa rugosa (rugosa rose)
Vaccinium oxycoccos (European cranberry)
Viburnum dentatum (arrowwood viburnum)
Viburnum trilobum (American cranberrybush viburnum)
Zenobia pulverulenta (zenobia)

Trees and shrubs for dry areas. If your site is on the dry side, choose from among these adapted plants:

Eucalyptus spp. (eucalyptus)
Juniperus spp. (junipers)
Lavandula spp. (lavenders)
Microbiota decussata (Siberian carpet cypress)
Pinus spp. (pines)
Prunus besseyi (western sand cherry)
Prunus maritima (beach plum)
Prunus tomentosa (Nanking cherry)
Sarcococca spp. (sweet boxes)
Sophora japonica (Japanese pagoda tree)
Syringa spp. (lilacs)
Taxus spp. (yews)

Trees and shrubs that will tolerate hardpan or heavy soil.
Here are some plants that can grow on a site with tight, clayey soil:

Acer rubrum (red maple)
Cornus sericea (red-osier dogwood)
Cydonia oblonga (common quince)
Picea spp. (spruces)
Rhododendron spp. (azaleas and rhododendrons)
Salix spp. (willows)
Sambucus canadensis (American elder)
Tsuga spp. (hemlocks)

If you're plagued with hardpan or heavy soil, consider a tolerant red maple
(*Acer rubrum*).

How to Plant a Tree

Keep your new tree or shrub well-watered and in the shade while you prepare the planting hole. If you're planting a bareroot tree, soak the roots for a day beforehand in a solution of fish emulsion and seaweed extract, and then use that same solution when watering it in.

DIG A HOLE THE RIGHT WAY

Researchers now say that traditional instructions calling for digging an extra-large hole are unnecessary. The hole needs to be only as deep as the root ball and twice as wide. Measure the height of the root ball with a yardstick. Check the depth of the hole by laying a board across the top of the hole and measuring the distance from the board to the bottom of the hole. Avoid lifting the tree or shrub in and out of the hole to check for depth; this disturbs the roots and can be hard on your back, too!

To make it easier for the tree's roots to spread outward, use a garden fork to loosen the soil surrounding the hole within a radius of 5 to 10 feet, as shown in the illustration on page 232. There's no need to loosen the soil beneath the roots: Most of a tree's feeder roots are within the top 8 inches of soil, and the unloosened soil beneath the root ball will prevent settling of the tree. Rough up the sides of the hole with a rake or other implement. If you have poor drainage, make the hole a little shallower, so that the top of the root ball ends up 1 or 2 inches above the ground line.

SETTLING IN

The natural tendency is to enrich the soil you use to fill the hole with nutrients to get the new tree off to a good start, especially if your soil is on the poor side to begin with. This, we now know, is the wrong approach. A rich backfill mix discourages the roots from growing out and down in search of nutrients. In extreme cases, roots can form a dense clump inside the confines of the hole, just like a rootbound houseplant. Backfilling with unenriched soil leads to a sturdier tree, better supported by spreading roots.

If you are planting in a highly developed urban area, or an area where soil has been rearranged by machinery, the "natural" soil may

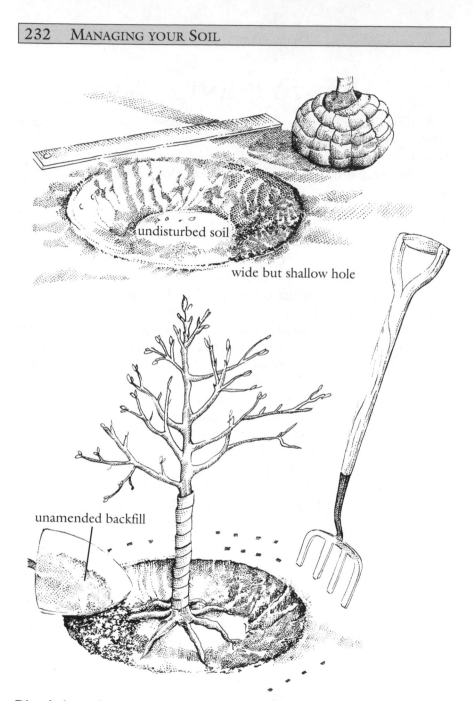

undisturbed soil

wide but shallow hole

unamended backfill

Dig a hole no deeper than necessary, wider at the top than at the bottom. Measure the depth with a yardstick instead of lifting the tree in and out of the hole. Scratch the soil on the sides of the hole to loosen it and make penetration easier. Fill the hole with the same soil you removed. Enriching the backfill discourages the roots from growing out in search of nutrients.

have disappeared. If you suspect your soil is poor, contact your local Cooperative Extension Service for suggestions of tough, adaptable trees and information on tree-planting techniques for difficult sites.

Because of its importance for root development, phosphorus is the one nutrient you should add liberally to each planting hole, along with a little lime if your pH is below 6.0. A cup of bonemeal or a pint of rock phosphate should suffice for most soils.

Remove your plant from its container or binding, position the roots in your hole, and finish filling it in with the same soil you removed. Avoid the impulse to stomp down the soil with your feet. The best way to eliminate air pockets around the roots is to stop when the hole is nearly full and pour in enough water to make a slurry. Then gently wiggle the trunk to encourage the muddy soil to ooze its way between the root branches. Then fill in the rest of the hole, leaving a slight depression to trap moisture. If your drainage is poor, slope the soil away from the trunk. Use a fish and seaweed solution or compost tea for the final watering.

Finish by spreading a layer of compost around the base of the plant. Place the compost in a circle extending 2 to 3 feet beyond the drip line (the point to which the branches reach). This extended circle encourages rapid formation of healthy feeder roots. Then apply a 1- to 2-inch layer of mulch to conserve moisture and keep weeds down, taking care to leave a space between the mulch and the trunk to prevent rot and rodent problems.

FERTILIZING AND MULCHING

Many trees need extra fertilizing during their first year or two, until root systems are well-established. Once established and growing well, annual renewal of an organic mulch, such as hay or bark, is all that most ornamentals or shade trees need, with occasional applications of compost as quantities on hand permit. To apply compost, pull back any existing mulch and spread an even layer of compost over the soil at least as far as the drip line. Then replace the mulch and, if necessary, add to it. For moderate or heavy feeders, apply a 3- to 6-inch layer of compost yearly. If your soil is poor or the tree is growing too slowly (you observe no new shoots or increase in height from one year to another), spring and fall compost applications may be in order.

TREES CAN BE LEGUMES, TOO

As we know from the vegetable garden, legumes are a pretty valuable type of plant. Because of the *Rhizobium* bacteria that live on their roots, legumes are able to use nitrogen from the air. You know that garden beans and soil-loving crops like clover and vetch are leguminous, but so are many other plants. In fact, no matter what your climate or soil conditions, you can find a plant that belongs to this nitrogen-fixing family. Some of these useful trees and shrubs are woody ornamentals that might fit nicely into your home landscape.

Many of these specimens help enrich the soil for other nearby plants, whether through direct root contact or by dropping nitrogen-rich leaf litter. Let the leaves lie where they fall to enrich the soil, or rake them up for your compost pile. These plants are generally troubled by few pest and disease problems, and most of them will flourish on poor soils. Some, in fact, are used to reclaim abused land such as abandoned strip-mine sites. As a bonus, many produce berries or seeds that attract birds and other wildlife to your yard.

Not all nitrogen-fixing plants are legumes. Some, such as alder and Russian olive, depend on nitrogen-fixing actinomycetes rather than the bacteria that live on legume roots.

Try these nitrogen-fixing woody plants in your landscape:

Alnus cordata (Italian alder)
Alnus rugosa (speckled alder)
Caragana arborescens (Siberian pea shrub)
Ceanothus americanus (New Jersey tea)
Ceratonia siliqua (carob)
Comptonia peregrina (sweet fern)
Cytisus scoparius (Scotch broom)
Elaeagnus angustifolia (Russian olive)
Eleagnus multiflora (cherry eleagnus)
Gleditsia triacanthos (honey locust)
Lespedeza thunbergii (lespedeza)
Myrica pensylvanica (northern bayberry)
Robinia pseudoacacia (black locust)
Shepherdia argentea (buffalo berry)
Sophora japonica (Japanase pagoda tree)
Tamarindus indica (tamarind)
Wisteria spp. (wisterias)

Mid-season fertilizing is rarely needed for most woody plants. Let the nutrient demands of the plant, coupled with knowledge of your soil conditions, guide you in deciding whether supplemental

Leguminous trees and shrubs, such as the sweetly fragrant black locust (*Robinia pseudoacacia*), use nitrogen from the air just like peas and beans in the garden. They're generally untroubled by pests and disease, and they flourish on poor soils.

fertilization is needed. If you notice pale leaves on a heavy nitrogen feeder, you can spread a high-analysis organic material or blended organic fertilizer. (See "Fertilizer or Amendment?" on page 101 for information on choosing a suitable fertilizer.) Work the fertilizer into the soil and water it in well, especially if conditions have been dry. Make sure you cover the area at least as far as the drip line. Since feeder roots are known to extend as far as two to three times the area of the tree's canopy, it is beneficial to fertilize as wide an area as you can. Cover with mulch. A foliar spray of fish emulsion will also give underfed trees a boost.

If you suspect some other type of nutrient deficiency, particularly micronutrients, the best approach is to have a laboratory test a leaf sample and give you recommendations for adding amendments based on their results. To provide for most normal micronutrient needs, spray with seaweed solution two or three times a season and use compost. Use a fine-mist sprayer and apply the seaweed solution in the morning, in the evening, or on a cloudy day.

Once established, most woody plants have little need for additional phosphorus. Supplemental potassium is often beneficial, particularly if soil levels, as indicated by a soil test, are marginal. Apply potassium late in the season to help trees and shrubs harden off for winter.

Scattering fertilizer aboveground might not get it to tree roots, due to competition from grass. To feed trees, poke holes around the drip line and fill with compost or a blended fertilizer, watering it in with fish emulsion or compost tea.

If you live in a humid climate, where minerals may be lost through leaching, regular monitoring of soil pH is important. Test pH levels every three to four years. Broadcast lime in accordance with recommendations to bring pH to between 6.2 and 6.8, unless your tree is an acid lover. If your soil has tested low in magnesium, use dolomitic lime.

A Shot in the Roots

If your shrubs or trees are growing in a thick lawn and are not mulched, broadcasting fertilizer may have little effect due to competition from the grass. In such cases, an injection may be called for (see the illustration on the opposite page). Use an auger or steel pipe to poke holes in the ground every 1 or 2 feet around the drip line; make them about 1½ inches in diameter and 1 foot deep. Fill the holes with compost or a blended organic fertilizer, and water it in with a solution of fish emulsion and seaweed extract or compost tea.

Fertility for Fruits and Nuts

If there's a particular area of your property where you'd like to put a berry patch or orchard, some advance planning will make a big difference in your results. Plant a cover crop the season before the trees or shrubs are to be planted, to help suppress weeds and improve soil tilth. Have your soil tested at the same time. Add any recommended soil amendments when you till in the cover crop.

Fruits and nuts generally need more care and feeding than ornamentals. Nut trees, for example, need adequate nitrogen (a major constituent of protein) to produce their protein-rich nuts. Use compost and bonemeal liberally when planting fruits and nuts. Sprinkle about 1 cup of bonemeal in the hole at planting time. Top-dress with a 1-inch layer of compost after planting, 2 to 3 feet beyond the drip line. Weed competition can set back fruit production, so use a heavy, low-nitrogen mulch such as wood chips to suppress weeds. "Soil Needs of Fruits, Nuts, and Berries" on page 238 will give you specific information on the requirements of many common crops.

Make a yearly application of compost out to the drip line. In

Soil Needs of Fruits, Nuts, and Berries

Key: 1 = Tolerates a wide range of soils; soil must be well-drained
2 = Needs deep, rich, well-drained soil
3 = Apply compost yearly or spring and fall; mulch
4 = Needs little fertilizing; mulching is enough
5 = Needs fertilization during the season to produce well
6 = Other special nutrient/pH needs (see Comments)

Plant	Requirements	Comments
Almond	1, 4	—
Apple	2, 3	—
Apricot	1, 3	Avoid overfeeding
Avocado	2, 3, or 5, depending on location	Sensitive to deficiencies of trace elements, especially iron
Blueberry	3, 6	Needs pH of 4.0–5.2; needs iron and magnesium
Bramble fruit	2, 3	—
Cherry	1, 4	—
Chestnut	1, 3	—
Citrus	2, 5, 6	Sensitive to deficiencies of trace elements
Currant	1, 4	—
Elderberry	2, 3	—
Fig	1, 4	Doesn't like rich soil
Filbert	2, 4	—
Gooseberry	1, 4	—
Grape	1, 3	Avoid nitrogen late in season
Hickory	2, 3	—
Kiwifruit	2, 5	—
Mulberry	1, 4	—

(continued)

SOIL NEEDS OF FRUITS, NUTS, AND BERRIES—CONTINUED

Plant	Requirements	Comments
Nectarine	2, 3	Needs supplemental nitrogen early in season
Olive	1, 4	—
Peach	2, 3	Needs supplemental nitrogen early in season
Pear	2, 4	Tolerates poor drainage; avoid excess nitrogen
Pecan	2, 5, 6	High nitrogen demand; sensitive to deficiencies of zinc
Persimmon	1, 4	Avoid excess nitrogen
Pistachio	2, 4	Prefers alkaline soil; occasionally requires supplemental nitrogen
Plum	2, 3	Sensitive to deficiencies of nitrogen
Quince	2, 4	Tolerates poor drainage; avoid excess nitrogen
Strawberry	2, 5	—
Walnut	2, 3	—

northern climates, avoid applying compost or other fertilizers after midsummer to avoid stimulating succulent growth, which is prone to winter injury. This is especially crucial for pears, which become more susceptible to fire blight if given too much nitrogen. Many fruits, especially apples, cherries, and peaches, are also heavy potassium feeders. Applying 1 cup per tree of langbeinite (Sul-Po-Mag) or potassium sulfate with the annual compost application is a good idea, except if soil tests show high potassium levels.

Many fruits are sensitive to micronutrient deficiencies. Citrus and avocados are most susceptible, but apples, pears, cherries, and other common fruits can also suffer from deficiencies of boron, zinc, manganese, and iron. If you suspect a micronutrient deficiency, based on the symptoms listed in the table "Nutrient Deficiency

Symptoms" on page 91, confirm it with a leaf tissue analysis before applying any single element. Consult your local Cooperative Extension office for information about leaf tissue analysis.

Corrective micronutrient applications are most effective when sprayed directly on the leaves, since nutrient uptake through tree roots is very slow, and sometimes soil imbalances prevent uptake of necessary micronutrients. All fruits benefit from foliar spraying two or three times a season with seaweed solution, which is rich in micronutrients. Follow directions on the package. Fish emulsion may also be beneficial for species with a heavy nitrogen demand.

SEASONAL SOIL CARE FOR TREES AND SHRUBS

Below are general guidelines for maintaining soil fertility for trees and shrubs. New trees and shrubs can be planted at any time, as long as they have a chance to get established before severe weather sets in.

SPRING

In spring, pull back old mulch from around your trees and shrubs, and make a fresh application of compost or other natural fertilizers (depending on the plants' needs). Replace the mulch and add to it as needed, being careful to leave a few inches of space between the mulch and the trunk of the plant.

SUMMER

During the summer, spray plant leaves two or three times with seaweed emulsion to provide balanced micronutrients. Include fish emulsion for heavy nitrogen feeders but not after midsummer in the North (so plants can harden off for winter). If you suspect nutrient deficiencies, collect leaf samples for laboratory analysis.

FALL

Repeat spring mulching and fertilizing, if necessary. To prevent winter injury, avoid adding high-nitrogen fertilizers. If the soil is dry, thoroughly irrigate around trees and shrubs before the ground freezes to make sure the roots can get adequate water.

SOIL NEEDS OF PLANTS IN POTS

CHAPTER 12

It's no wonder container gardening is so popular. You can beautify your home with houseplants, enjoy home-grown citrus fruits in a northern climate, grow fresh herbs on the kitchen windowsill, or create a garden on a suburban deck or city rooftop. Many gardeners are finding that it's less expensive—and more fun!—to start their own tomatoes and other seedlings than to buy them at the local garden center. Do-it-yourself seed starting also gives you a selection of thousands of species and cultivars, instead of limiting your choices to the big sellers on the six-pack table.

MAKING POTTING MIXES

Indoor and container-grown plants have special needs. Houseplants are asked to grow under circumstances vastly different from their natural home. And container plantings must depend totally on you for nourishment. If you garden in a home greenhouse, the growing bed is more ecologically balanced than a restricted container, but soil needs still are different from an outside garden.

You can use homemade or commercial potting mixes in your containers. If you have a good supply of the main ingredients, or if you need to mix a large amount, it's more economical to make your

241

Mix up a big batch of potting medium in a wheelbarrow, using a coffee can as a scoop. Measure and mix dry ingredients, then moisten well and let the water soak in before you fill containers.

own. It's also satisfying and fun, especially since you don't have to be precise about measurements. Mixing and filling pots is a good activity to share with children, too. Homemade mixes create a healthy medium for container-grown plants—one that nourishes them as well as providing physical support for their roots. Commercial potting and growing mixes are widely available, but some are laced with chemical fertilizers. If you decide on store-bought, look for compost-based mixes.

The first priority for healthy container-grown plants is good aeration and drainage. Feeding is best accomplished by including a slow-release source of nutrients, such as compost. Plants need just a little food at a time; highly soluble plant foods tend to concentrate harmful salts in the soil.

You can blend a small batch of soil mix in a large bowl, using a cup for a scoop. For larger quantities, a coffee can or sturdy quart-size yogurt container makes a great scoop, and a wheelbarrow makes a handy mixing bowl. Precision is less important than using quality

POTS: PRACTICAL OR PRETTY?

Consider your caretaking habits when choosing a pot. If you tend to be a bit heavy-handed with the watering can, opt for more-porous clay pots or wood barrels so you are less likely to drown the roots. Clay and wood will breathe, allowing air to infiltrate the soil all around, and allowing water to evaporate. If you've been known to forget about watering till the plants wilt before your eyes, nonporous plastic might be the wiser choice for you.

Picking a pot is just as much a matter of aesthetics as it is of practicalities like size and cost. If you find clay pots more appealing but want to keep watering chores to a minimum, there's an easy solution. Plant in plastic, and then slip the plastic pot into a slightly larger clay pot. The double wall will slow evaporation even more and will keep the plant roots cooler. Use this pot-in-a-pot trick inside wicker baskets, copper washtubs, or any other favorite containers.

ingredients. Measure and mix ingredients dry. (Mix up more than you think you'll need—when you add the water, the volume will decrease.) Moisten the dry ingredients well, and let the water soak in before you fill your containers with the mixture.

SOIL MIX INGREDIENTS

Your custom mixes are only as good as the ingredients you start with. The basic ingredients are topsoil, sand, and compost: a recipe that suits all kinds of container-grown plants. You can add other materials to fine-tune the mix, provide nutrients, or improve texture or soil chemistry. For example, leaf mold or peat moss help retain water in the mix. Vermiculite or perlite lighten the mix in texture and in weight—something to consider if you're filling large containers. Amendments like lime and bonemeal provide necessary nutrients and minerals.

Topsoil

Put aside a bagful or two of your best garden soil to use for potting mixes. Soil in which onions have grown is said to have a beneficial effect on seedling growth. Purchased topsoil is another alternative. For potting mixes, a medium-textured loam is best. If your topsoil is either very sandy or very clayey in texture, amend it by adding compost, peat moss, or leaf mold. If your soil is sandy, cut back on the sand in the final mix. If your soil is clayey, increase the proportion of sand and use an additional measure of an aerating material such as perlite or vermiculite or both.

Compost

Good-quality screened compost is an essential ingredient of any potting mix, but contrary to what you might think, pure compost isn't recommended as a growing medium. Pure compost is far too rich for most ornamentals, and regular watering would cause plants to take up an unhealthy dose of soluble salts from the compost. But combined with topsoil, sand, and other ingredients, compost is a must. It supplies food for the container plants and improves drainage, aeration, and nutrient-holding qualities of the mix. The biological activity taking place in the compost is also important, even in small containers. It even includes organisms that help suppress fungal diseases.

Always save your very best quality compost for potting mixes. It is crucial that compost used in potting mixes, especially for starting seedlings, be thoroughly decomposed and well-aged. If the compost is still "working," certain compounds released during organic decomposition will suppress germination. Sift compost to remove large pieces of undecomposed material.

Sand

Buy sharp sand, also known as builder's sand, for your soil mixes. The coarse kind sold at building supply stores for mixing concrete works just fine. Avoid using play sand, which usually has much finer grains. Sand has no nutrients, but it improves drainage and helps hold roots.

Leaf Mold

Leaf mold—decomposed leaves—is an excellent source of humus in a potting mix. Although it offers negligible quantities of major plant nutrients (like nitrogen, phosphorus, and potassium), leaf mold is a good source of micronutrients. Depending on the species of tree, leaf mold can be fairly acid and affect the pH of your soil mix.

If you don't own a piece of woodland, make your own leaf mold in an out-of-the-way corner of your yard. Simply make a pile

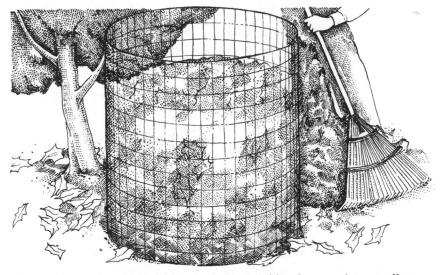

Pile your leaves into a wire-fence enclosure, and let them rot into excellent humus.

of leaves at least 3 feet long on each side, protect it from blowing around (a wire fence works well), and leave it to decompose for a year or two. In a dry climate, you may have to wet down the pile every so often. Use the leaf mold from the bottom of the pile first. It should be soft and crumbly and should smell like compost. You can add more leaves to extend the pile into a long, narrow windrow, and remove broken-down material from the oldest sections first.

Leaf mold is becoming available through some municipalities. Leaves collected from streets in fall are dumped into big compost piles, and the resulting leaf mold is often given away to residents. Call your local department of streets or city hall to find out whether

LIVE COMPOST IS BEST

Many people erroneously believe that it is necessary to sterilize soil for germinating seedlings. Quite the opposite is true. Research has shown that seedlings grown in mixes containing compost are more disease-prone when the mix has been sterilized. Antifungal organisms are killed off in the sterilization process, and fungal spores are always floating around, waiting to land and grow in the right conditions. Also, the high temperatures of sterilization can make certain nutrients more soluble and therefore more easily taken up by plants, which can lead to a problem of nutrient imbalances.

your municipality gives away leaf mold. (If you discover that they collect leaves but do *not* compost them, you can write your mayor or city council a letter suggesting that the municipality start such a program.)

Peat Moss

Peat moss consists of anaerobically decomposed plants—mostly sphagnum moss—mined from bogs. It takes thousands of years of decay to produce peat moss, making it a limited natural resource. Although as of now peat moss is readily available, a better ecological choice is to use easily renewable resources, such as leaf mold, in place of peat. However, if you do choose to use peat, it helps to know the differences between the two types—brown and black.

Brown peat is the standard fluffy peat moss, taken from the upper layers of the bog. It improves aeration but contributes little to nutrition and serves to lower the pH. The lower layers of a peat bog consist of darker, more thoroughly decomposed residues, called black peat or peat humus. This material contributes more body to a soil mix than brown peat, and it holds more moisture. It may also contain some significant nitrogen and has a more neutral pH than brown peat.

Both types of peat are dusty to work with, and they shrink and repel water when they dry out. To improve water retention and alleviate dust problems, thoroughly moisten any type of peat before adding it to potting mixes. It's also important never to let plants growing in peat-based mixes dry out completely. If the mix dries out, it shrinks away from the sides of the pot, and any water you add just runs right out without getting absorbed. If this happens to your plants, use warm water to gradually moisten the surface of the mix, until the mix absorbs enough to fill out the pot again. Or stand the pot in warm water, and let the water slowly wick upward through the peat.

Perlite

Perlite looks like Styrofoam beads, but it is actually a natural product, formed when volcanic minerals are exposed to high temperatures and popped like popcorn. It is extremely light, only weighing 8 pounds per cubic foot in comparison to 60 to 95 pounds per cubic foot for most soils, making it a terrific aerator. Perlite has a pH between 7.0 and 7.5. Handle it very carefully—it's dusty and abrasive, and it's not good to breathe.

Vermiculite

Shiny, flaky vermiculite is mica that has been heated to cause the sheets to expand and separate. Be sure to buy the horticultural grade; vermiculite sold at building supply stores is coarser and alkaline. Light-textured vermiculite all by itself is an excellent medium for starting seeds. It soaks up moisture and nutrients and slowly releases them to plants. Like perlite, its pH is between 7.0 and 7.5. It contributes a tiny amount of potassium and magnesium to the soil.

Fertilizers and Amendments

Slow-release rock powders such as rock phosphate, greensand, and lime all may have their place in a potting mix, especially if it is used for producing edibles. Small amounts of bonemeal (for phosphorus and calcium) and kelp meal (for micronutrients) can likewise be beneficial. Supplementary nitrogen sources such as blood meal or alfalfa meal can be used if your supply of compost is limited. You can make up a fertilizer for your potting mix containing nitrogen, potassium, and phosphorus by mixing together equal portions of blood meal, rock or colloidal phosphate, and greensand. Add about ½ tablespoon of this mix per quart of finished potting soil.

A SAMPLING OF SOIL MIXES

To get the best results from your container plants, you can tailor the ingredients in the growing medium to match the needs of your particular plants. In the following pages, you'll find recipes for some of the most basic growing mixes. As you gain more experience in growing container plants, you can fine-tune the mixes to fit your conditions.

ALL-PURPOSE POTTING MIX

The simplest all-purpose potting formula is based on equal portions of garden soil, well-aged compost, and coarse sand, with a dash of supplemental plant nutrients. An additional measure of perlite or vermiculite ensures good aeration. Add a portion of leaf mold for plants that need extra humus, such as bleeding hearts (*Dicentra* spp.), and acid lovers, such as African violets. Give cacti and succulents twice as much sand and little or no compost. The recipe below will give you a good basic soil mix for most plants. As you become experienced with different materials, you will feel more confident about making changes to improve drainage or adjust the nutrient supply.

Basic Soil Mix

    1 part garden soil
    1 part well-aged compost
    1 part coarse sand
    1 part vermiculite or perlite

To give your basic mix an extra dose of nutrients, add the following combination in a ratio of about 80:1. For example, if you have mixed up 20 quarts (5 gallons) of basic soil mix, add 1 scant cup of Supplemental Nutrient Mix (see recipe below).

Supplemental Nutrient Mix

    1 part blood meal
    1 part rock or colloidal phosphate
    1 part greensand or granite dust

SEED-STARTING AND PROPAGATION MIXES

Media for starting seeds or rooting cuttings don't need to supply nutrients, but they must provide excellent aeration and drainage. Many people use some combination of sand, peat, vermiculite, and perlite, leaving out the soil. Vermiculite alone makes a fine seed-starting mix; damp sand has long been popular for rooting cuttings. Brown peat by itself is not a good idea because it is acidic and is difficult to water when it dries out. If seedlings may be held past the first-true-leaves stage before transplanting, add a small amount of compost to the mix. Biologically active compost may also help suppress damping-off, a disease that often plagues small seedlings. Use the following recipe to create a light, well-balanced growing mix for your seedlings.

Seed-Starting Mix

2 parts sand
2 parts vermiculite or perlite
1 part well-aged compost

To root cuttings, you'll need a slightly different medium. The following mix will give good results with most plants.

Propagation Mix for Cuttings

1 part sand
1 part vermiculite or perlite
1 part leaf mold or peat

Containerless Seed-Starting

How would you like to never have to buy seed-starting pots again? With a simple hand tool, you can press out perfect seed-starting soil blocks as easily as you pop ice cubes out of an ice cube tray. This wonderful tool is called a soil block maker. Soil block makers come in several sizes, generally 1½ to 2 inches square and 2 inches deep. Some mail-order sources of soil block makers are listed in "Soil-Care Supplies" on page 260.

To make soil blocks, your growing mix will need to be substantial enough that it can hold its form until the plant roots are big enough to knit the ingredients together. Black peat or peat humus provides an extra binding quality. The trick to successful soil block making is to get the mix wet enough to hold its shape and not crumble when you touch it—much wetter than you would want for soil going into a pot or cell. The following recipe gives the ideal amounts of each dry component needed to make good, sturdy soil blocks.

Soil Block Mix

2 parts brown peat
2 parts black peat
2 parts sand
1 part garden soil
1 part compost

For each quart of mix, add 1 scant teaspoon of lime and 2 teaspoons of Supplemental Nutrient Mix (see the opposite page for the recipe).

Fill your soil block maker with the mix, and press out the finished blocks.

A soil block maker is a handy tool for turning loose potting mix into individual planting cubes. Use a mix wet enough to hold its shape when you touch it.

Besides not needing seed-starting pots anymore, soil blocks provide another benefit—the new plant's roots are "air-pruned" as they grow. The roots stop growing when they reach the edge of the block, which is separated from its neighbors by an air space. The plants can't become rootbound—a situation that interferes with their growth once they are transplanted. However, if held in soil blocks too long, roots will jump the gap and grow into neighboring blocks. If this happens, slice (don't tear) them apart, and plant as quickly as possible. The drawbacks of soil blocks are that they take up quite a bit of space, and the blocks consume larger quantities of soil mix than do containers with a more tapered shape.

ORNAMENTALS AND EDIBLES
IN CONTAINERS

Many plants you would normally find growing outdoors can be successfully grown in containers. If you are an urban gardener, are physically challenged, or just want extra greenery indoors or on a patio, consider growing your favorites in containers. Look for bush cultivars of vegetables, and dwarf trees. Most culinary herbs lend themselves to container growing and will offer fresh-cut kitchen delights all year. Follow the recipe below to create a light, fertile, well-drained growing medium that is suitable for a wide range of container plants.

Container Mix

> 2 parts garden soil
> 1 part compost
> 1 part leaf mold or peat
> 1 part sand
> 1 part perlite or vermiculite

Add supplemental nutrients in an 80:1 ratio. For example, if you have mixed up 20 quarts (5 gallons) of basic soil mix, add 1 scant cup of Supplemental Nutrient Mix (page 248). If your garden soil is on the acidic side, add one-quarter part of dolomitic lime.

HOUSEPLANTS

Houseplants need a growing medium that allows good aeration and root penetration but doesn't dry out too fast. Include a very modest nutrient source, and houseplants can be happy for a long time in the right-size pot. Use the following as a basic houseplant soil recipe. For very demanding plants, add some Supplemental Nutrient Mix. (See page 248 for the recipe.)

Houseplant Mix

> 1 to 2 parts garden soil
> 1 part sand or perlite
> 1 part compost, leaf mold, or peat

Cacti need special treatment. For a soil mix that suits their unique needs, use the following recipe.

Cactus Mix

> 1 part garden soil
> 1 part compost
> 2 parts sand
> 1 part perlite or vermiculite

To make a potting mix for the houseplant-lover's favorite, the African violet, use the recipe on page 252.

African Violet Mix

> 1 to 2 parts garden soil
> 1 part sand or perlite
> 2 parts leaf mold or peat
> For each quart of mix, add 1 tablespoon of bonemeal.

FERTILIZING CONTAINER PLANTS

How much and how often you fertilize depends on how quickly the plant grows and what its stage of development is. Seedlings need supplemental feeding when they have reached the limits of the containers they are in—as quickly as 10 days for fast-growing lettuce in 1-inch cells. Extra nutrients won't do a dormant plant much good, but they can be critical when a plant is emerging from dormancy or setting buds. A plant newly potted in a good compost-based mix usually won't need supplemental fertilization for several weeks.

The easiest way to feed plants in pots is with a fertilizer in liquid form. Fish and seaweed solutions are the backbone of the non-chemical plant-feeding program. Add them as you water, or spray them on foliage with a hand-mister. Compost tea is another rich source of nutrients. Make up small quantities of compost tea by placing a cloth bag of compost right in your watering can. Let it set overnight to steep, then apply the tea as though watering.

HOW MUCH IS ENOUGH?

Once your plants use up the nutrients in the original mix, you'll need to put them on a regular feeding schedule. An easy way to do this is to water with a diluted fertilizer such as manure tea every other watering. Repeat feedings at intervals of two weeks to a month, depending again on growth rate and stage of development. Plants growing in small pots need feeding more often than those in large pots. Seedlings that have exhausted their containers need feeding twice a week until transplanting. Container gardens in full sun that need daily watering will benefit from a weekly application of fish emulsion, mixed according to package directions.

Feed houseplants only during their active growth period. If they bloom once a year, stop fertilizing after the blooms die back. Those with bulbs, corms, or tubers need feeding for a few weeks after flowering to prepare for dormancy. A light dusting of wood ashes on the surface will help by providing an extra shot of potassium. Feeding is rarely needed in wintertime, when growth slows or stops altogether.

Extra phosphorus encourages root growth. Add some to newly repotted plants, to flowering plants just prior to blooming, and to cacti and succulents during rapid growth stages. Adding too much phosphorus to established plants can cause them to become root-bound prematurely. If you notice phosphorus deficiency symptoms like purple undersides of leaves (assuming the leaf isn't supposed to be purple), a dose of fish emulsion and a surface dusting of bone-meal should take care of it.

Long-lived plants, especially those in large containers, can also be fed by top-dressing, illustrated on page 254. Dig away the top layer of soil, up to one-quarter of the total depth of the root ball. You may cut away some fine root hairs in this process, but be careful to avoid disturbing any main roots. Then replace the removed soil with fresh potting mix, adding a slightly larger amount of supplemental nutrients than you would for repotting.

AVOID OVERFEEDING

Overfertilization can be just as big a problem for container-grown plants as underfertilization. As is true with garden plants, the weak, lank growth caused by too much nitrogen will attract aphids and other pests and will increase disease susceptibility. Algae growing on the outside of a clay pot is an indicator of excessive fertilization. If you have been feeding a plant because it was looking sickly and it continues to decline, chances are that its problem is disease and not a nutrient deficiency.

Salt buildup, which shows up as white deposits on the inside of the pot, is one consequence of overfertilization. Watering habits play a role in this problem, too. Light, frequent watering makes salts concentrate in the upper layers of the pot as the water evaporates. The best course is to water thoroughly only when needed. If you find salts building up on your pots, one solution is to repot and then water thoroughly. You can also place the whole pot in the bathtub

To top-dress large container plants, dig away the top layer of soil, up to one-quarter of the total depth of the root ball, being careful to avoid disturbing any main roots. Fill with fresh potting mix amended with supplemental nutrients.

and keep pouring water through the soil to wash out the salts, a process known as leaching. Since this process also washes out plant nutrients, you will need to add some supplemental fertilizer after you're finished.

GLOSSARY

Absorption: The taking up of elements or compounds in solution as part of the stream of solvent (such as plant nutrients in water).

Aerobic: A process that requires the presence of free oxygen, or a condition in which free oxygen is present.

Aggregate: A collection of soil particles that holds together, forming the basis for soil structure.

Allelopathy: Suppression of one plant species by another through secretion of phytotoxic exudates.

Anaerobic: A process that does not require free oxygen, or a condition in which free oxygen is excluded.

Anion: A negatively charged chemical element or radical that is acid-forming.

Bio-Dynamics: A school of agricultural thought, based on the spiritual teachings of Rudolph Steiner, that views the living interrelationships of soil, farm, and community as an organic whole.

Biomass: The total weight of vegetation growing on a given area of soil.

Bioregion: A geographic area defined by common ecological characteristics, such as climate, soil types, topography, predominant vegetation, and water system.

Capillary action: The ability of soil to wick up moisture from deeper levels as it is needed, made possible by good soil structure.

Carbon:nitrogen ratio: The proportion of carbon to nitrogen by weight in any organic matter. The optimum level for biological activity in raw organic matter is between 20 and 30 parts carbon to 1 part nitrogen.

Cation: A positively charged chemical element or radical, usually alkaline-forming.

Cation exchange capacity (CEC): The capacity of the colloidal particles in a given soil to hold positively charged ions (cations).

Chelate: A compound consisting of a metallic element bound within a complex organic molecule, or the process of forming such a compound.

Colloid: A mass of very fine particles having a high ratio of surface area to weight and characterized by a gooey consistency. Examples include protoplasm, clay, humus, and mayonnaise.

Compost: A process that uses any one of several methods to speed up the decomposition of raw organic matter, usually by piling, aerating, and moistening. Also, the crumbly, nutrient-rich product of this process.

Consumers: Organisms that obtain nourishment by consuming the products or remains of other living organisms.

Cover crop: A crop used to protect soil from erosion, at the same time building organic matter and controlling weeds.

Decomposers: Organisms, usually soil bacteria, that derive nourishment by breaking down the remains or wastes of other living organisms into simple organic compounds.

Exudates: Biochemical compounds secreted by plant roots.

Fertilizer: Any material added to the soil for the purpose of providing essential nutrients to plants.

Fixation: The binding of a nutrient into a more stable form that may be either less available to plants or more available to plants.

Foliar-feed: To apply liquid fertilizers directly to plant leaves, generally as a fine spray over the entire leaf surface.

Green manure: A crop that, before it reaches full maturity, is incorporated into the soil for the purpose of soil improvement.

Hardpan: A heavily compacted subsoil layer, sometimes naturally occurring but usually created by poor soil management practices.

Horizon: A distinct layer of soil (parallel to the surface) that has particular characteristics due to the soil-forming process in a given locale.

Humus: The fragrant, spongy, nutrient-rich material resulting from decomposition of organic matter.

Immobilization: The conversion of an element to a form that is not available for biological processes or chemical reactions. Soil nutrients may be immobilized in microbial or plant tissues or in very stable chemical complexes.

Inoculant: The spores of the desired strain of *Rhizobium* bacteria, applied in powder form to the appropriate legume seed when planted. Also, any material of high microbial content added to soil or compost to stimulate biological activity.

Leaching: The downward movement through soil of chemical substances dissolved in water.

Legume: A member of the plant family Leguminosae (including clover, alfalfa, beans, and peas), whose roots host nitrogen-fixing bacteria in a symbiotic relationship.

Nitrogen fixation: The conversion of atmospheric (gaseous) nitrogen into complex chemical compounds that can eventually be used by plants.

Macronutrient: A plant nutrient needed in substantial quantities, including carbon, hydrogen, oxygen, nitrogen, phosphorus, sulfur, calcium, magnesium, and potassium.

Metabolism: The sum of the biochemical processes of growth, maintenance, and energy transformation carried out by a living organism.

Micronutrient: A plant nutrient needed in very small quantities, including copper, chlorine, zinc, iron, manganese, boron, and molybdenum.

Mineralization: The release of soluble minerals and simple organic compounds through the decomposition of organic matter.

Mucigel: A gelatinous material surrounding the root, created by the interaction of the root, the soil, and the microbe community directly adjacent to the root.

Mycorrhizal association: A symbiotic relationship between mycorrhizal fungi and plant roots, in which soil phosphorus is made more available to plants.

NPK analysis: The ratio of nitrogen (N), phosphorus (P), and potassium (K) in an organic soil amendment. For example, the NPK analysis for steamed bonemeal is 1-11-0.

Organic matter: The remains, residues, or waste products of any living organism.

Parent material: The raw material—native rock or organic matter—from which topsoil is created through biogeochemical processes and weathering.

Pathogen: An organism capable of causing disease in other organisms.

pH: The concentration of hydrogen ions in a solution, which determines the solution's level of acidity or alkalinity. A pH of 7.0 is neutral. Lower numbers indicate acid conditions, and higher numbers indicate alkaline conditions.

Phytotoxin: A substance that is toxic to plants.

Pore space: The space between soil particles where air and water circulate.

Producers: Organisms, generally green plants, that can make their own food from inorganic materials, usually through the use of radiant energy in photosynthesis.

Raw manure: Manure that has not yet decomposed, containing highly soluble nitrogen and potassium.

Rhizobia: Nitrogen-fixing bacteria that live in symbiosis with legumes.

Rhizosphere: The area immediately surrounding plant roots, where the highest level of soil biological activity exists.

Soil amendment: Any material added to the soil in order to enhance soil biological activity.

Structure: The physical arrangement—shape, size, and stability—of soil particles.

Symbiosis: A mutually beneficial relationship between two living organisms, such as plant roots and rhizobia.

Synergy: The mutual combined enhancement of two or more factors (such as soil nutrients) that exceeds the expected sum of individual effects.

Texture: The proportions of sand, silt, and clay in a particular soil.

Tilth: The physical quality or condition of soil, similar to the concept of health in a living organism.

Volatilization: The escape of chemical elements into the atmosphere.

RESOURCES

General Soil Information

A & L Agricultural Laboratories
7621 Whitepine Road
Richmond, VA 23237
Also has branches in TN, NE, IN, TX, CA, and FL.

ATTRA (Appropriate Technology Transfer for Rural Areas)
P.O. Box 3657
Fayetteville, AR 72702

Biosystem Consultants
P.O. Box 43
Lorane, OR 97451

Cook's Consulting
R.D. 2, Box 13
Lowville, NY 13367

Council on Soil Testing & Plant Analysis
University of Georgia Station
P.O. Box 2007
Athens, GA 30612

Erth-Rite
R.D. 1, Box 243
Gap, PA 17527

Soil Conservation Service
Check your phone directory under "United States Government."

Plant Information

American Horticultural Society
7931 East Boulevard Dr.
Alexandria, VA 22308

Center for the Development of Hardy Landscape Plants
Dr. Harold Pellet
P.O. Box 39
Chenhassen, MN 55317

Planetary Design Corp.
2601 East Airport Dr.
Tucson, AZ 85706
Supplies information on salt-tolerant landscape plants.

Soil-Care Supplies, Soil Test Kits, and Composting Supplies

A. M. Leonard, Inc.
P.O. Box 816
Piqua, OH 45356

Earthly Goods Farm & Garden Supply
Route 3, Box 761
Mounds, OK 74047

Ecology Action/Bountiful Gardens
19550 Walker Road
Willits, CA 95490

Four Winds Farm Supply
N8806 600th St.
River Falls, WI 54022

Gardener's Supply Company
128 Intervale Road
Burlington, VT 05401

Harmony Farm Supply
P.O. Box 460
Graton, CA 95444

Johnny's Selected Seeds
Foss Hill Road
Albion, ME 04910

Necessary Trading Company
703 Salem Ave.
New Castle, VA 24127

North Country Organics
Depot St.
Bradford, VT 05033

Peaceful Valley Farm Supply
P.O. Box 2209
Grass Valley, CA 95945

Smith & Hawken
25 Corte Madera
Mill Valley, CA 94941

Worms

Cape Cod Worm Farm
30 Center Ave.
Buzzards Bay, MA 02532

Carter's Worm Farms
P.O. Box 99
Plains, GA 31780

Dolche-Vita Earthworm Products Co.
P.O. Box 445
Willow Creek, CA 95573

Flower Field Enterprises
10332 Shaver Road
Kalamazoo, MI 49002

Wiggle Worm Haven, Inc.
7802 Old Spring St.
Racine, WI 53406

The Worm Concern of America, Inc.
1450 Tierra Rejada
Simi Valley, CA 93065

Environmentally Friendly Products

Eco Design Company
1365 Rufina Circle
Santa Fe, NM 87501

Real Goods
966 Mazzoni Street
Ukiah, CA 95482

Seventh Generation
Colchester, VT 05446

Organic Certification Program Information

California Certified Organic Farmers
P.O. Box 8136
Santa Cruz, CA 95061

Organic Certification Program Information — Continued

Farm Verified Organic, Inc.
R.R. 1, Box 40A
Medina, ND 58467

Natural Organic Farmers Association
411 Sheldon Road
Barre, MA 01005

Organic Crop Improvement Association
3185 Township Road 179
Bellefontaine, OH 43311

Organic Foods Production Association of North America
P.O. Box 1078
Greenfield, MA 01301

Organic Growers & Buyers Association
1405 Silver Lake Road
New Brighton, MN 55112

FURTHER READING

Appelhof, Mary. *Worms Eat My Garbage*. Kalamazoo, Mich.: Flower Press, 1982.

Bradley, Fern Marshall, ed. *Rodale's Chemical-Free Yard and Garden*. Emmaus, Pa.: Rodale Press, 1991.

Bradley, Fern Marshall, and Barbara W. Ellis, eds. *Rodale's All-New Encyclopedia of Organic Gardening*. Emmaus, Pa.: Rodale Press, 1992.

Coleman, Eliot. *The New Organic Grower: A Master's Manual of Tools and Techniques for the Home and Market Gardener*. Chelsea, Vt.: Chelsea Green Publishing Co., 1989.

Creasy, Rosalind. *The Complete Book of Edible Landscaping*. San Francisco, Calif.: Sierra Club Books, 1982.

Ferguson, Nicola. *Right Plant, Right Place*. New York: Summit Books, 1984.

Fukuoka, Masanobu. *The One-Straw Revolution*. Emmaus, Pa.: Rodale Press, 1978.

Gershuny, Grace, and Joseph Smillie. *The Soul of Soil: A Guide to Ecological Soil Management*. St. Johnsbury, Vt.: Gaia Services, 1986.

Howard, Sir Albert. *The Soil and Health*. New York: Schocken Books, 1947.

Hyams, Edward. *Soil and Civilization*. London: Thames and Hudson, 1952.

Jeavons, John. *How to Grow More Vegetables (Than You Ever Thought Possible on Less Land Than You Can Imagine)*. Berkeley, Calif.: Ten Speed Press, 1982.

Loewer, Peter. *Tough Plants for Tough Places*. Emmaus, Pa.: Rodale Press, 1992.

Martin, Deborah L., and Grace Gershuny, eds. *The Rodale Book of Composting*. Emmaus, Pa.: Rodale Press, 1992.

Mollison, Bill. *Permaculture: A Practical Guide for a Sustainable Future*. Washington, D.C.: Island Press, 1990.

Sarrantonio, Marianne. *Methodologies for Screening Soil-Improving Legumes*. Kutztown, Pa.: Rodale Institute, 1991.

Schultz, Warren. *The Chemical-Free Lawn*. Emmaus, Pa.: Rodale Press, 1989.

Storl, Wolf. *Culture and Horticulture: A Philosophy of Gardening*. Wyoming, R.I.: Bio-Dynamic Literature, 1979.

Stout, Ruth, and Richard Clemence. *The Ruth Stout No-Work Garden Book*. Emmaus, Pa.: Rodale Press, 1971.

INDEX

Note: Page references in *italic* indicate illustrations.
Boldface references indicate tables.

A

Acer rubrum, 230
Achillea, 161
Achillea millefolium, **20**
Acid soil, 96, 163–67. *See also* Soil pH
    correcting acidity, 166–67
    humus for, 166
    liming materials for, **166**
    plants tolerant of, 164–65
    problems, 164–65
    United States map, *163*
Actinomycetes, *29,* 30
    in compost, *69,* 70
African violet mix, recipe, 252
Agropyron repens, **18,** 54
Agrostis, **219**
Air
    for lawns, 216–17
    for soil health, 38
Alfalfa, 50, *52,* 53, 55, **60–61**
Alfalfa hay, carbon:nitrogen ratio for,
    79
Alfalfa meal, 121, **124–25**
Algae, 33
Alkaline soil, 96, 167–70. *See also* Soil
    pH
    correcting alkalinity, 169–70
    plants tolerant of, 168
    salinity of, 168, 169
    United States map, *167*
All-purpose potting mix, 247–48
Almond, **238**
Amaranthus retroflexus, **19**
Animal manures, 64–65
    composition and use of, 118–20
Animals, 34–35, *34*
Anions, 97, 98–99
Annuals, 205
Apple, **238**
Apple pomace, **79, 124–25**
Apricot, **238**
Aragonite, **124–25,** 133, **166**
Arsenic, **176, 179**
Ascophyllum nodosum, 132, 135
Asparagus, **193**
Avocado, **238**
Axonopus compressus, **219**

B

Bacteria, 28–30, *29,* 31
    aerobes and anaerobes, 29
    in compost, 69–70, *69*
    hoeing and, *47*
Bahiagrass. *See Paspalum notatum*
Bark, as mulch, 206
Barley, as green manure, **60–61**
Bat guano, **124–25**
Beans
    as green manure, 56, **60–61**
    soil needs of, **193**
Beets, **193**
Bentgrass. *See Agrostis*
Benzoic acid herbicides, **179**
Bermudagrass. *See Cynodon dactylon*
Berries, **238–39**
Bindweed, field. *See Convolvulus
    arvensis*
BioActivator, **124–25**
Blood meal, 121, **124–25**
Blueberry, **238**
Bluegrass, Kentucky. *See Poa pratensis*
Bluegrass hay, **124–25**
Bonemeal, 123, **124–25**
    for flowers, 202, *204*
Borax, **124–25,** 135
Boron
    deficiency symptoms, **92**
    desired amount in soil, and
        function in plants, **102**
    as soil contaminant, **176**
Bracken, Eastern. *See Pteridium
    aquilinum*
Bramble fruit, **238**
Brassica, **19, 194**
Brassica hirta, **19**
Brassicas, as green manures, 55,
    60–61
Broccoli, **193**
Bromegrass, smooth, as green manure,
    60–61
Brush, shredded, as mulch, 208
Brussels sprouts, **193**
Buchloe dactyloides, **219**
Buckwheat
    couchgrass elimination with, 54